ENCHANTMENTS

UNIVERSITY PRESS OF FLORIDA

Florida A&M University, Tallahassee

Florida Atlantic University, Boca Raton

Florida Gulf Coast University, Ft. Myers

Florida International University, Miami

Florida State University, Tallahassee

New College of Florida, Sarasota

University of Central Florida, Orlando

University of Florida, Gainesville

University of North Florida, Jacksonville

University of South Florida, Tampa

University of West Florida, Pensacola

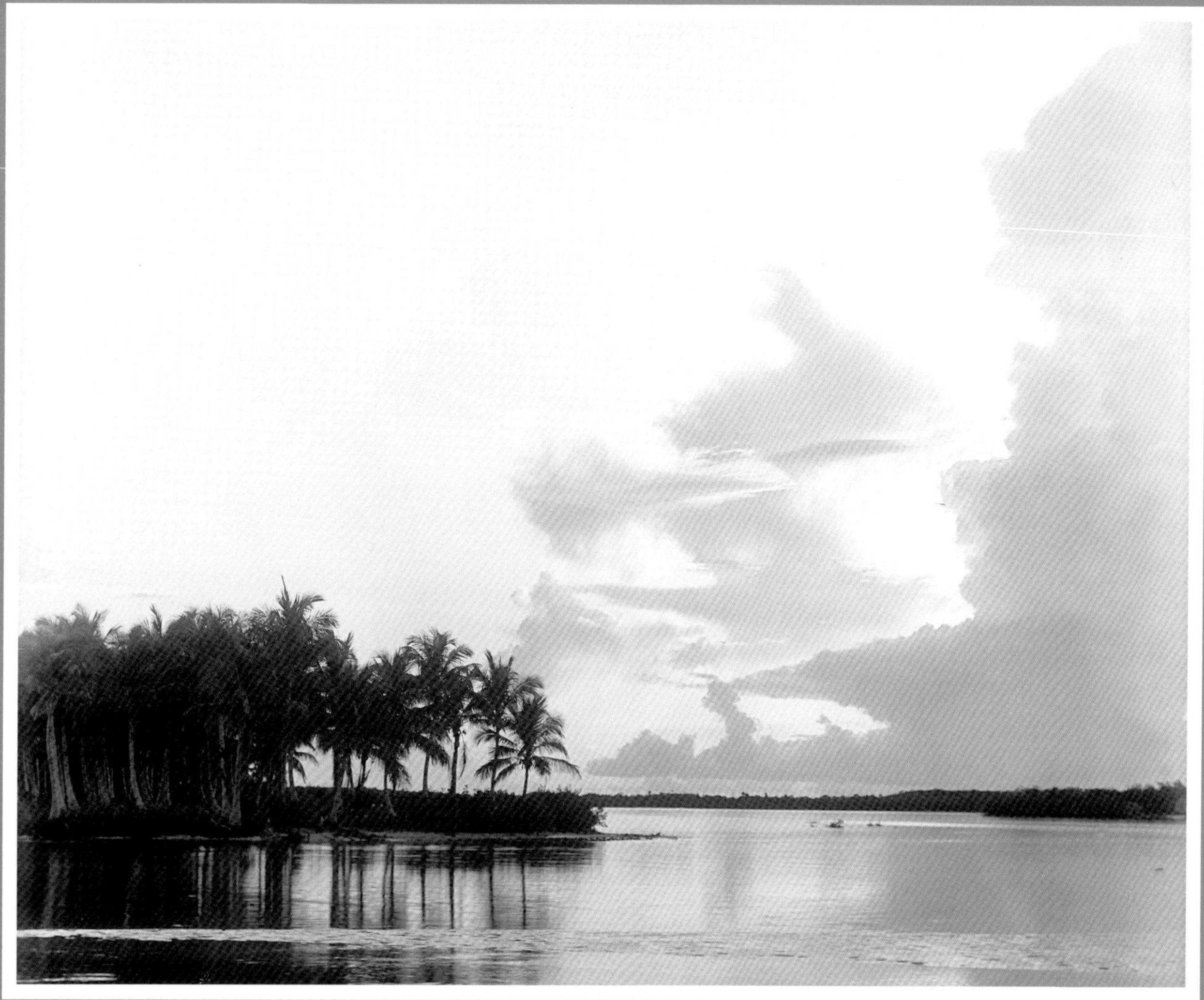

ENCHANTMENTS

Julian Dimock's Photographs of Southwest Florida

Jerald T. Milanich and Nina J. Root

University Press of Florida

Gainesville · Tallahassee · Tampa · Boca Raton
Pensacola · Orlando · Miami · Jacksonville · Ft. Myers · Sarasota

VIVA FLORIDA 500.
1513-2013
A Florida Quincentennial Book

Frontispiece: Over a three-year period (1904–7), Julian Dimock took four photographs of this same point of land on Marco Island. He labeled this one "Marco Palms—Sunset." The coconut palms probably were planted by William D. Collier. June 17, 1904; 48369.

All photographs courtesy of the Research Library, American Museum of Natural History, New York City.

Publication of this book was made possible in part by a grant from the Everglades Society for Historic Preservation.

EVERGLADES SOCIETY FOR HISTORIC PRESERVATION
Dedicated to our Unique History

Printed in China on acid-free paper

Book design by Louise OFarrell · This book may be available in an electronic edition.

18 17 16 15 14 13 6 5 4 3 2 1

Library of Congress Cataloging-in-Publication Data

Milanich, Jerald T.
Enchantments: Julian Dimock's photographs of Southwest Florida / Jerald T. Milanich and Nina J. Root.
p. cm.
Includes bibliographical references and index.
ISBN 978-0-8130-4928-1 (alk. paper)
1. Dimock, Julian A. (Julian Anthony), 1873–1945—Photograph collections.
2. Florida—Pictorial works. 3. Florida—Description and travel I. Root, Nina J. II. Title.
F312.M55 2013
975.90022'2—dc23
2013015085

University Press of Florida
15 Northwest 15th Street
Gainesville, FL 32611-2079
http://www.upf.com

The coast

the mainland

the in-between

no beginning

no end

only enchantments

CONTENTS

ENCHANTMENTS

Introduction

BETWEEN 1904 AND 1913, Julian Dimock and his father, A. W. Dimock, traveled through southwest Florida taking pictures and writing stories about their adventures. During those ten years, they made at least ten trips to the area, often spending several months at a time.

New York financiers who had been discredited by A. W.'s legal and financial problems, the Dimocks had left Wall Street for the wilds of Florida. Using Marco Island as their base, they motored and sailed the Gulf littoral in their houseboat, the *Irene*, on which they carried or towed a skiff, canoe, and small powerboat. Using the smaller craft, they traversed many of the rivers flowing into the Ten Thousand Islands. On occasion, they canoed well into the Everglades and the Big Cypress Swamp, twice going all the way to Miami. Julian and A. W. also traveled overland via oxcart and mule-drawn wagon to reach places like Deep Lake Plantation on the mainland. They frequently camped out, sometimes for days or weeks at a time. On all of these adventures, Julian used his cameras to take photographs.

When they were done, Julian Dimock had amassed nearly two thousand photographs of Florida, all on glass negatives. His photographs illustrated nearly eighty magazine and newspaper articles on Florida written by him and/or his father for *Collier's*, *Field and Stream*, *Harper's*, *Scribner's*, and other periodicals (a listing can be found at the end of this book). Some of the articles were reprinted in A. W.'s 1908 book *Florida Enchantments* (an expanded and revised edition was issued in 1915). A. W. also authored several books for young adults, including *Dick in the Everglades* (1909) and *Be Prepared, or the Boy Scouts in Florida* (1912). All of the books featured Julian's photographs. Julian also supplied photographs to magazines to illustrate articles written by others.

By the time A.W. died in 1918 at age seventy-six, Julian had married and moved to Vermont, where he had taken up farming (Julian died at seventy-three in 1945). In 1920, Julian gave his collection of exposed-glass plates to the American Museum of Natural History. Julian's photographs, especially when viewed in the context of the articles and books written by him and his father, provide an extraordinary record of southwest Florida in the early 1900s.

Southwest Florida in the First Decade of the Twentieth Century

Twentieth century? The words sound very modern. But in the spring of 1904, when A.W. and Julian Dimock traveled to Marco Island and began to amass their trove of photographs, the island lay on the southern edge of the United States' frontier. Following the Civil War, the frontier had crept down the Gulf coast until it hit the Ten Thousand Islands, an untamed, verdant labyrinth of mangroves, shell mounds, small islands, and innumerable streams. Settlements on Marco Island, at Henderson Creek just to the north on the mainland east of Rookery Bay, and at Everglades City (then known only as Everglade) to the south on Chokoloskee Bay marked the boundary between Anglo "civilization" to the north and the Ten Thousand Islands and the wetlands of the Big Cypress Swamp and the Everglades to the east. Farming and settling lands along the Caloosahatchee River, where Fort Myers was located, or on Marco Island was one thing; wresting a living from the Ten Thousand Islands was another.

In one sense, the Ten Thousand Islands were a barrier to further expansion down the Gulf coast. But they also were an "in-between," a region whose unique physiography separated Marco Island and the other islands and the mainland in and around Charlotte Harbor and Pine Island Sound in the north from the vast wetlands of the Big Cypress Swamp and the Everglades to the south and east. Those wetlands spread across south Florida from the Gulf coast to Miami and the nascent settlements on Florida's lower Atlantic coast. Far to the south, at the tip of the Florida Keys, lay the "metropolis" of Key West, south Florida's largest town. Key West's founding had leapfrogged the relatively unfriendly (to Anglos) Ten Thousand Islands and the wetlands of interior south Florida.

In a cultural sense, too, the Ten Thousand Islands were an "in-between." Anglos were living from Marco Island north along the Gulf coast, localities they had settled in the mid-nineteenth century or earlier, while the Big Cypress and the Everglades were home to Seminole Indians whose ancestors first had made their homes there in the nineteenth century. The Ten Thousand Islands themselves were sparsely populated.

A glance at the U.S. census from 1900 supports the contention that the frontier reached down the Gulf coast only to southwest Florida at the time the Dimocks were there. In that year, all of south Florida below Lake Okeechobee—then comprised of only three counties: Dade, Lee, and Monroe—had a total population of 26,000 people, of whom 18,000 were in Key West (Monroe County), 4,955 in Dade County, and 3,071 in Lee County, including fewer than 1,000 in Fort Myers. At the same time, Florida's total population was 528,000, while New York City held a whopping 3.44 million residents.

In 1900, southwest Florida was the sticks and Fort Myers was a frontier town, though its citizens probably would have contested that characterization. The Dimocks, on the other hand, would have agreed. In "A Summer Florida Vacation," a magazine article he published in July 1905, Julian wrote that though he loved Marco, if one wanted a newspaper, one had to go all the way to Sarasota, a town with regular railroad connections and other "superfluities of the modern day." Fort Myers apparently did not enter into his thinking as an outpost of civilization.

The Dimocks would discover that the Ten Thousand Islands, the "in-between," served as a common ground where Anglos and Seminole Indians came in contact with one another. At places like Storter's trading post and store in Everglades City at the north end of the Ten Thousand Islands, white settlers and tourists came face to face with Seminole Indians who brought hides, feathers, and other goods to sell and trade for the items they wanted. Otter pelts, buckskin, and alligator hides moved west; cloth, guns, ammunition, pails, ceramic jugs, and tobacco went back east; photographs of Seminoles Indians went back north.

Photographing Southwest Florida

It was at Storter's store in April 1905 that Julian Dimock and his father first met and photographed Seminole Indians. That initial meeting would lead to the Dimocks making forays into the Big Cypress and Everglades to document the Seminole people in their traditional camps. Sometimes they were guided, not always successfully, by local residents of Everglades City. Other times they employed Seminole Indian guides to lead them and introduce them to the native inhabitants of the Big Cypress and Everglades, people still smarting from the horrific attempts by the U.S. government and its armies to forcibly resettle them in Indian Territory west of the Mississippi River.

The Seminole Indians had not forgotten the wars of the 1830s and early 1840s and the mid-1850s, when federal and state troops had invaded interior south Florida. Understandably, the Seminoles remained extremely suspicious of white people like the Dimocks who traveled there, thinking they might be federal agents. It is a tribute to both the Seminoles and to Julian and A. W. that the latter were allowed to travel reasonably freely to Seminole camps and take photographs. As a consequence, Julian's photographs of Seminole Indians provide an unparalleled visual record of the Seminole people just prior to the time when the United States' frontier moved into southern Florida, bringing with it efforts to drain, ditch, and dike large portions of the area, altering the centuries-old water regime. A selection of those Seminole Indian photographs, each with Julian's information about the individuals depicted and the date and place each photograph was taken, can be found in our book *Hidden Seminoles: Julian Dimock's Historic Florida Photographs* (2011).

Julian not only used his camera to document the Seminole Indians; he also photographed white and African American people and their activities on Marco Island and at Henderson Creek and Deep Lake Plantation on the mainland. In the Ten Thousand Islands, he spent considerable effort photographing rookeries of the birds then being threatened by plume hunters. Several of his illustrated articles decried the slaughter of thousands of birds to satisfy the demands of haute couture in New York and Europe.

Julian also sought to record information about other southwest Florida animals, including manatees, alligators, and crocodiles. Mangroves and other plants caught his camera's eye as well. The most photographed resident of southwest Florida, however, one that Julian and his father spent literally months taking pictures of, was *Megalops atlanticus*, the Atlantic tarpon. To photograph a tarpon, one first had to catch the animal—not an easy task—and then wait for him to jump. Julian and his father both became expert tarpon fishermen, and Julian became an even more expert tarpon photographer, taking hundreds of shots of leaping tarpon and even writing magazine articles on how best to capture a tarpon in midleap. His father went one better. In 1911, he published *The Book of the Tarpon* (illustrated by Julian), which, a century later, is still in print and a favorite of anglers.

Julian was a gifted photographer whose father dubbed him "the camera-man." A. W., whose skill was writing, called himself "the scribe." His magazine articles and Julian's photographs together are an enchantment, a fascinating record of a time and place that still delights us today.

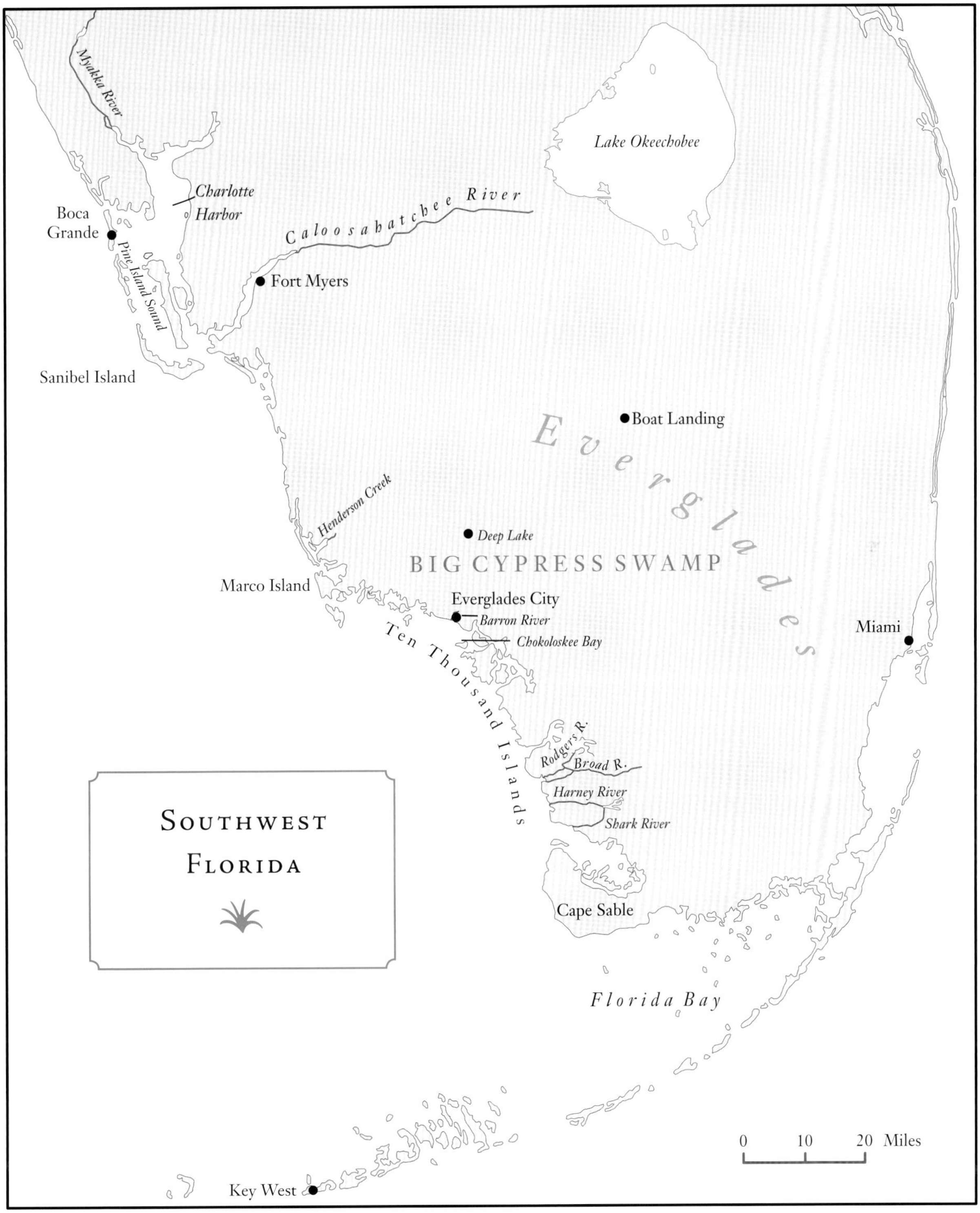
Southwest
Florida
Myakka River
Charlotte
Harbor
Boca
Grande
Pine Island Sound
Caloosahatchee River
Lake Okeechobee
Fort Myers
Sanibel Island
Boat Landing
Everglades
Henderson Creek
Deep Lake
BIG CYPRESS SWAMP
Marco Island
Everglades City
Barron River
Chokoloskee Bay
Ten Thousand Islands
Miami
Rodgers R.
Broad R.
Harney River
Shark River
Cape Sable
Florida Bay
0
10
20
Miles
Key West

Southwest Florida Travels

When Julian and A. W. Dimock traveled to southwest Florida, they apparently spent little or no time in Fort Myers, which was simply their jumping-off place for Marco Island and southwest Florida. To reach Fort Myers from their homes in New York, Julian and his father took a train or steamship to Jacksonville, then a train to Fort Myers. At Punta Rassa at the mouth of the Caloosahatchee River west of Fort Myers, they bought a ride on the mail boat that took them and their supplies—including Julian's cameras, tripod, boxes of glass plates, and chemicals needed for processing the plates—to Marco Island 40 miles south. The total cost of the round trip from New York to Marco and return was $71 (New York to Jacksonville and back, $50; train to Fort Myers and back to Jacksonville, $16; round-trip mail boat to Marco, $5). Still another alternative was to travel from New York to Key West by sea and then take a smaller boat to Marco Island, but the Dimocks clearly did not relish that itinerary, noting that the boats from Key West to Marco were home to hordes of cockroaches. They also preferred taking a steamship to Jacksonville because the trains from New York were uncomfortable and often hot. Either way, the transition from life in New York City to the Florida frontier must have been jarring at best.

On Marco Island, the Dimocks likely stayed at the twenty-room Marco Hotel, owned by William D. "Bill" Collier, that was located in the small settlement on the northern end of the island (known today as Old Marco Village). The Dimocks, however, nowhere provide information about their accommodations or what the village was like, and Julian did not take a single photograph in the village.

Julian's earliest photographs of southwest Florida are from late May 1904. That summer, he and his father apparently stayed on the island for two and a half months before returning north, a pattern that modern snowbirds, who prefer winters in Florida, might find perverse. During that time, they traveled around Marco Island and its nearby waters, probably in rented boats or with local residents, exploring, learning, and photographing. Returning to Marco in November and staying into February 1905, they traveled to the mainland, first to the small Henderson Creek settlement and then to Deep Lake Plantation in the Big Cypress Swamp. Julian, perhaps with his father, also traveled north to the St. Johns River Valley to photograph orange groves. Julian may have been on assignment for *Country Calendar* magazine, whose first issue would be published in 1905. It was about this time, late 1904, that the Dimocks decided to buy a boat so they could travel farther afield on their own.

The *Irene*, as they named their 37-foot houseboat, was well suited to the shallow waters of the coast. After hiring a captain who knew the local waters and one or two crew members (the latter called "boys" by the Dimocks), Julian and his father spent a month in April and May 1905 on a shakedown cruise through the Ten Thousand Islands and on down the coast past Cape Sable to Florida Bay. It was on that initial cruise that they first met Seminole Indians at Storter's store in Everglades City. From late May into June, they traveled north to Pine Island Sound and Charlotte Harbor and then returned to New York. They were back again in January 1906 and spent the first five months of the year largely aboard the *Irene* sailing the coast from Marco to Cape Sable with many stops in between in the Ten Thousand Islands.

In June and perhaps early July of that year, the Dimocks had the *Irene* retrofitted to better serve their needs. A larger tank for fresh water was added, along with a darkroom for Julian. To accommodate the darkroom, the cabin was enlarged by removing the *Irene*'s aft mast. By late July, the *Irene* was ready for a trip down into the Ten Thousand Islands.

Initially the plan was for the Dimocks, a local guide (Harrison), and two of the *Irene* "boys" to download a canoe, skiff, and the small motorboat from the *Irene* near the mouth of Rocky Creek in the Ten Thousand Islands north of Rodgers River. Then the motorboat was to tow the skiff and canoe up Rocky Creek until they reached a small seasonal Seminole camp they knew of. There they would leave the motorboat (which would be taken back to the *Irene* by some of the men), and the others would then paddle and pole their way east across the Everglades to Miami, photographing the Seminole Indians they met along the way.

As recounted in *Hidden Seminoles*, the plan went bad from the beginning. One of the *Irene* crew refused to go, and they replaced him with George Storter, owner of Storter's store at Everglades City. He apparently intended to guide them into Rocky Creek and return with the motorboat. When they could not find the Seminole camp, it was decided that the water in the Glades was deep enough to continue on east with the motorboat towing the other two craft. Several days later, they could see smoke from Miami. What they did not see, though, were any Seminole Indians. The Seminoles, unsure of the motives of the five white people, simply hid.

After spending a short time in Miami, the Dimocks and their companions boarded their craft and traveled southward from Miami, through the Upper Keys, then up the Gulf coast to Everglades City and on to Marco Island. The entire journey took less than two weeks.

In September, in search of more adventures and land and seascapes to photograph, Julian and A.W. sailed the *Irene* north to Pine Island Sound and Charlotte Harbor. They did some fishing and also went up (and back down) the Myakka River.

In May 1907, the Dimocks returned to Florida and continued their explorations of the coast. Intent on again crossing the Everglades, in mid-August they returned to Storter's store, where they hired Charley Tommy, a Seminole Indian, as a guide. Charley Tommy was well aware that it had been a dry year and that there was not enough water in some parts of the Everglades to float a canoe. Despite his admonitions, the two-canoe flotilla set out from Storter's south into the Ten Thousand Islands before turning east into the Everglades. Just as Charley Tommy had predicted, the expedition was forced to abort after several days when it became clear that the water was too shallow to allow them to reach Miami. Even so, with Charley Tommy as guide, the Dimocks were able to gain entry into several Seminole camps and take photographs.

Unable to move east, they instead went north to Brown's Boat Landing, a store near the boundary of the Big Cypress Swamp and the Everglades (about 35 miles southeast of present-day Immokalee). There Julian took more photographs of Seminole Indians.

Bidding adieu to Charley Tommy and a man from Everglades City who had accompanied them, the Dimocks rented oxen and a cart from William Brown, owner and operator of Boat Landing, and, guided by Brown's adult son Frank, loaded up their two canoes and equipment and traveled overland to the Caloosahatchee River several days to the north. Once there, they took leave of Frank Brown and the oxen, put their canoes in the river, and paddled back to Marco Island.

Early June 1908 saw the Dimocks back at Marco Island, again engaged in fishing and photography expeditions up and down the coast aboard the *Irene*. For the next three months, they traveled from Boca Grande down through the Ten Thousand Islands and back to Marco. At that point, they had spent a total of more than twenty-five months in southwest Florida.

The Dimocks did not return to Florida again until February 1910, and then they did not travel to Marco Island. Instead, a month was spent photographing truck farms and the citrus industry in north central and east Florida, around McIntosh, Lake Weir, Ocala, Sanford, and Cocoa (it is not certain that A.W. was with Julian). During the month, Julian traveled south from Cocoa to Fort Lauderdale and perhaps farther south before turning back north into central Florida. Using photographs of the farms and groves that he had visited, Julian wrote four articles for *Country Life in America* that appeared between November 1910 and February 1911. Some of the published photographs were colorized.

Later that year, Julian was persuaded by the anthropologist Alanson Skinner to accompany him as photographer on an American Museum of Natural History expedition to southern Florida to make collections of Seminole Indian items for the museum. That expedition resulted in Julian's accumulating a collection of photographs, some showing Seminole people wearing or using clothing and other items that Skinner collected. Today, both the photographs and the objects, all well documented, are curated at the American Museum of Natural History, where some of the objects are on display in the Hall of North American Indians.

A. W. (whose first wife had died in 1901 and who remarried in 1909) and Julian would return to southwest Florida in mid-August 1913 with a small entourage that may have included their spouses. A. W., apparently wanting to impress some of his fellow members of the Camp Fire Club with the fishing amenities southwest Florida offered, invited William E. Coffin (president of the New York–based Camp Fire Club of which both Dimocks were members) and Gifford Pinchot (first chief of the United States Forest Service and governor of Pennsylvania in the 1920s and again in the 1930s and also a club member) along on the trip. Also with the Dimocks was Gilbert C. Demorest, a teenager whose father, William C., was a magazine publisher in New York and a club member.

The Dimocks and their guests took the train to Fort Myers, where a large houseboat—the *Kennesaw*—was rented to transport the group up and down the coast for a month. Julian again took photographs, the last he would take in Florida, and this time he also brought along a movie camera (though the whereabouts of any movies he made are not known). Five of the photographs he took of the men fishing were featured in an article in the *New York Times* on Sunday, February 1, 1914 ("Tarpon Fishing in Florida Waters Told in Pictures").

By 1913, the frontier had caught up to Fort Myers. Since 1900, its population had more than doubled to around 2,900 people, and Lee County held about 6,600 residents. The Ten Thousand Islands, however, remained largely unpopulated. Across the interior of south Florida, the Seminole Indians continued to live in a number of small settlements. Through their growing interactions with the outside world, the Seminoles were laying the groundwork for the relative prosperity they would earn later in the twentieth century.

Julian Dimock's photographs provide a valuable record of people and places that enables us to better understand and value our collective past and to appreciate southwest Florida's natural history.

How This Project Came to Be

Prior to 1978, Julian's glass-plate negatives were kept by the American Museum of Natural History's General Service Department. In that year, they were transferred to the museum's Research Library, where Nina Root, director, "discovered" them. Over the years, as time permitted, she became familiar with the thousands of images, and in August 1996 she published "Legacy of a Reluctant 'Camera Man'" in *Natural History* magazine, a project that led to the book *Camera Man's Journey: Julian Dimock's South* (2002), edited by her and Thomas L. Johnson.

In 2007, Root invited Milanich to join her in research on Julian's images from Florida, a collaboration that resulted in the book *Hidden Seminoles: Julian Dimock's Historic Florida Photographs* (2011) and this volume.

All of the photographs reproduced here are used courtesy of the Research Library, American Museum of Natural History, New York City. For each image, the date the photograph was taken and the Research Library image number are noted. Information on the Research Library and how to obtain copies of these and other photographs from the library's collections can be found at: http://library.amnh.org/special-collections/photograph-collection.

The Coast

Traveling with *Irene*

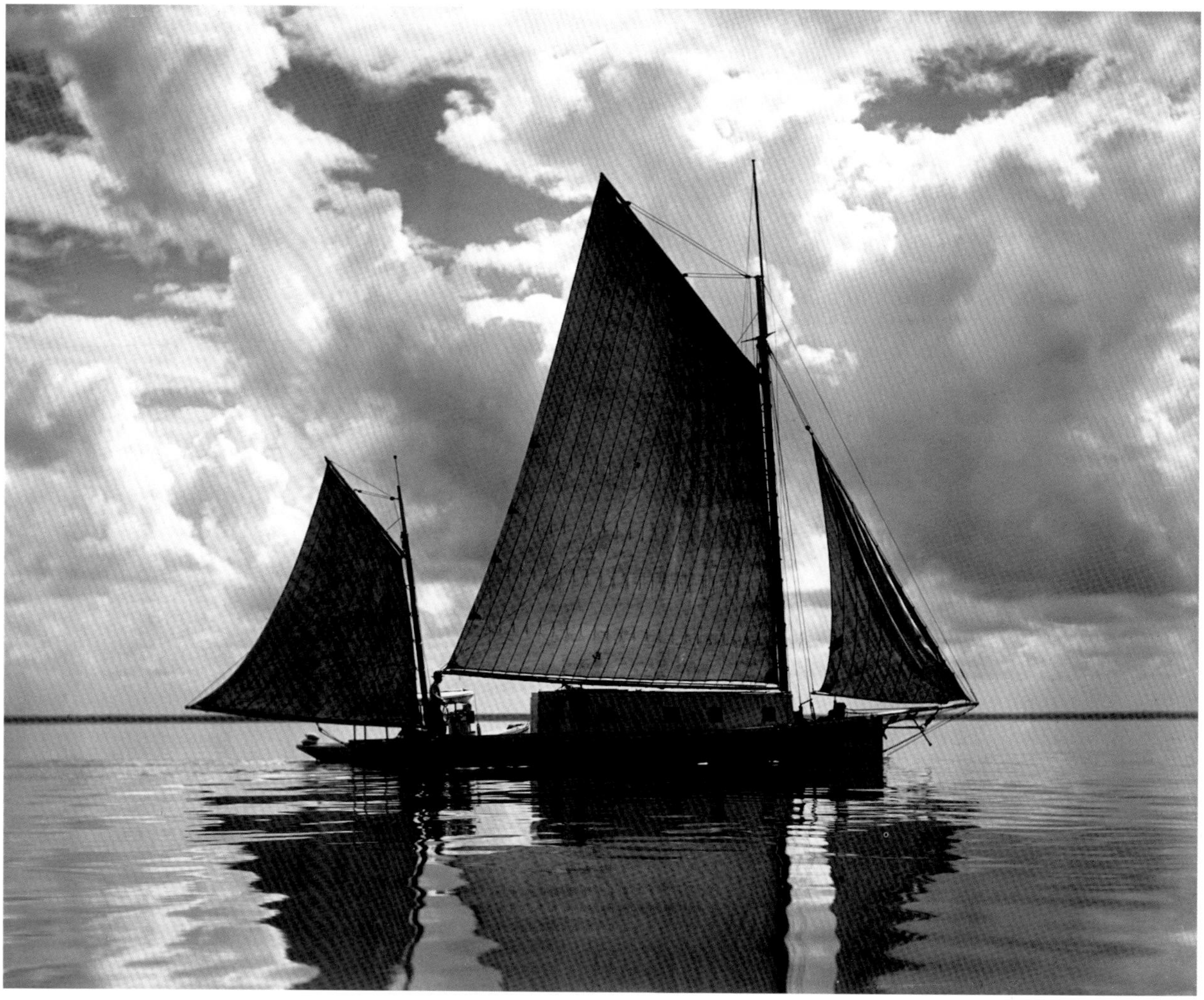

In early 1905, the Dimocks purchased the *Irene*, an 18-ton, 37-foot houseboat. The 14-foot-wide flat-bottomed craft with its 3-foot draft was well suited to the shallow inland waters of the coast. On their initial voyage from mid-April into early May 1905, they took the *Irene* south from Marco Island to Florida Bay at the southernmost tip of peninsular Florida. From late May into June, they explored Charlotte Harbor and Pine Island Sound. During the first five months of 1906, they again traveled the Ten Thousand Islands. Here the *Irene* is under way in the Gulf of Mexico off the Ten Thousand Islands. April 11, 1906; 48485.

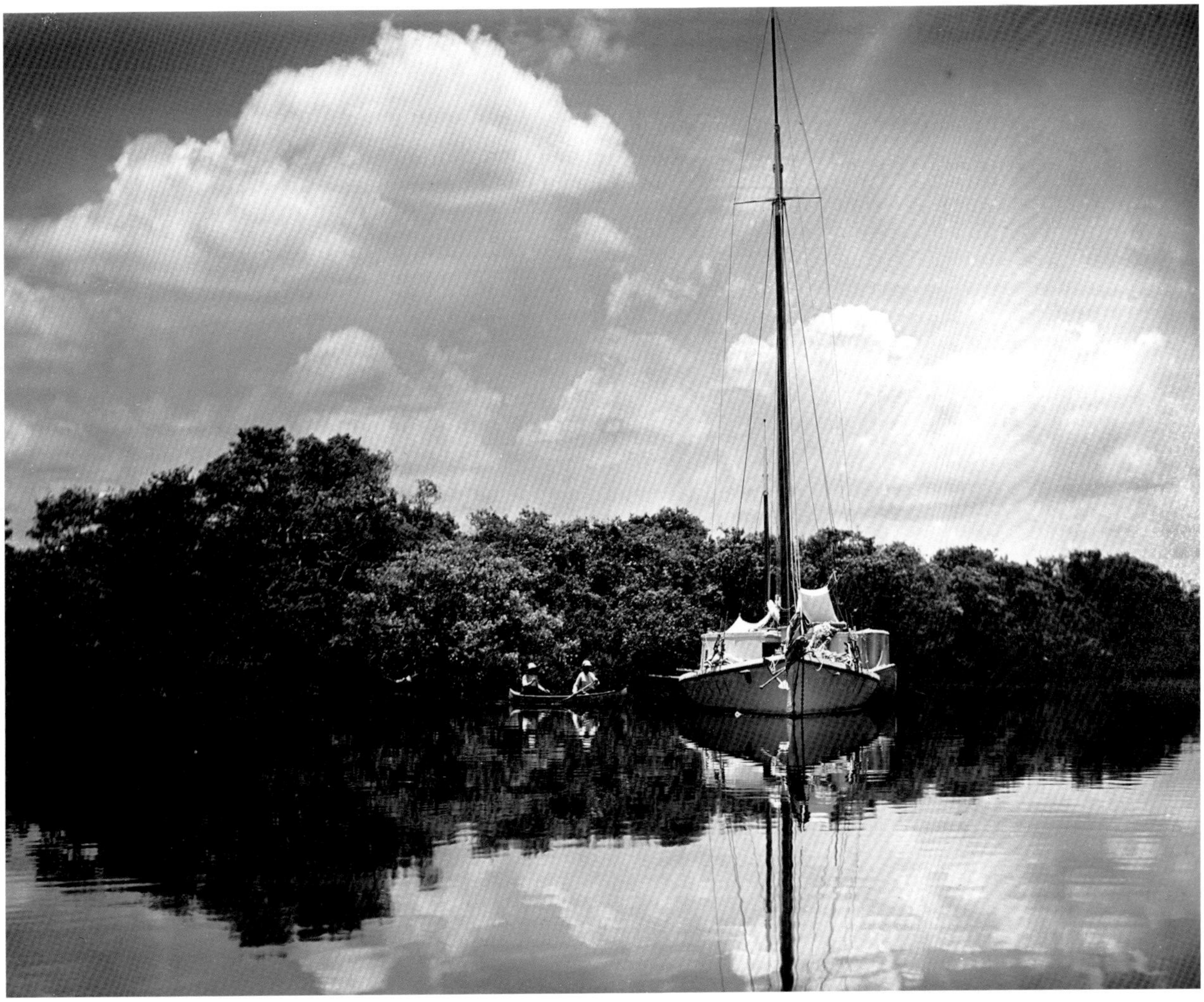

On the deck of the *Irene*, the Dimocks carried a small motorboat, a canoe, and a skiff (rowboat) or a second canoe. The smaller craft were used in waters that were too shallow for the *Irene* or where they simply wanted to use a smaller and quieter mode of transportation, such as on the Harney River in the Ten Thousand Islands, shown here. They also used the smaller craft for fishing. Their scenic adventures provided Julian and his father with inspiration for nearly eighty magazine articles and several books. May 30, 1906; 48384.

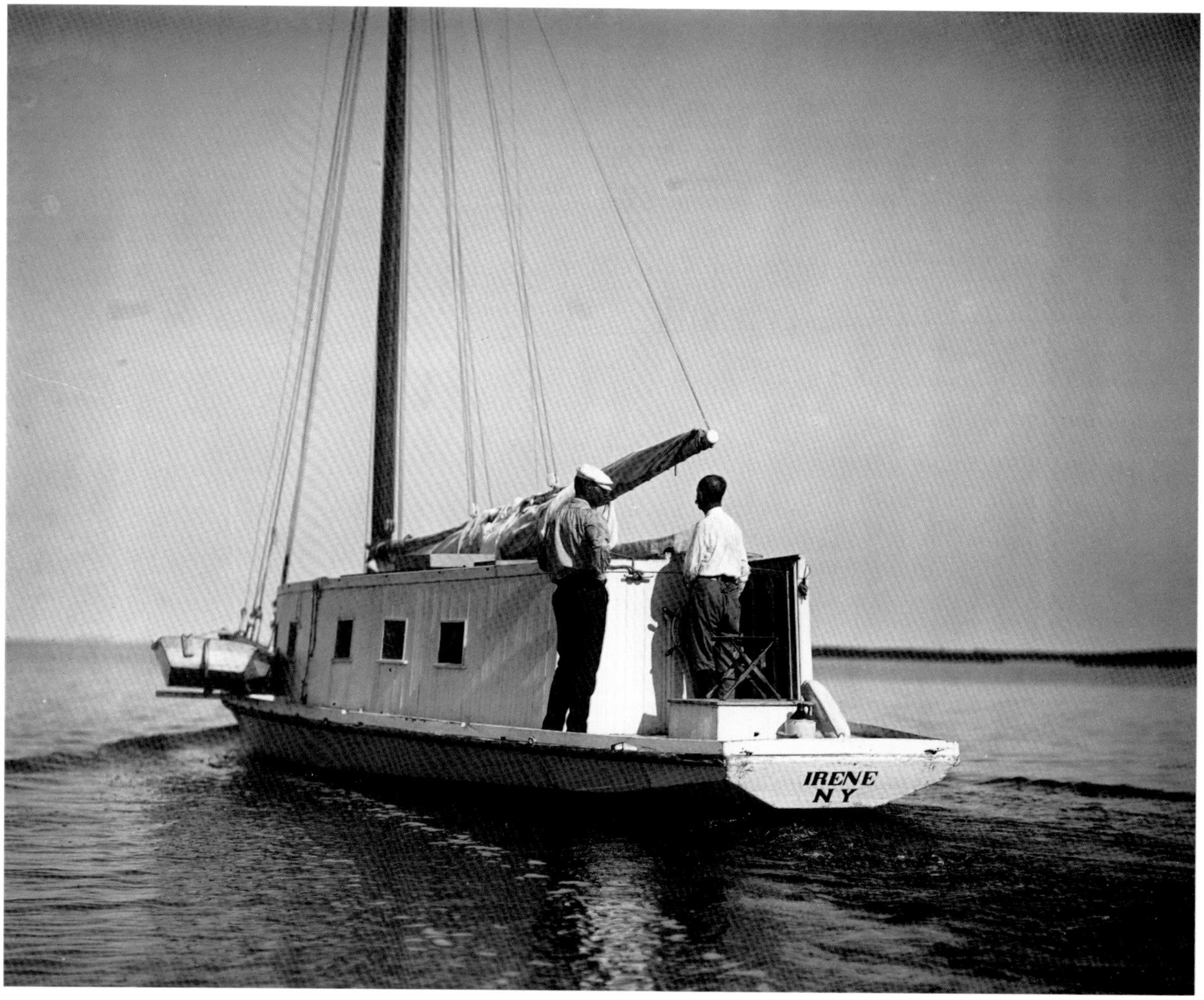

About a year and a half after buying the *Irene*, the Dimocks removed the aft jigger mast and enlarged the cabin, making space for a 200-gallon freshwater storage tank, an auxiliary engine, and a photography darkroom. They regularly employed two local men as ship hands and guides. In this photograph taken near Coon Key southeast of Marco Island, A. W. Dimock is on the right and one of the hired hands, probably the *Irene*'s captain, is on the left. September 16, 1906; 48489.

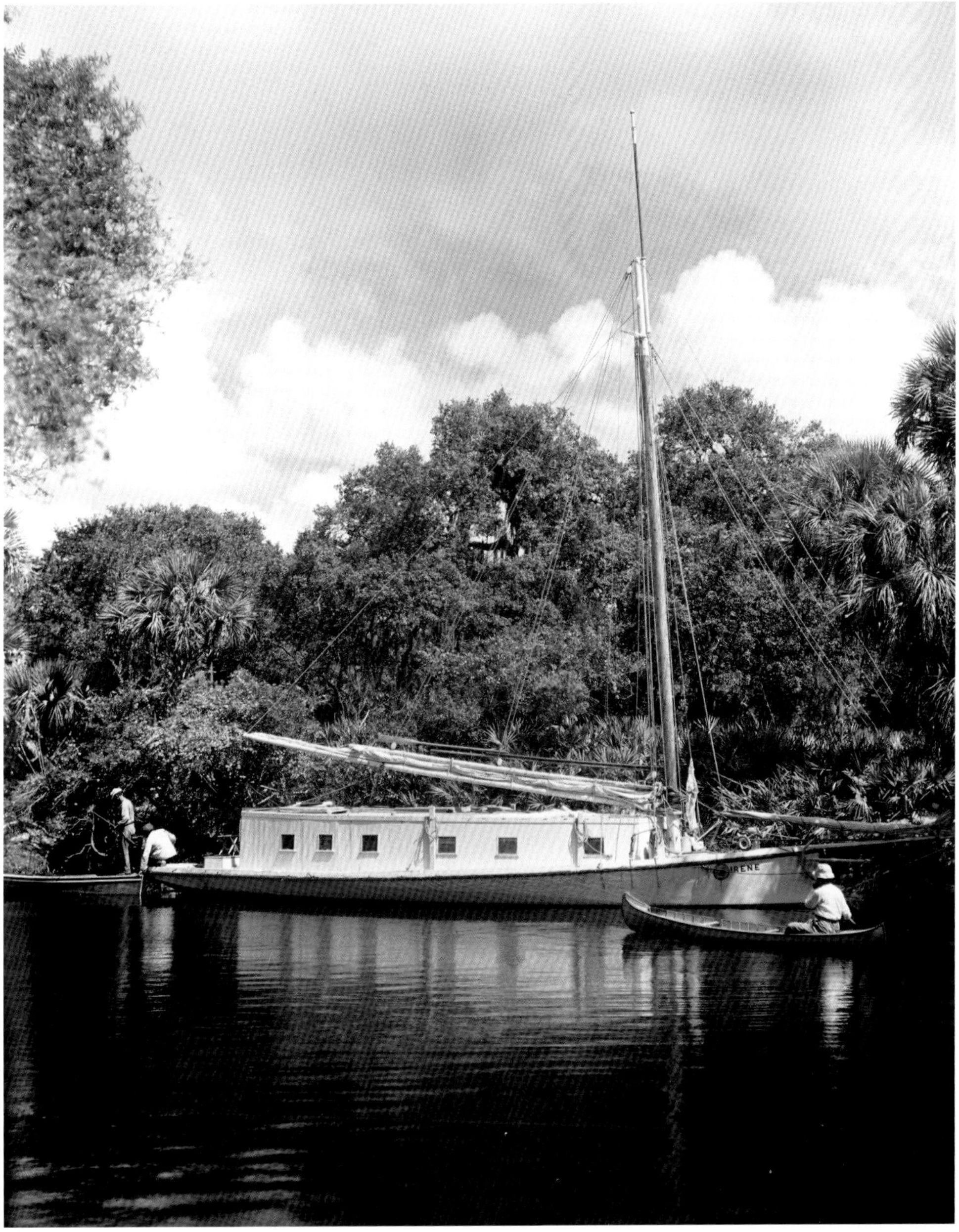

In September 1906, the Dimocks sailed north into Pine Island Sound and Charlotte Harbor, then continued up the Myakka River. When overhanging tree limbs prevented them from going farther upriver, they anchored the *Irene*, unloaded a canoe and the small motorboat, and continued upstream. The Dimocks' exploration of the river is recorded in an article by A. W. published in 1907, "An Overlooked River in Florida." September 23, 1906; 48404.

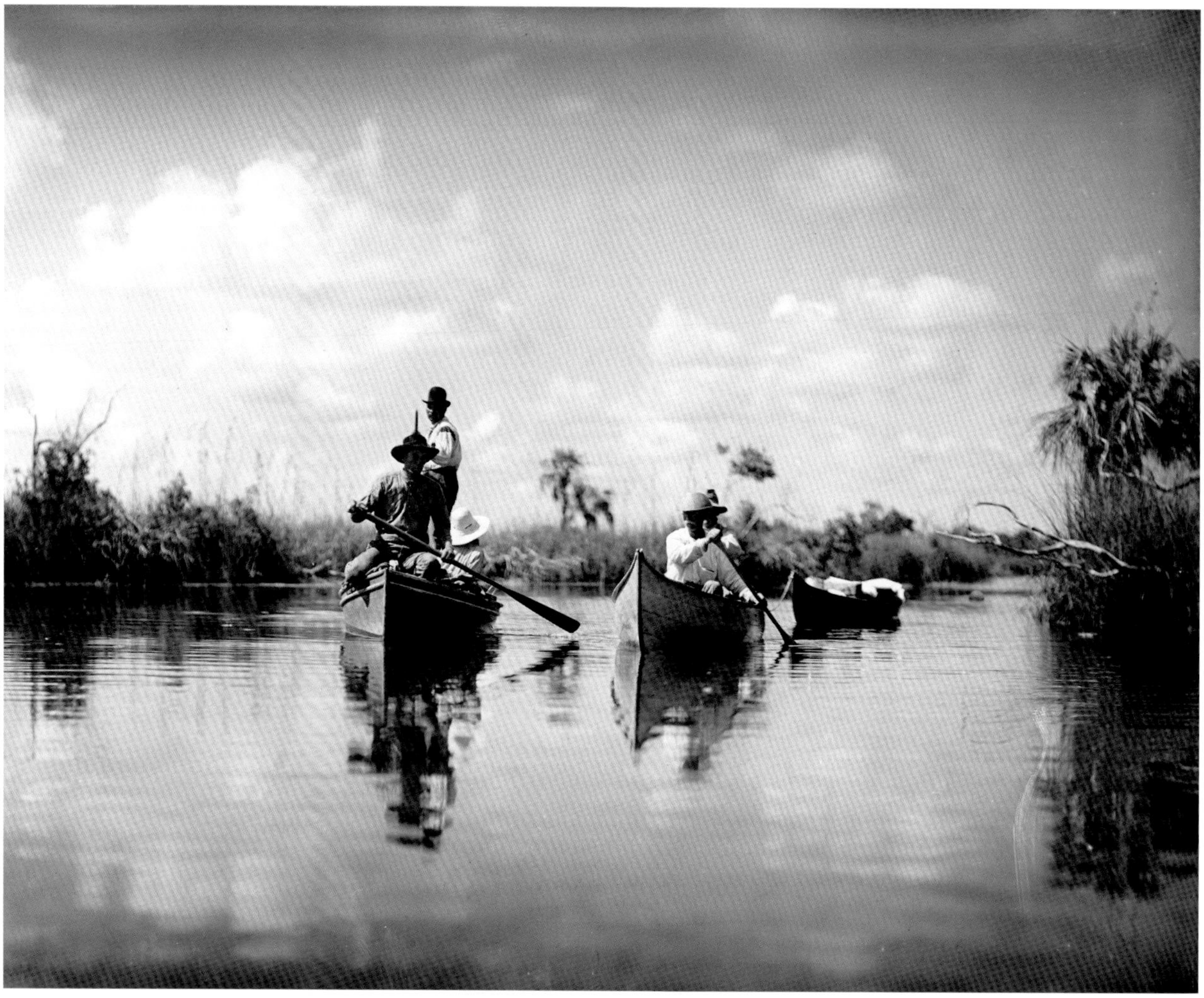

In August 1907 with Charley Tommy, a Seminole Indian man, as their guide (*standing on left*), the Dimocks planned to use canoes to cross the Everglades from the Ten Thousand Islands to Miami. They took the *Irene* south from Marco Island into the Ten Thousand Islands, anchored, and unloaded the small craft. The motorboat towed the canoes up Rocky Creek (*shown here*) as far as possible, and then the Dimocks set out to the east. The two crewmen from the *Irene* took the motorboat back to the houseboat and returned to Marco Island. Just as Charley Tommy had warned them, the Everglades were too dry to traverse even in canoes, and the expedition was abandoned nine days later. August 12, 1907; 48367.

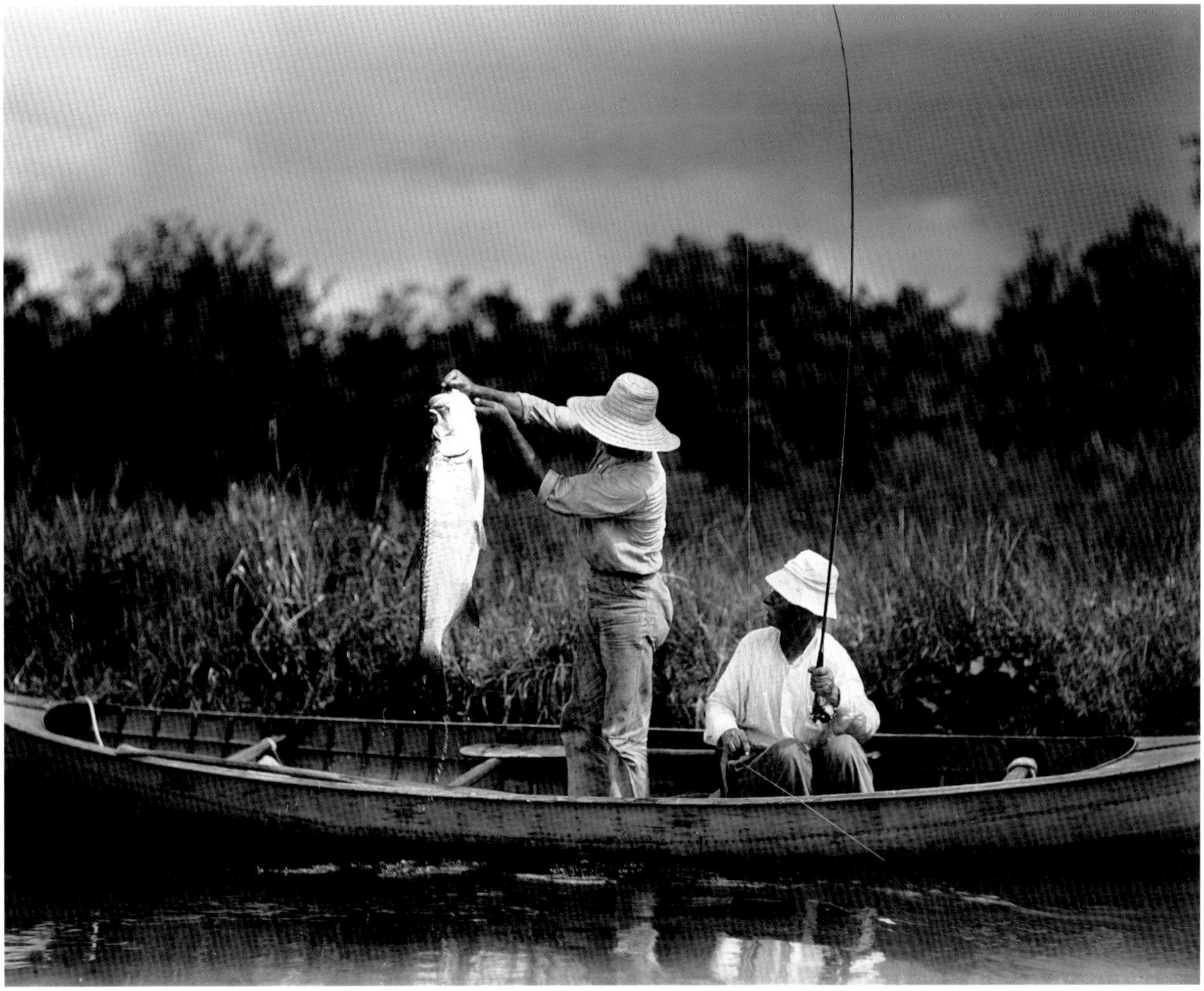

The Dimocks first experienced tarpon fishing while on the Homosassa River (on the Gulf coast about 165 miles north of Fort Myers) at least several years prior to 1904. A. W. took to the sport like a duck to water. *The Book of the Tarpon*, which he published in 1911 with ninety-three of Julian's photographs, is a classic on the subject and is still in print today. Julian, in his own book, *Outdoor Photography*, and in a 1907 article, "Photographing Tarpon," explains how one photographs leaping tarpon (the answer is: it's not easy). In all, Julian took almost five hundred photographs of tarpon fishing. Together father and son provided the standard references for catching and photographing Florida tarpon. This tarpon was caught with a fly rod from a canoe on Barron River (then called Allen's River) in the Ten Thousand Islands. September 5, 1908, 47394.

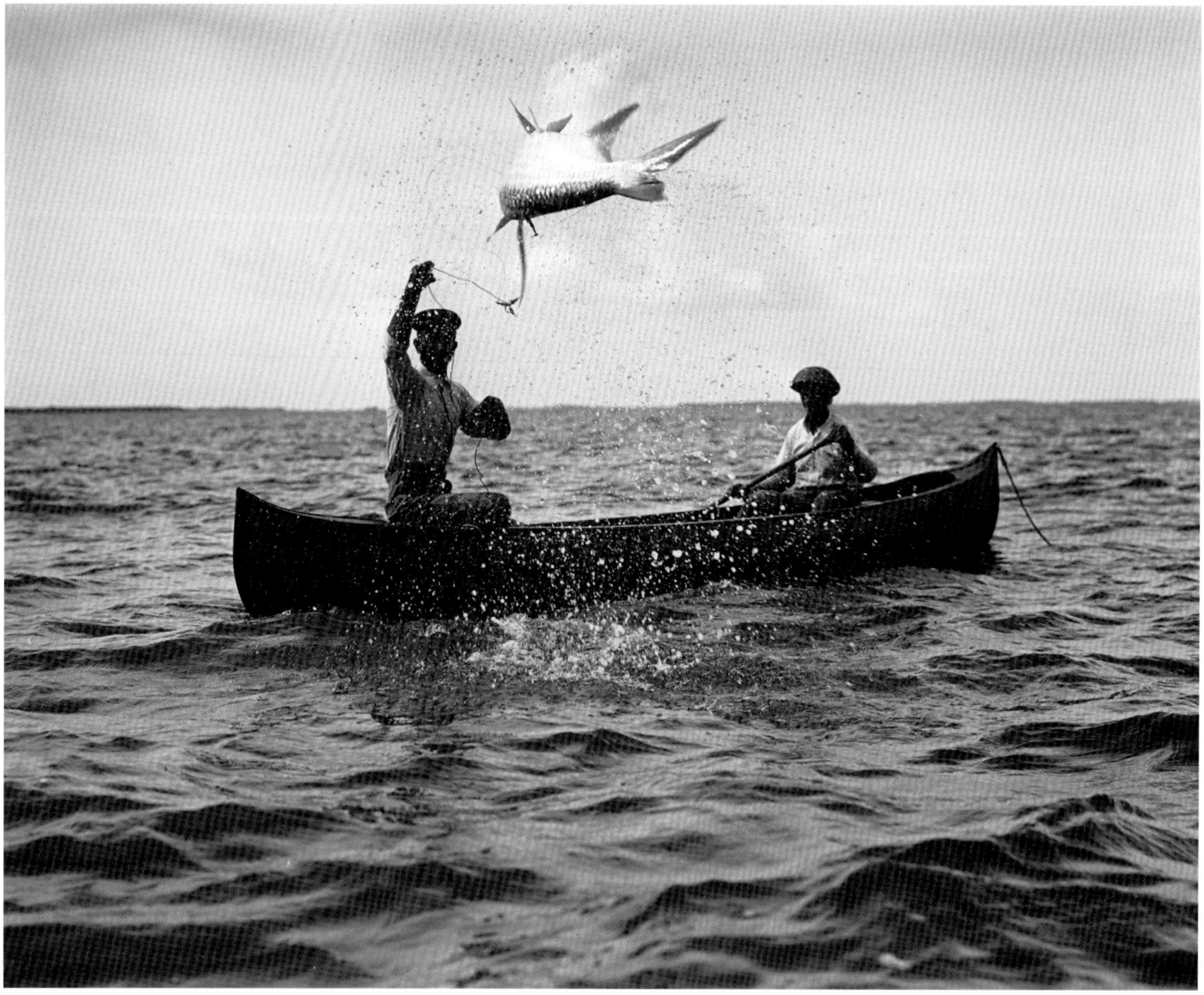

Aboard the *Irene*, the Dimocks set out on numerous fishing expeditions. One trip in the summer of 1908, when Julian perfected his technique for photographing tarpon in midleap, lasted for fifty-two days. On that outing, as reported in A. W.'s *Book of the Tarpon*, they fished from Boca Grande to Barron River in the Ten Thousand Islands. Along the way, they caught 334 tarpon, all from a canoe. Sixty-three were caught on an 8-ounce fly rod; some were caught with hand lines. The best fishing locales were: Boca Grande (84 tarpon in 15 days); Captiva Pass (66 in 14 days); and the Caloosahatchee River (35 in 5 days). A. W. wrote that the only reason they quit fishing was that Julian had exhausted his supply of glass negatives. This spectacular shot of *Irene*'s captain catching a tarpon on a hand line was taken off Boca Grande. It was used as the cover shot for *The Book of the Tarpon*. July 12, 1908; 47093.

Marco Island

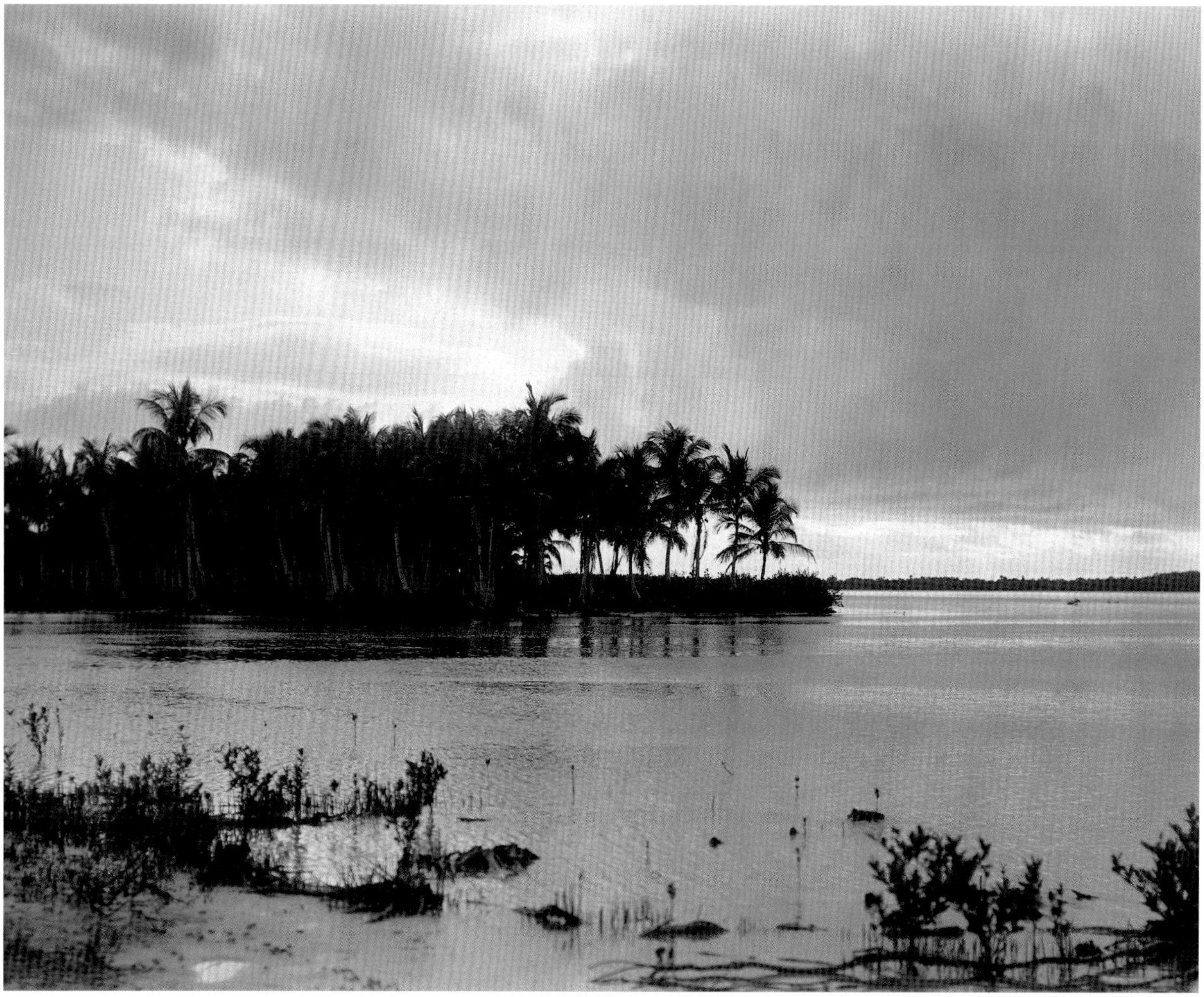

Julian Dimock took photographs of this point of land on Marco Island several times over a three-year period. He must have found it particularly scenic. This image, which he labeled "Cocoa Palms and Clouds," was used as an illustration in an article, "The Passing of a Wilderness," published by his father in 1907 in *Scribner's Magazine*. The legend for the published photograph reads, "Marco Point, Proposed site of a fashionable hotel." Most likely A.W. Dimock was referring to plans expressed by William D. "Bill" Collier, one of the island's well-known entrepreneurs and owner of the Marco Hotel established in 1896. The photograph used as this book's frontispiece was taken on the same day as this one. June 17, 1904; 48376.

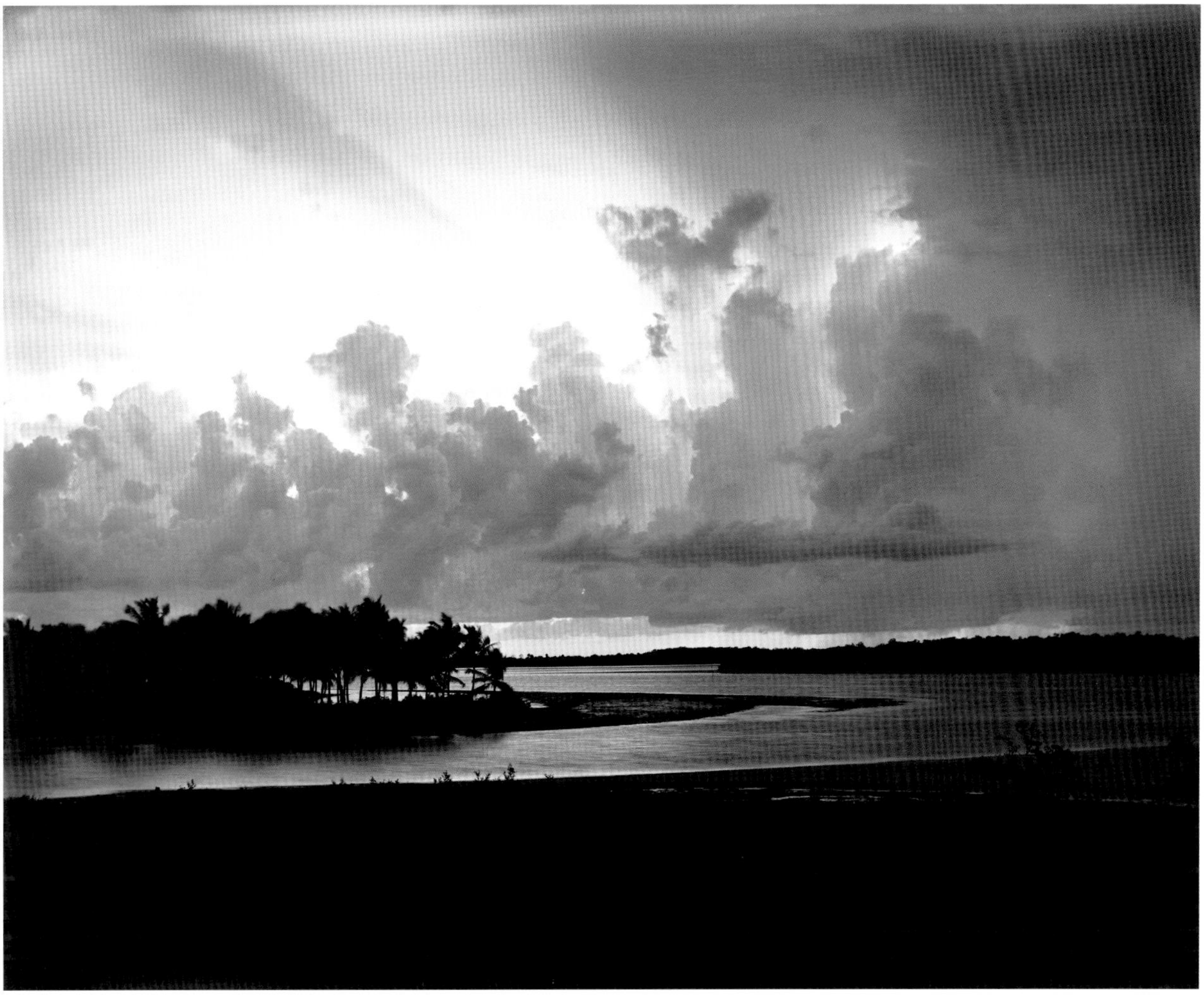

A third photograph of the point taken a month later. This one Julian Dimock called "Sunset." In 1908, his father used it as an illustration for his article "Yachting in a Canoe." The photograph, according to the article, showed the view from Marco's "piazza," suggesting that one could see the point of land and its palms from Marco Village looking north across Collier Creek, the entrance to Collier Bay. The coconut palms may well be a grove Collier had planted in the late nineteenth century. Julian Dimock's fourth photograph of the point, taken three years after this one, looks much the same as the other three; in that 1907 photograph, no construction is apparent on the point. July 24, 1904: 48374.

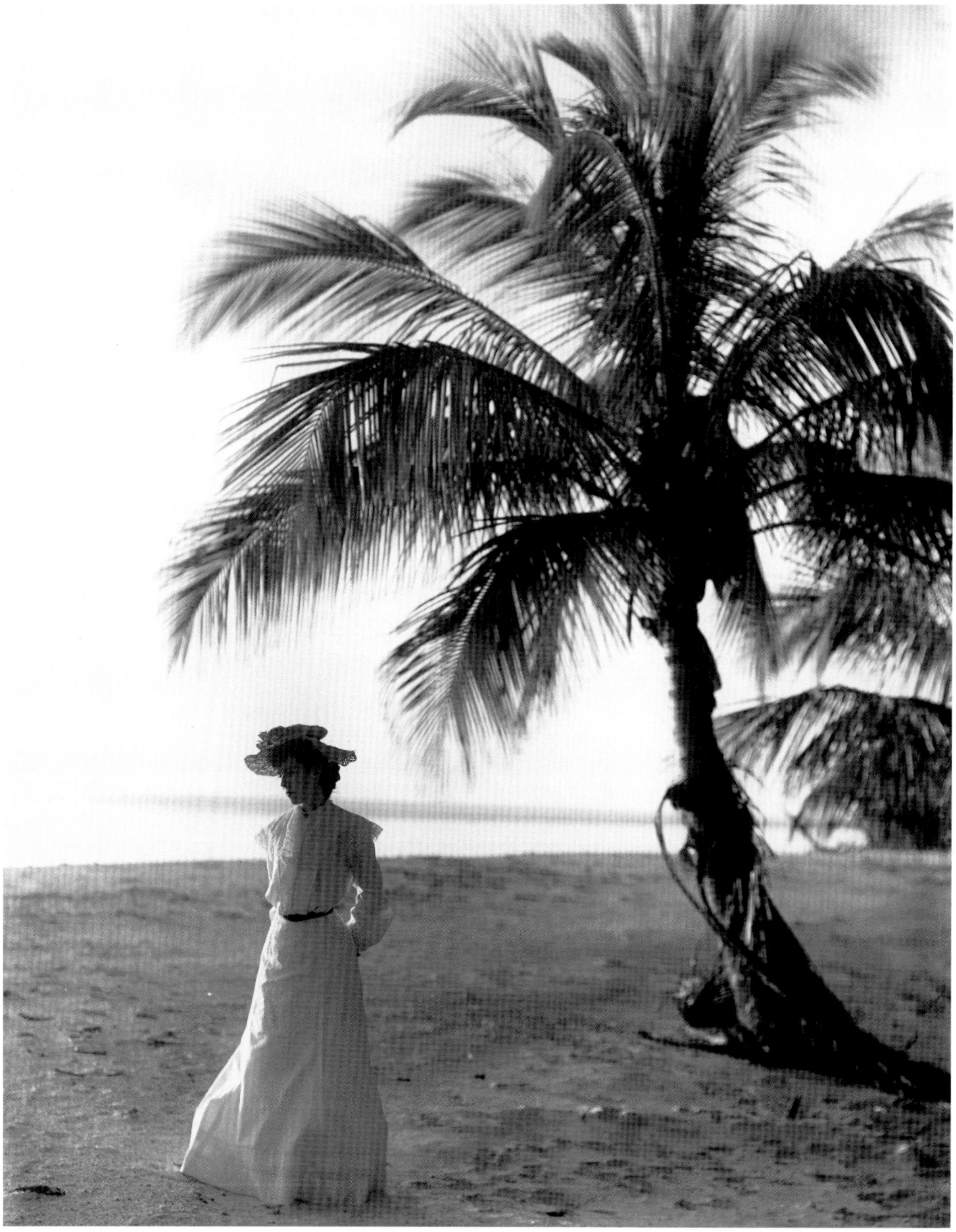

"Lonesome on Christmas Day," Marco Island. The woman shown here is not identified, though she is likely Julian's sister, Mabel, who appears in other of his photographs. December 25, 1904; 48479.

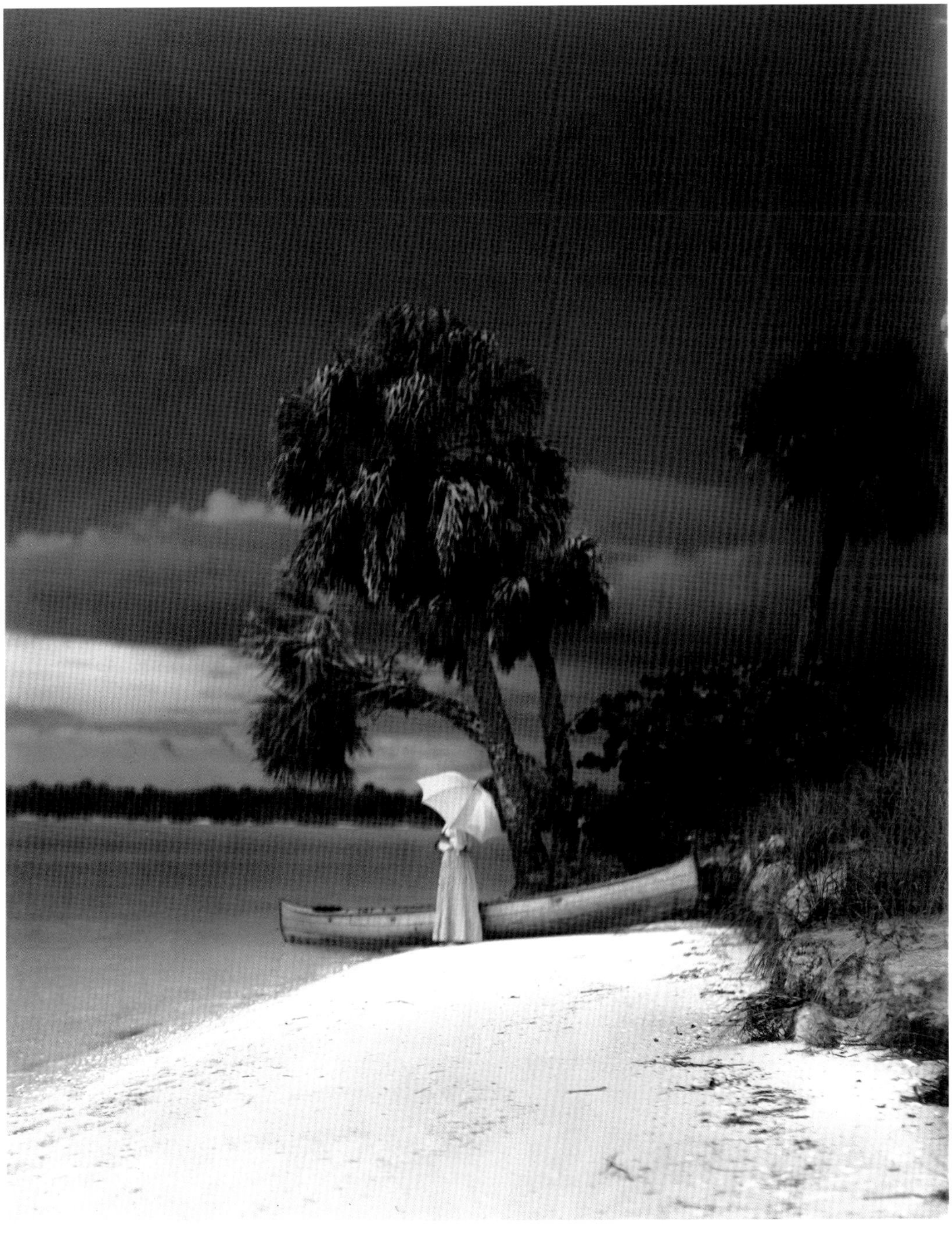

Mabel, Julian's older sister, sometimes came to Marco Island with her father and brother. A. W. referred to her as "the girl." August 14, 1908; 48530.

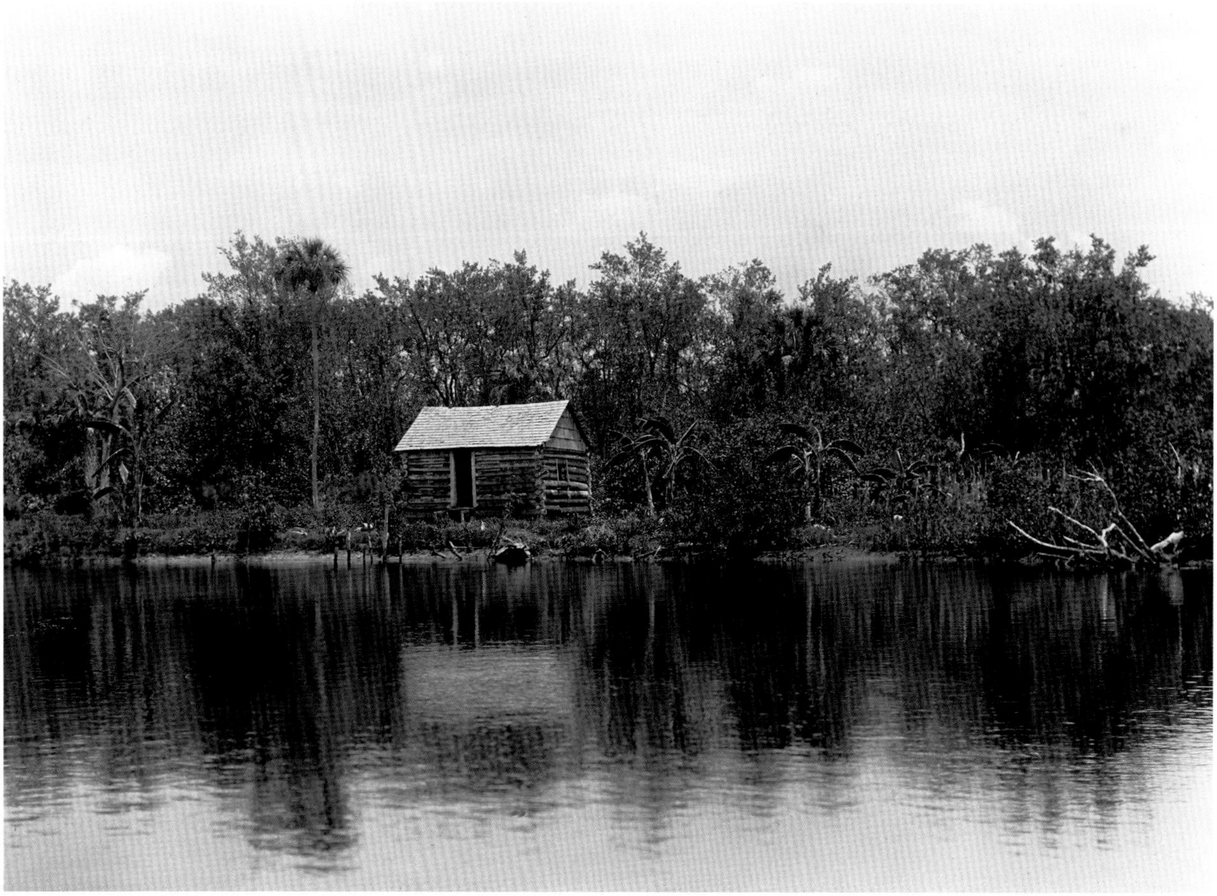

A "Crackers House," as Julian Dimock labeled it, either on Marco Island or on the mainland nearby. July 16, 1904; 48372.

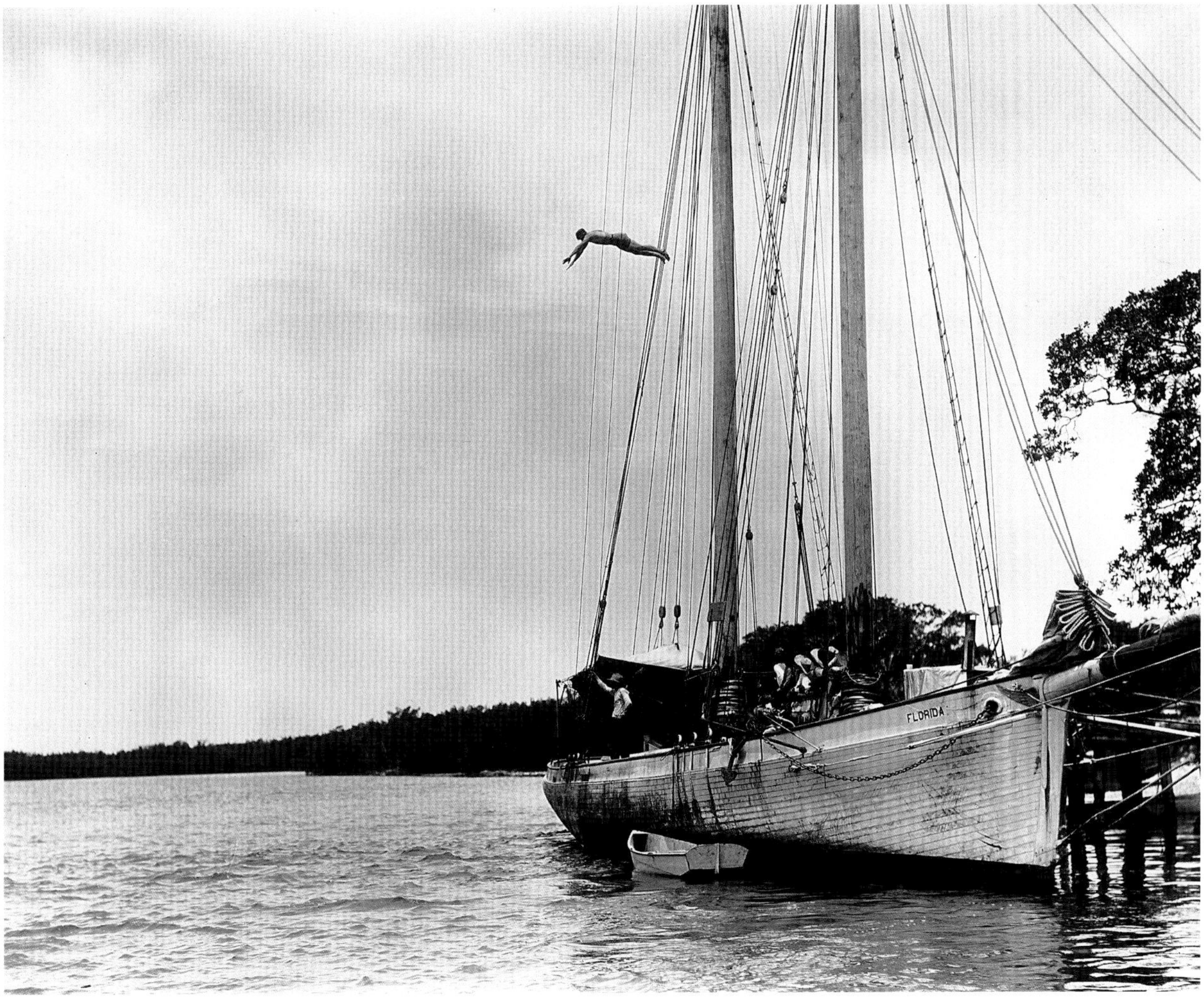

In "A Florida Family's Picnic," a chapter in *Florida Enchantments*, A.W. wrote that the diving boy was the son of the owner of a "Northern boat" tied up at the wharf at Caxambas. A.W. went on to say that on his first dive, the young man "ran fifty feet up the rigging to the cross-trees like a cat" before launching himself into space. On his second dive, "he again sprang far out, this time holding his body horizontally as he fell, until near the surface when he turned a quick somersault and plunged headfirst" into the water. The boat is almost certainly the *Florida*, a 49-foot sailing vessel out of Chatham, Massachusetts. July 1, 1904; 43871.

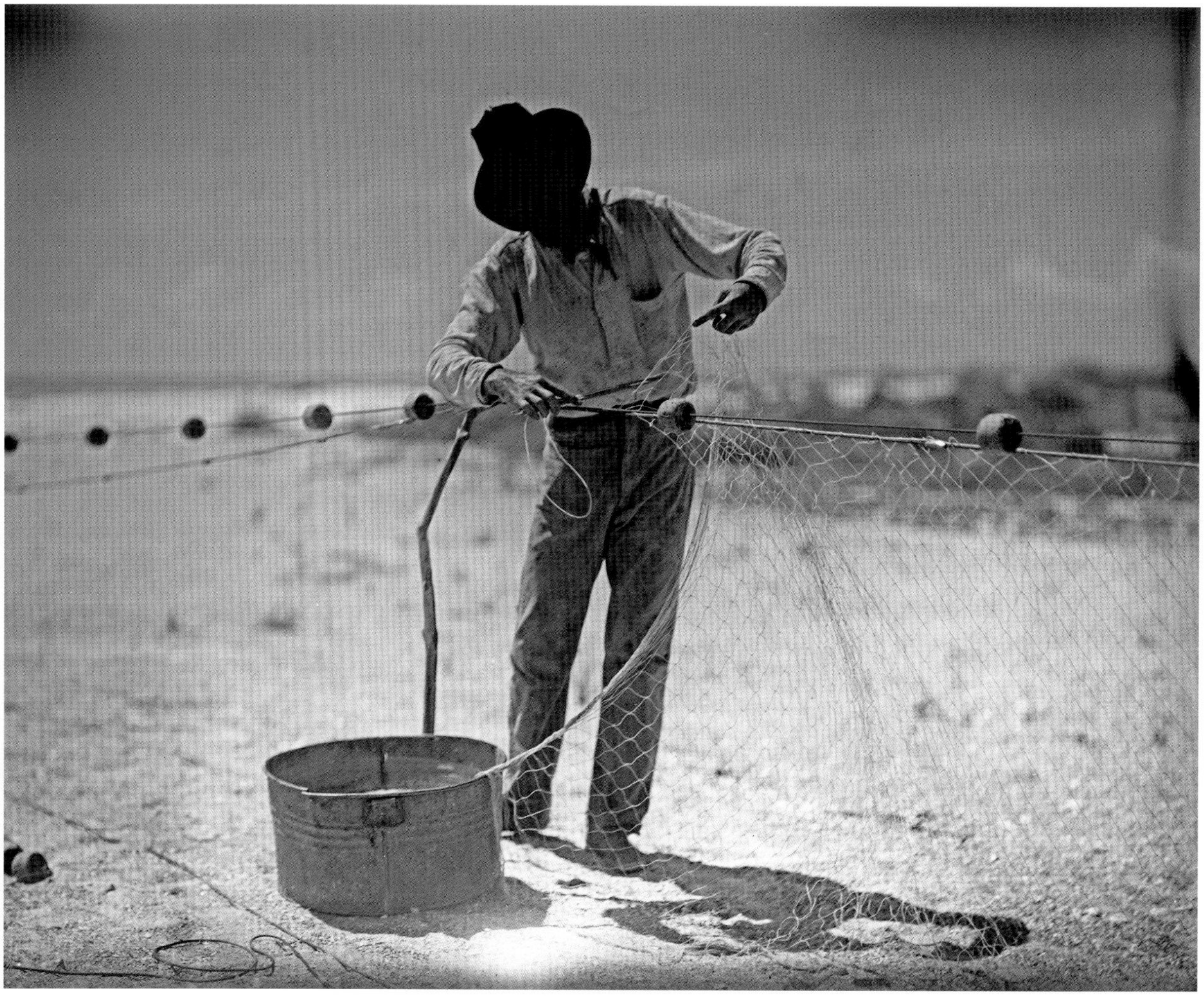

"Hanging Seine" on Little Marco Island north of Marco Island proper in Rookery Bay. At the time the island faced the Gulf of Mexico, but in recent times a sand bar has formed between the island and the Gulf. Fisherman once used nets to catch the runs of mullet along the (then) beach side of the island. July 23, 1907, 48861.

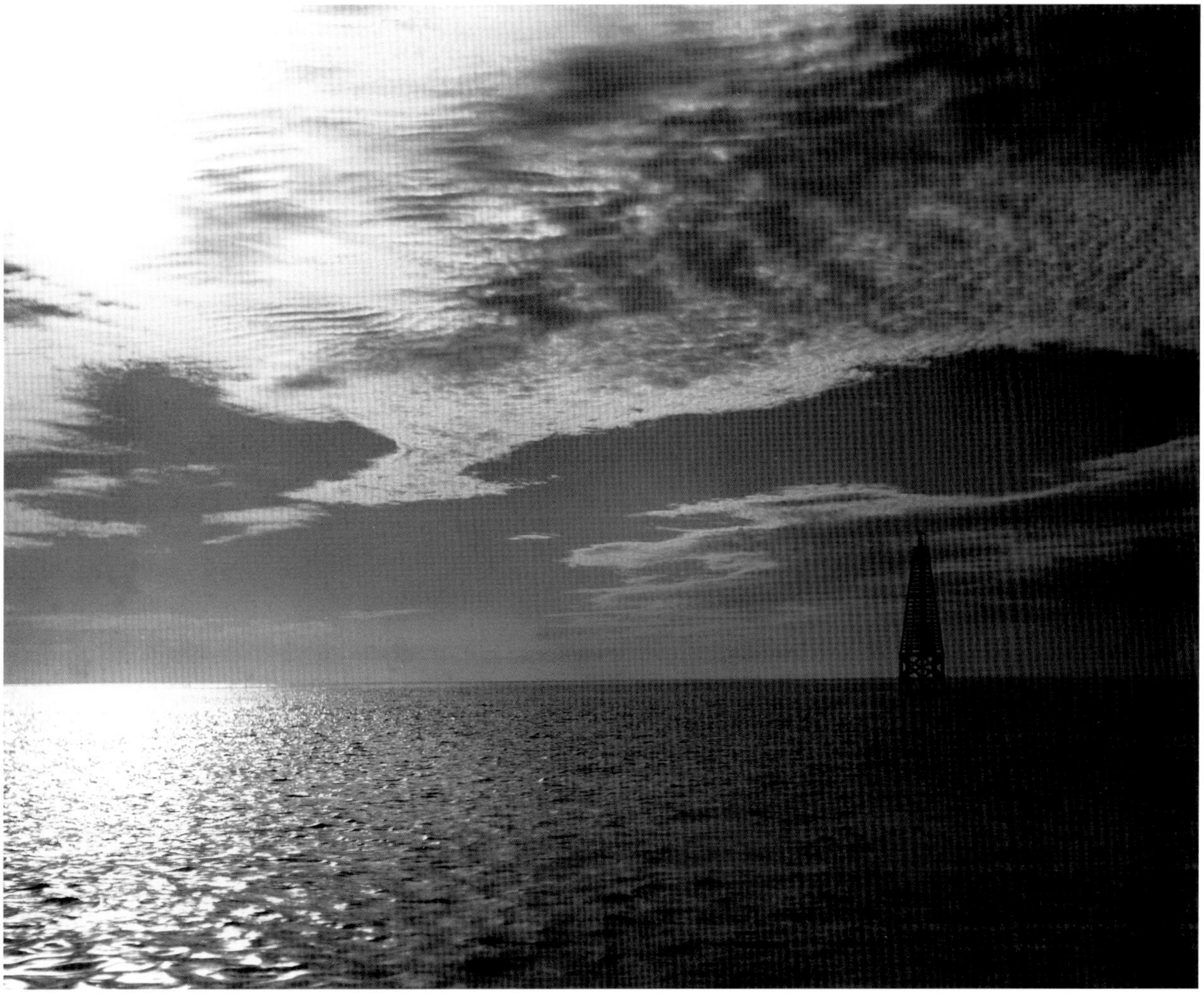

A navigation beacon off Marco Island. The lamp probably was fueled by oil.
November 15, 1904; 48470.

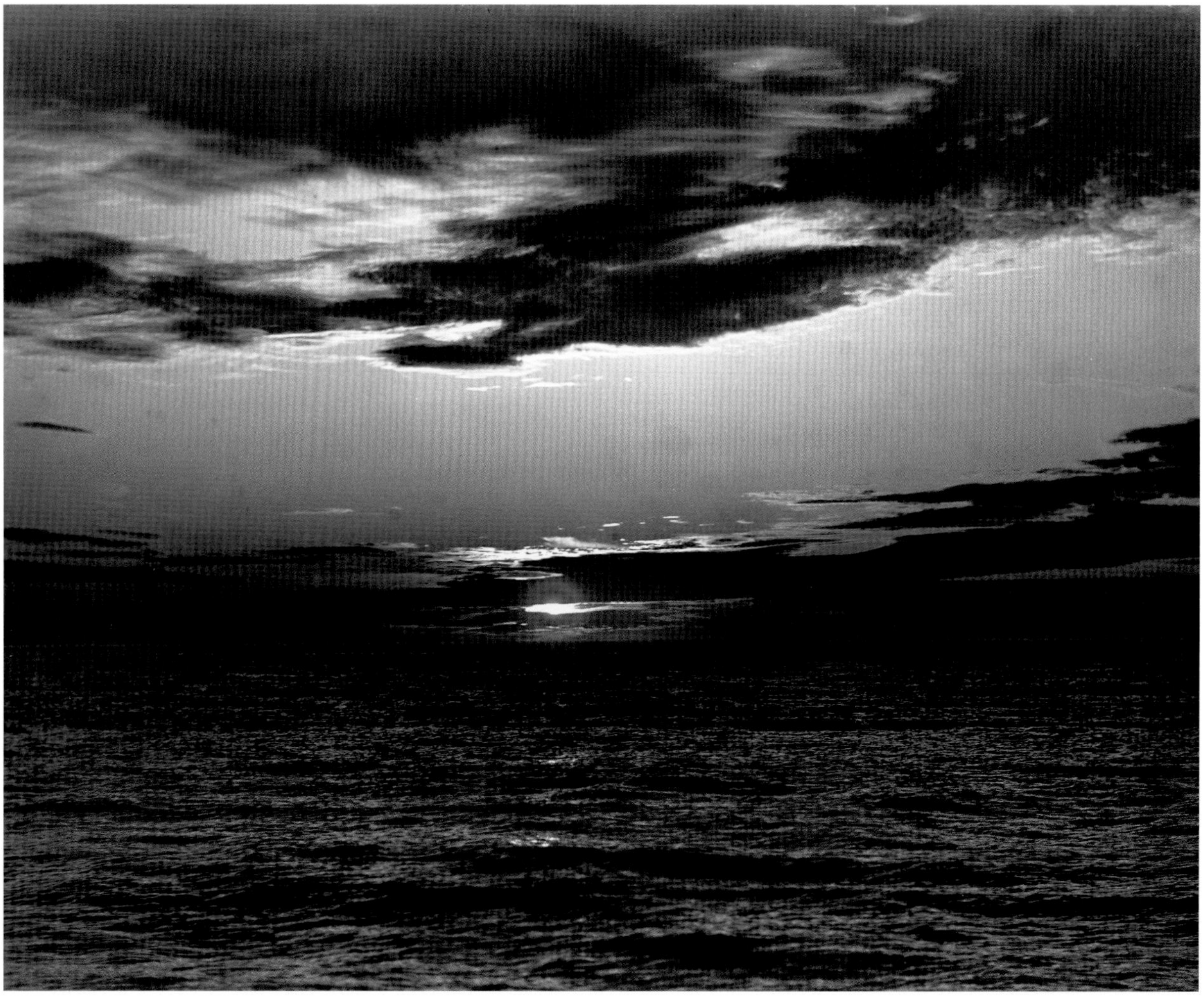

Sunset over the Gulf from Marco Island. In reference to the island and Collier's influence, A.W., writing in *The Book of the Tarpon,* noted: "Marco is the name of a post-office, but the place is called Collier's. . . . Island, bay, hotel, houses, boat-building plant, and even the atmosphere are, and always have been, Collier's. When Ponce de Leon was cavorting about the peninsula, pestering the inhabitants with his inquiries about a spring, he stopped at Collier's. Everybody who goes down the coast stops there." December 23, 1904; 48472.

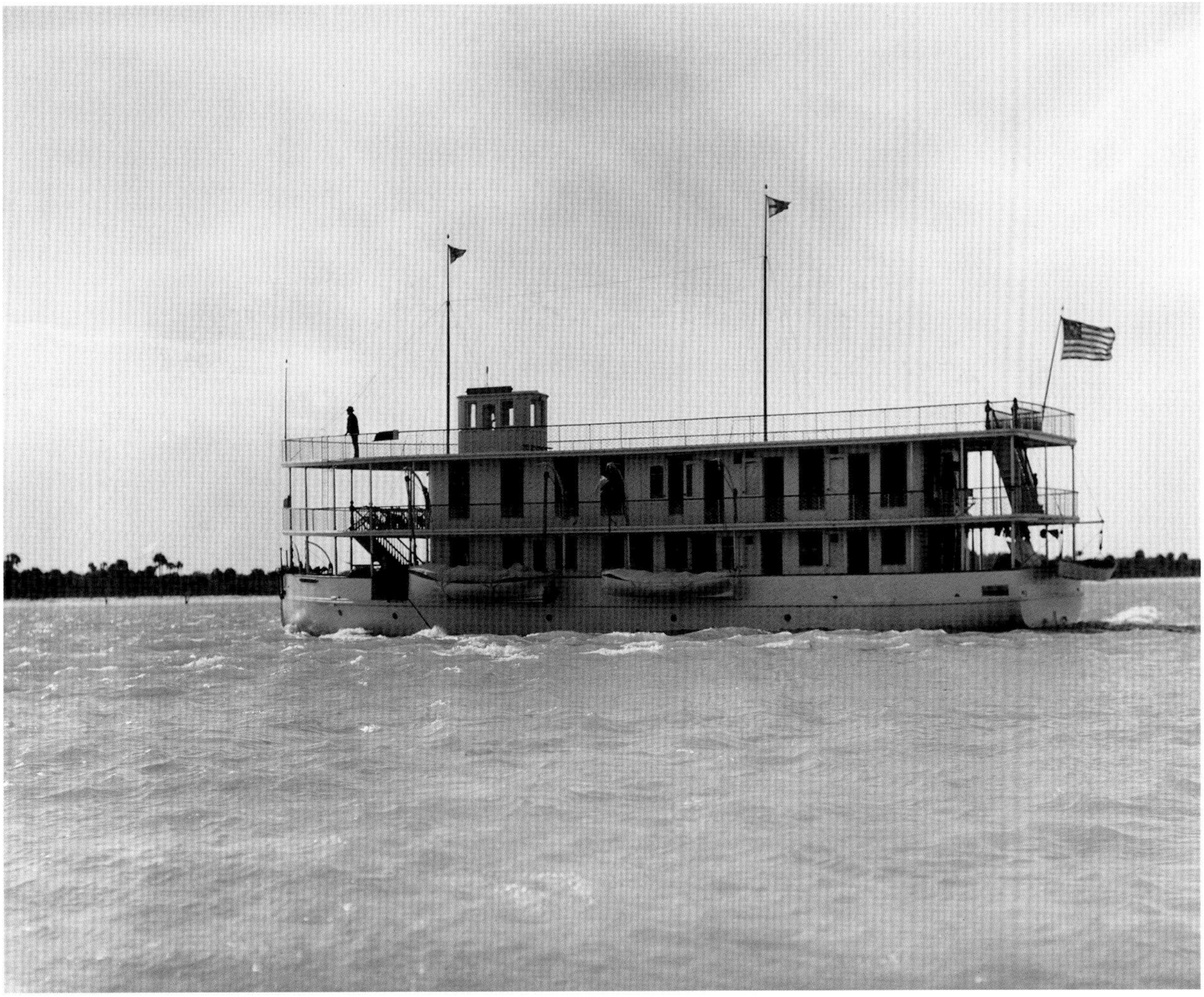

The houseboat *Whim Wham* off Marco Island. Built in Jacksonville especially for Florida's shallow waters, the hull was divided into twelve separate watertight compartments, each with its own pump to prevent sinking if the ship hit a snag. The *Whim Wham* and its owner, Dr. R.V. Pierce of Buffalo, New York (a member of the New York Yacht Club), were well known in Florida. According to a short review in *Outing* magazine (April 1898), the 91-foot-long houseboat featured a "deck house . . . divided into luxurious quarters for the owner and his guests, the cabins and staterooms being exceptionally light and large." The upper, hurricane deck was used for bicycling. February 20, 1905; 48480.

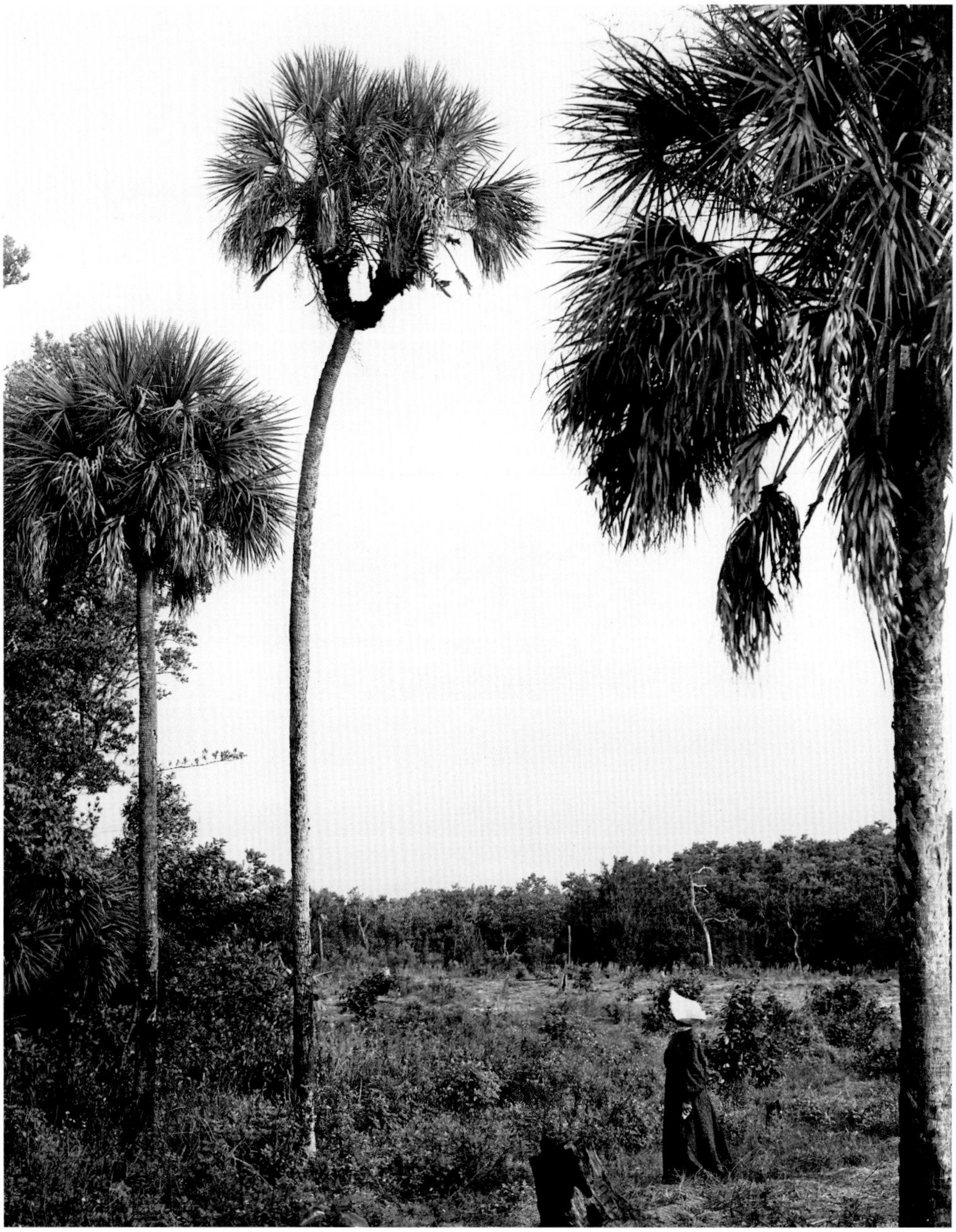

"Two-Headed Palmetto and Figure," Marco Island.
January 14, 1906; 48610.

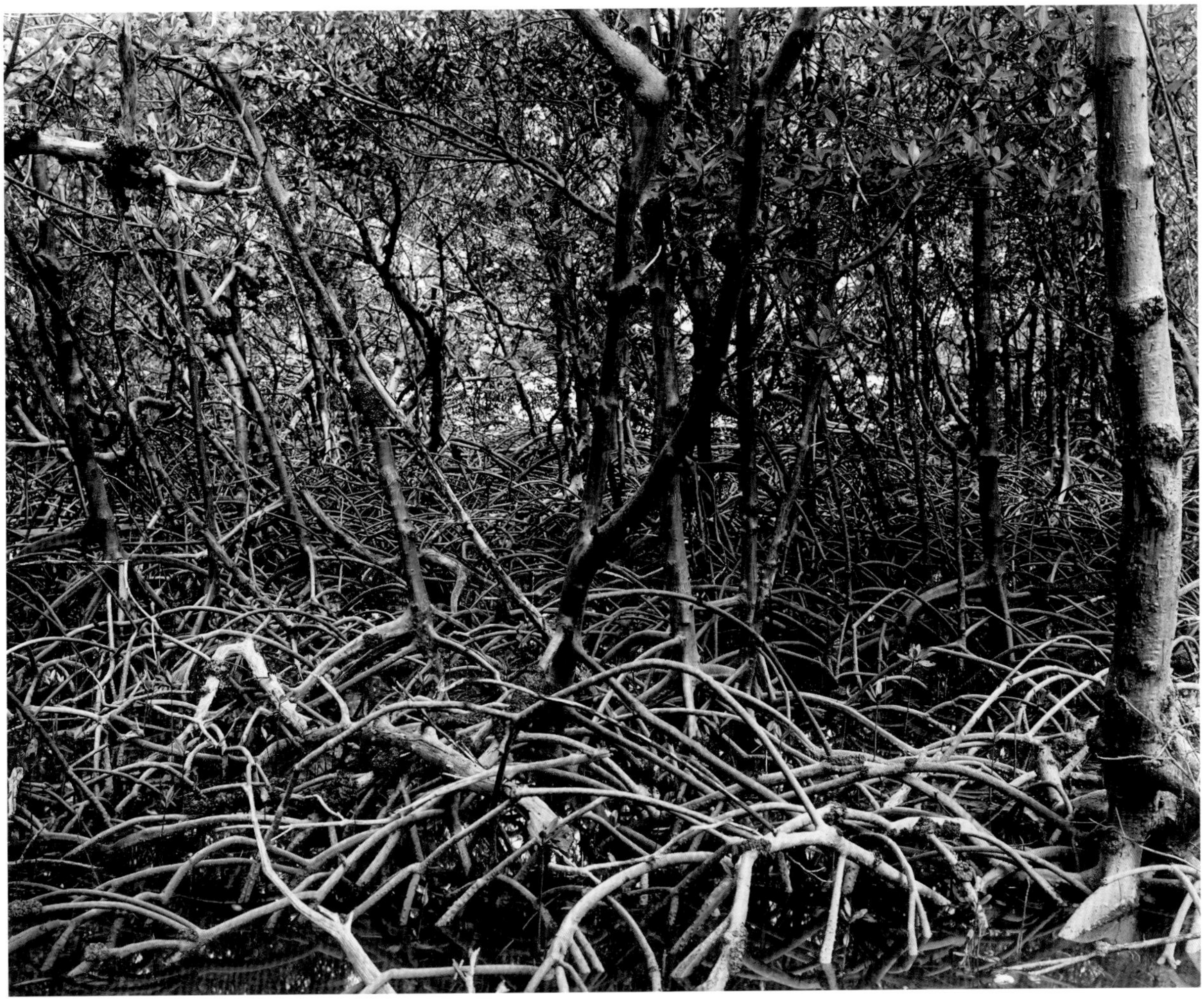

In mid-1904, the Dimocks began to explore the mangrove "thickets," as they called them, along the eastern edge of Marco Island. June 27, 1904; 48629.

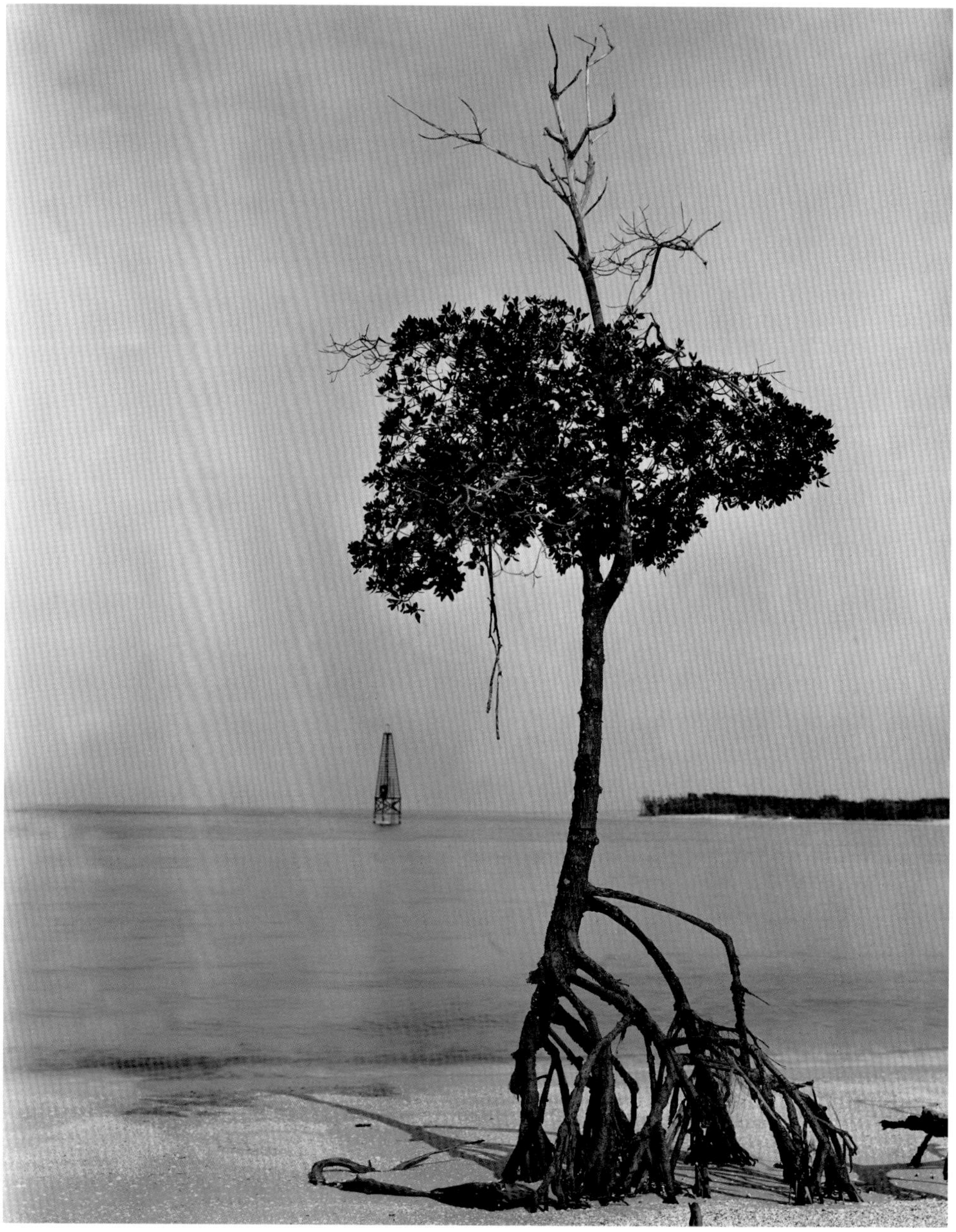

Julian and his father were both enamored with mangrove trees and their role in the formation of islands. In *Florida Enchantments*, A.W. wrote, "When Spring sets [the seeds] free[,] the waters are filled with pioneer mangroves which are borne by the tide over banks and shoals where, as the water recedes, roots take hold and extend, leaves unfold, and new colonies of mangroves are established in the shallows of the open water. Sometimes a single tree sets up an island of its own and sometimes a thousand begin housekeeping together. . . . Planted on shifting sands and unstable soil, the mangrove anchors itself and makes firm the land by sending forth a hundred aërial roots like cables from the branches to the earth beneath."
November 26, 1904; 48634.

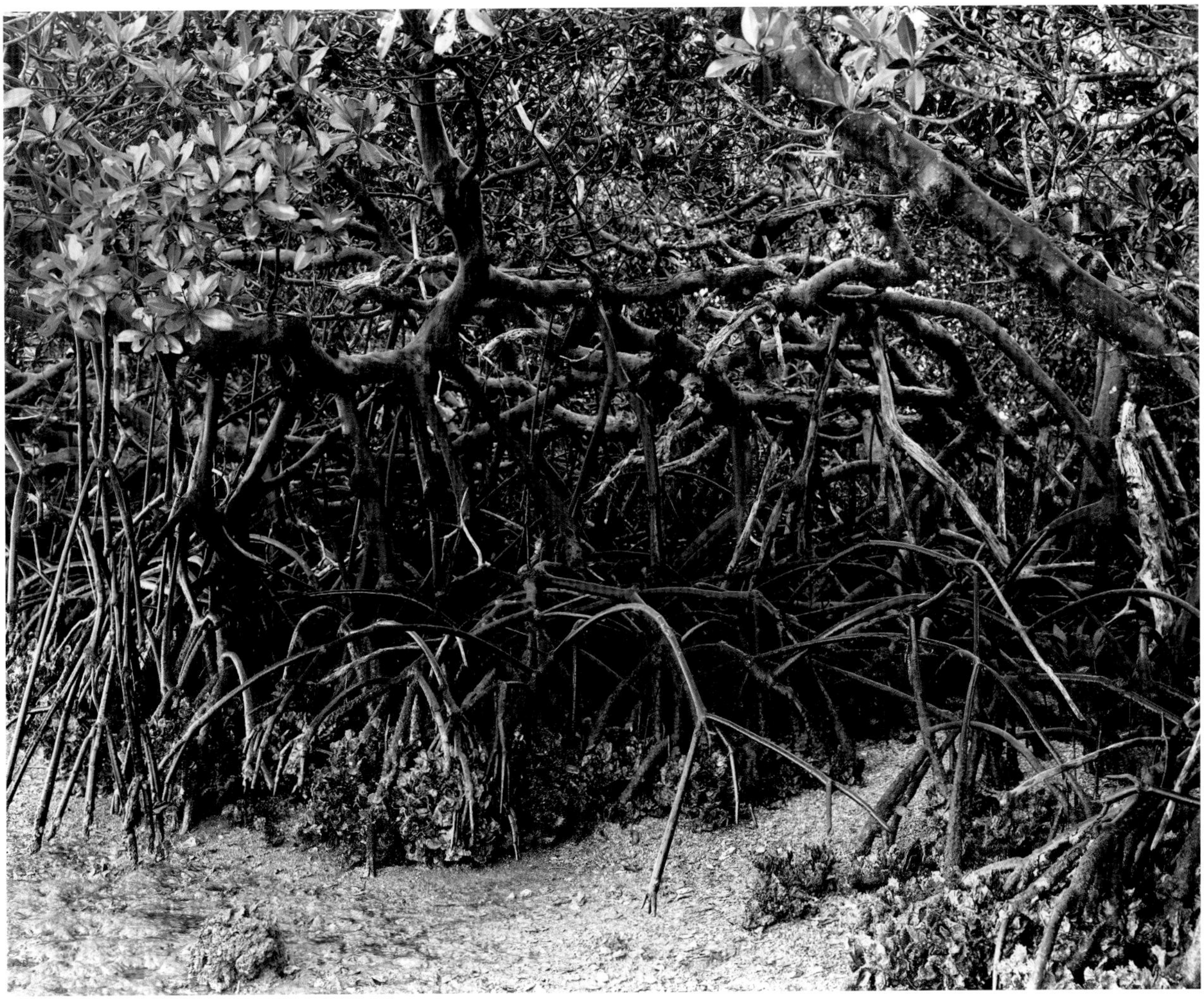

In 1905, Julian published a photographic essay, "The Mangrove as an Island Builder," in *Country Life in America* magazine. The article introduced a wide audience to Marco Island and its mangroves. January 25, 1905; 48630.

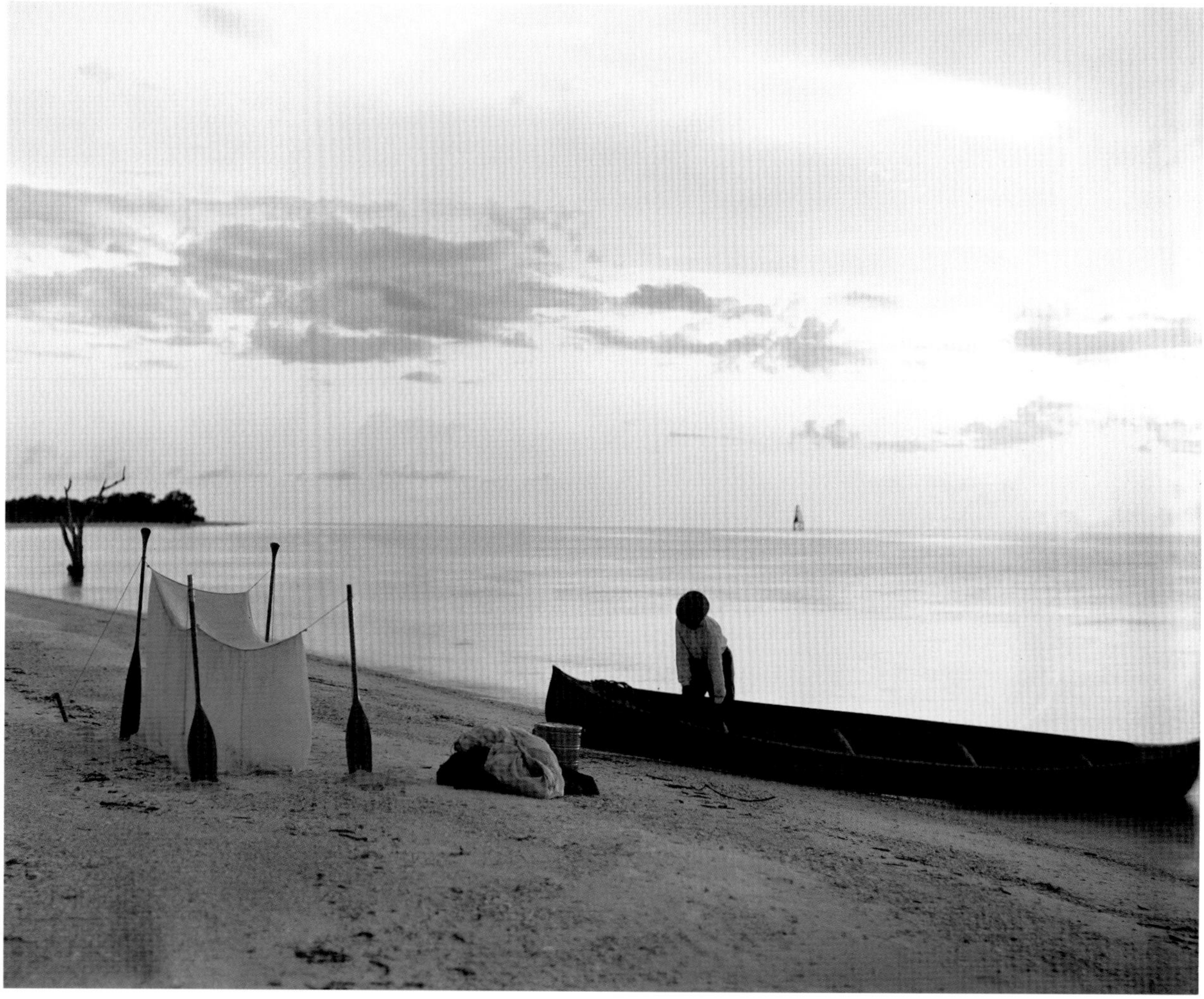

Together the Dimocks camped, sometimes for weeks at a time, in the Everglades, the Ten Thousand Islands, the Big Cypress Swamp, and the shores of islands in what today are Lee, Collier, and Monroe Counties. Wherever they camped, they were never without their "mosquito bar," the netting that protected them from the swarms of biting insects that greeted all visitors. Here A. W. is setting up his mosquito bar in preparation for a night on the beach on Marco Island after spending the day canoeing around the island's periphery. August 30, 1907; 48682.

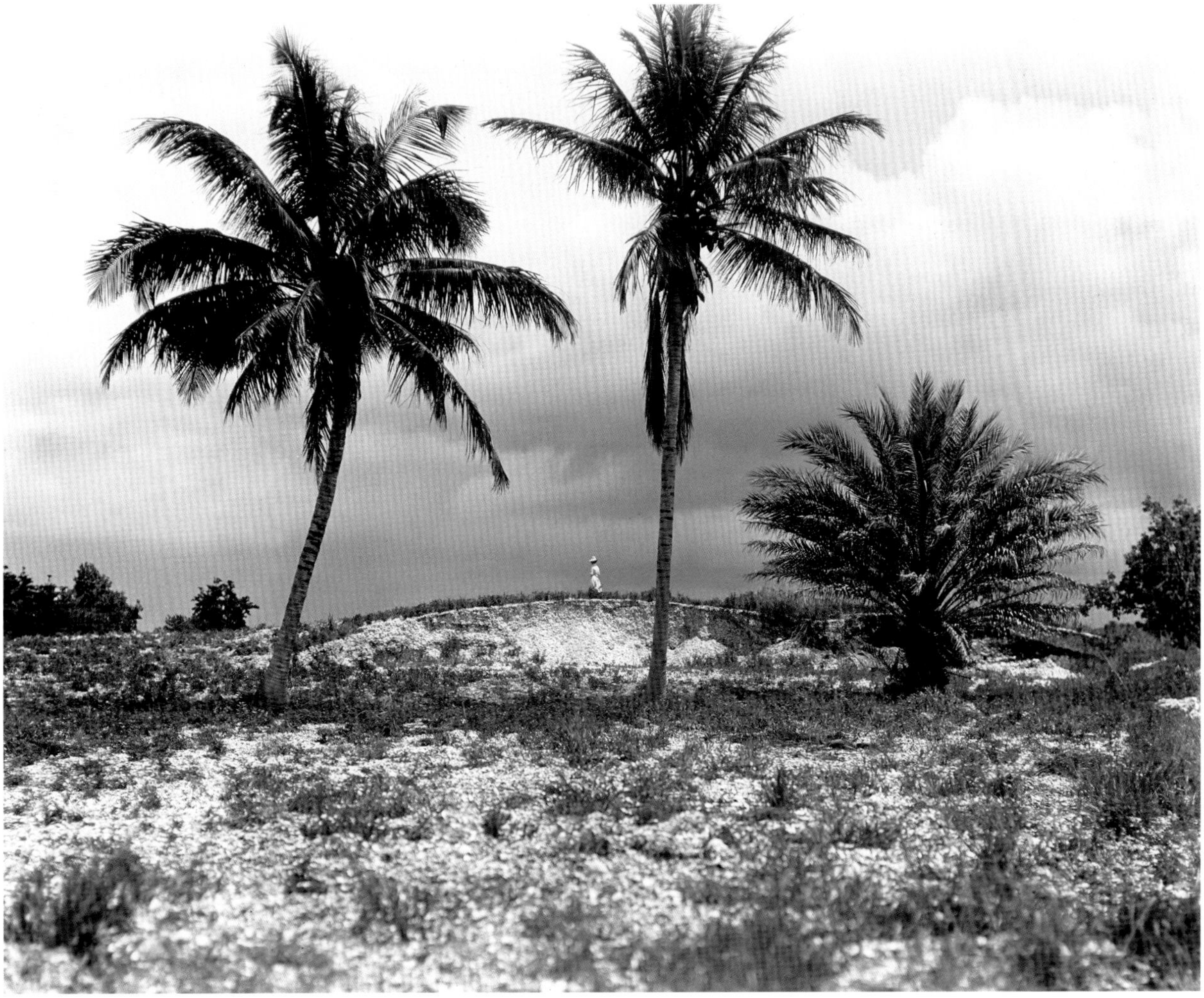

A pre-Columbian shell mound on Marco Island. The woman on the mound is identified as M.D., certainly Mabel, Julian's sister. Residents of the island likely had mined some of the shell to use in construction or for other purposes. Captain Collier used shell from Marco Island mounds to build a walkway from his hotel to the beach for the convenience of the hotel's guests, who previously had to use a boat to reach the beach. July 31, 1904; 48733.

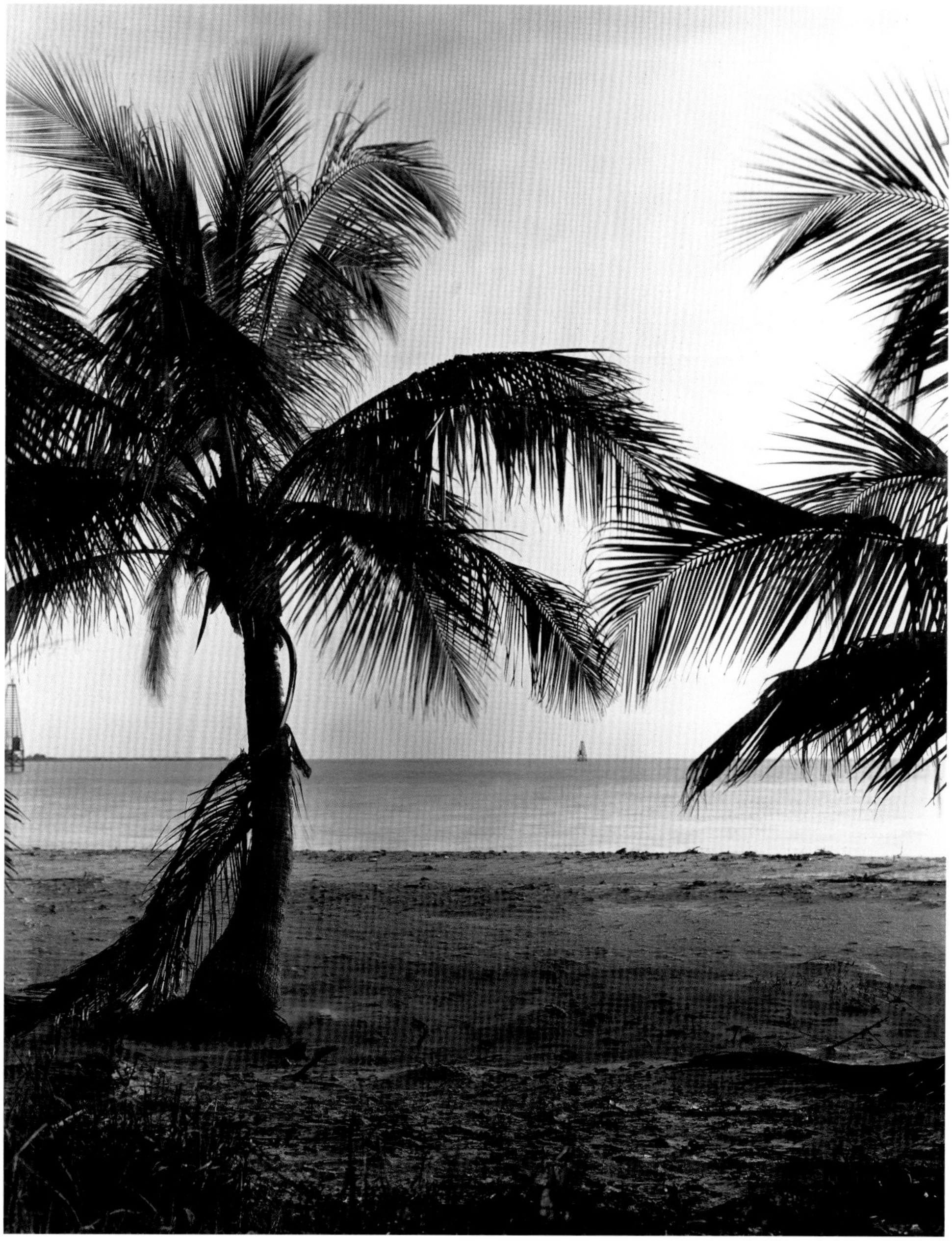

The beach at Marco Island. A navigation beacon can be seen on the left; a second one is farther out to sea. November 28, 1904; 48736.

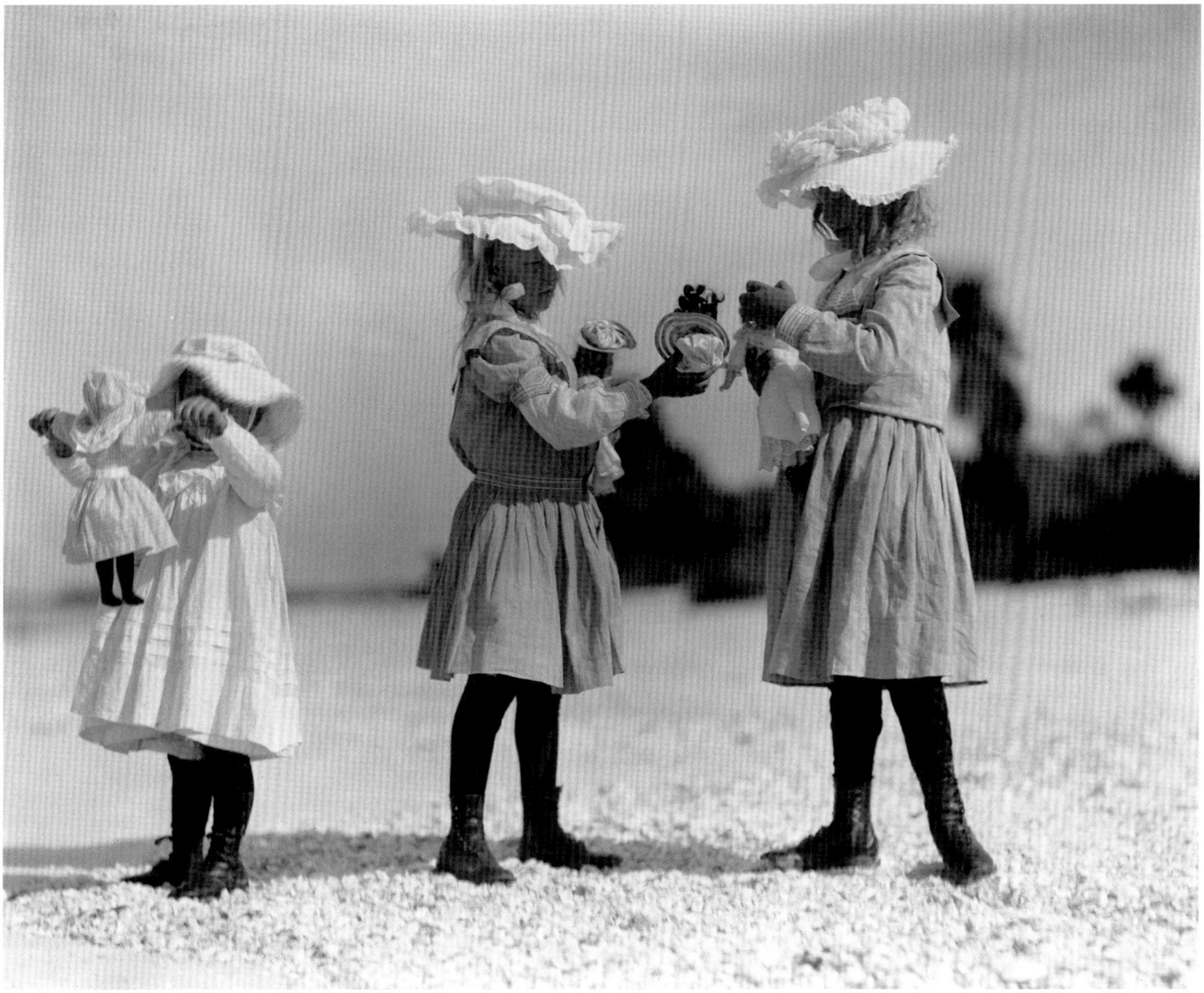

Rosalie (about 3 years old), Saloma (about 5), and Orida (about 8) Olds playing on the beach at Marco Island on Christmas Day. In her book *Island Voices: They Came to Marco Island* (2006), author Elizabeth McDonald Perdichizzi has a chapter about the Olds girls and their extraordinary life on the island in the early 1900s. December 25, 1904; 49476.

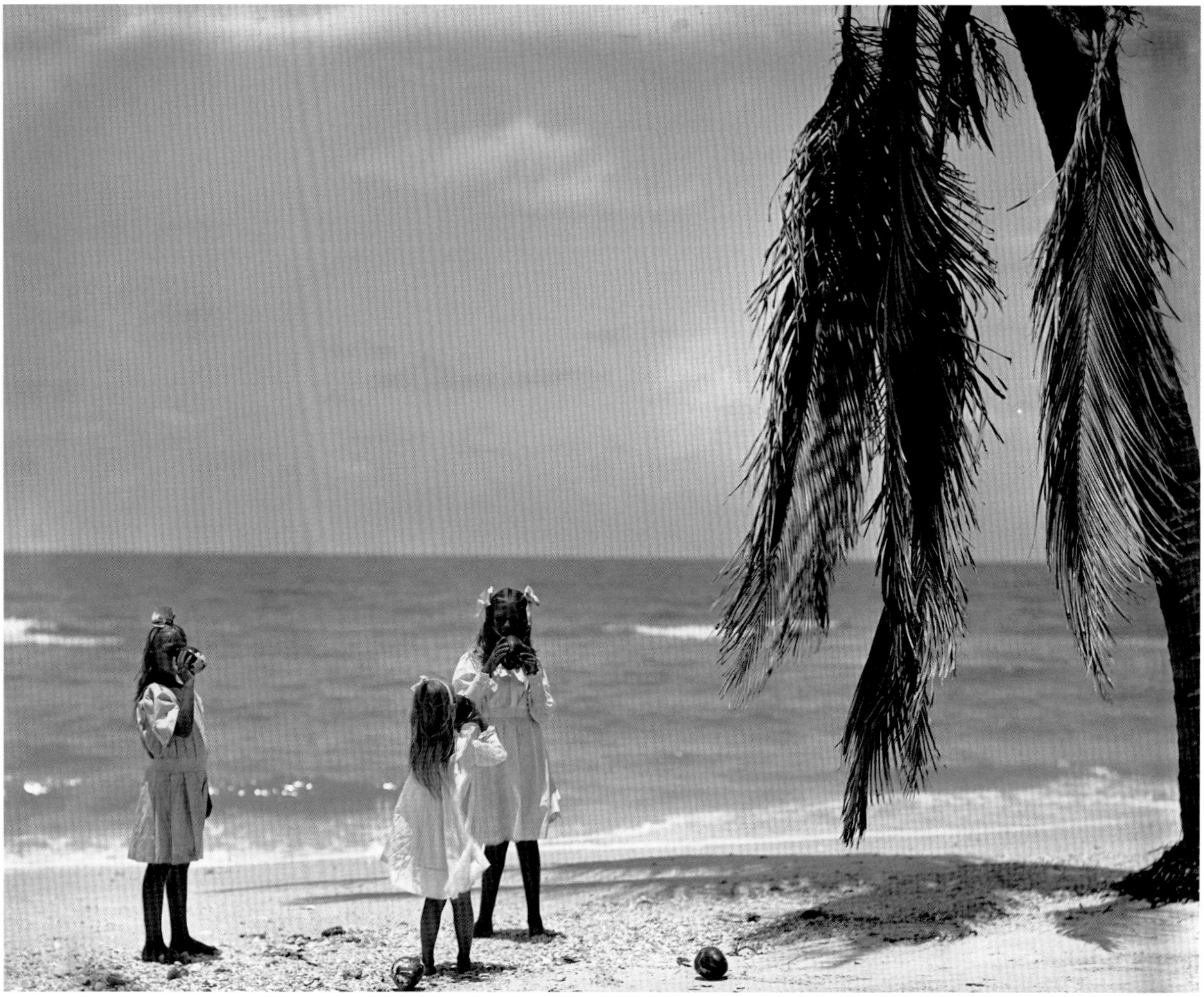

The three Olds daughters drinking from coconuts on the Marco beach two and a half years later. Their parents, Mary Johns Olds and Charles Louis Olds, were homeopathic doctors who had moved to Marco Island about 1901–2. The girls were home-schooled. June 6, 1907; 49490.

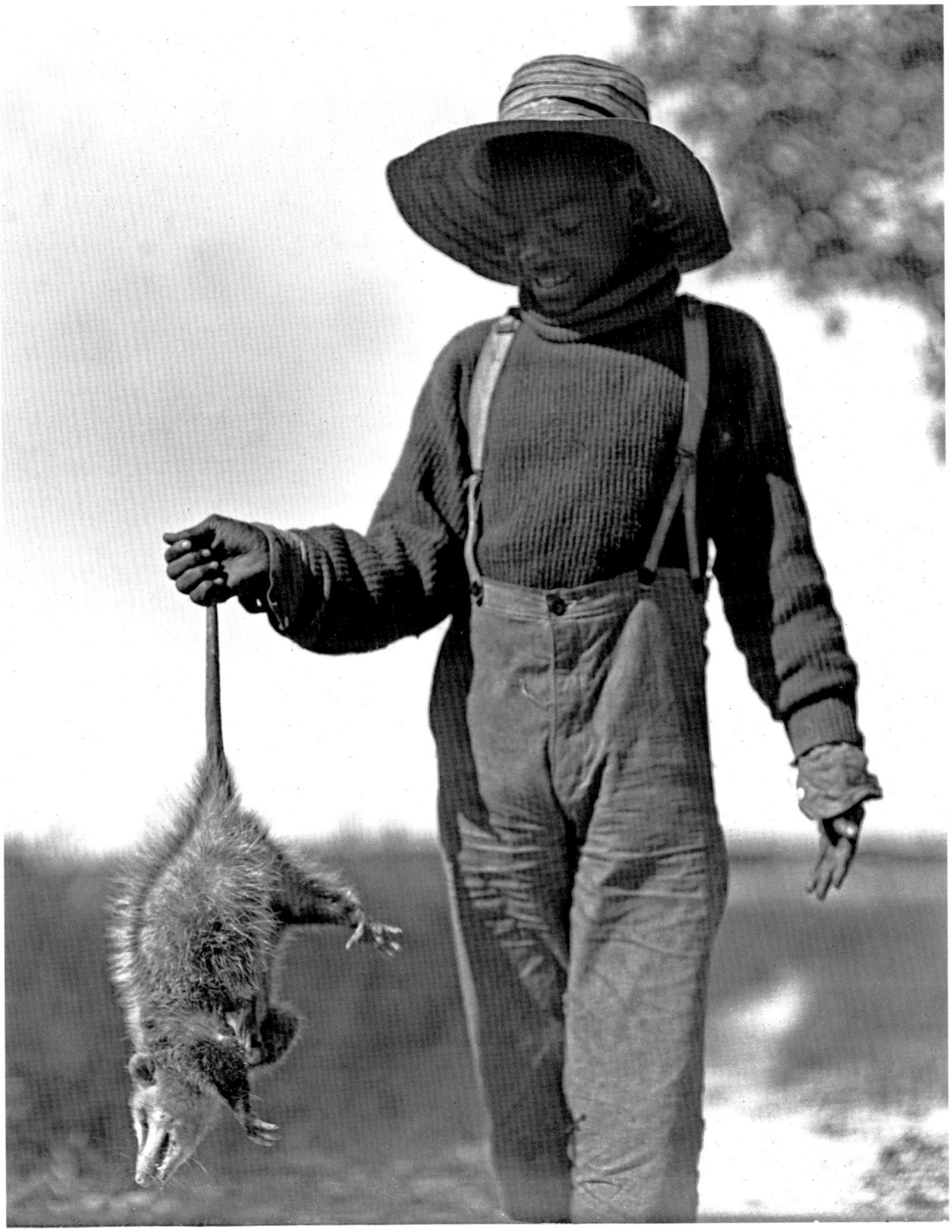

A young Marco resident with an opossum.
December 21, 1904; 47731.

Farming on Marco

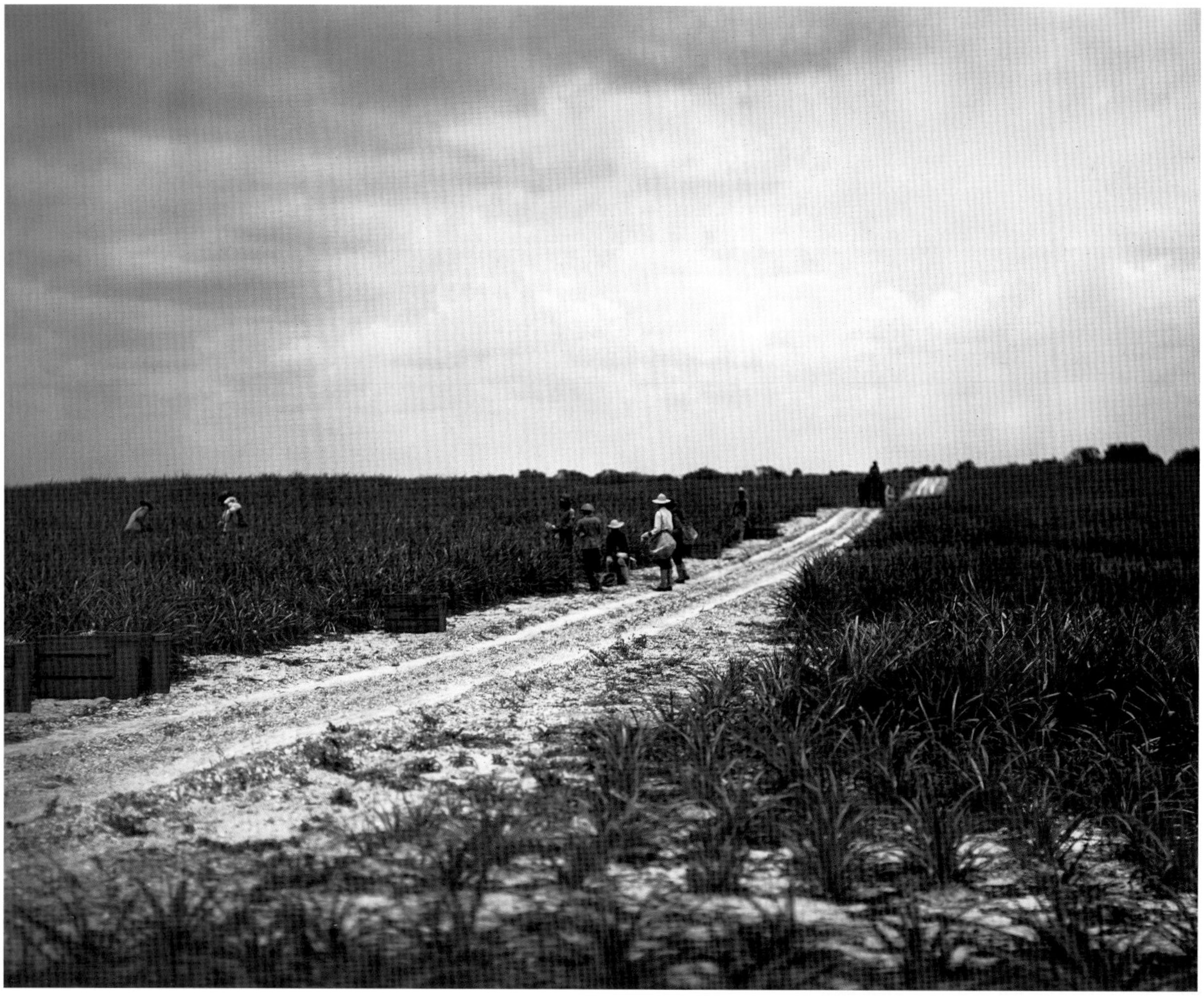

Pineapple fields blanketed portions of Caxambas (Julian and A. W. spelled it "Caximbas," as it appears on some early maps) on the south portion of Marco Island. The pineapples were shipped by boat to the railroad near Fort Myers or to steamships at Key West and then transported north. May 22, 1905; 48710.

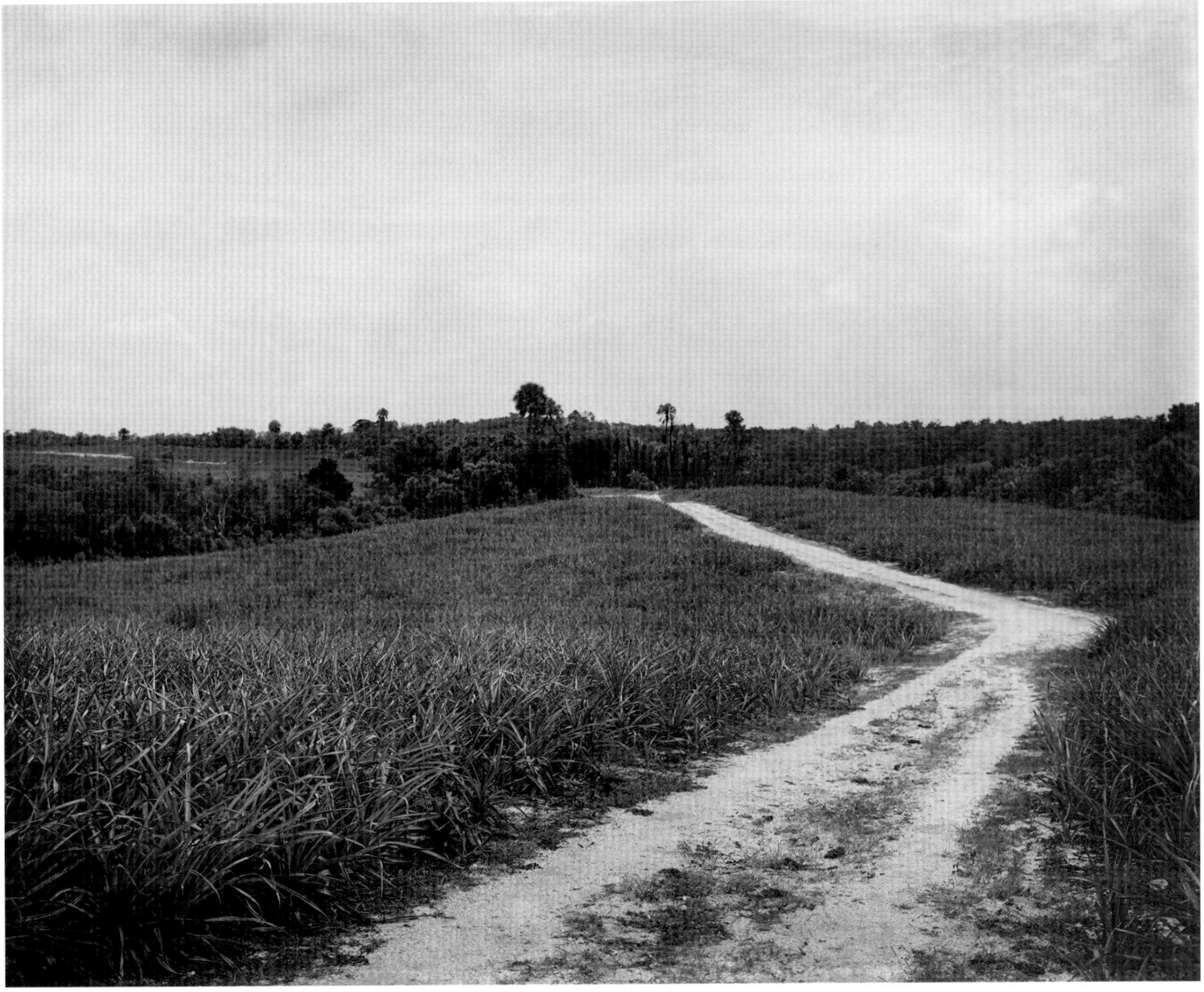

Julian aptly titled this photograph, taken at "Caximbas," "Field of a Million Pineapples." Likely these are the fields of Fred Ludlow, founder of the Ludlow Fruit Company. A hurricane in 1910 flooded the fields with salt water, killing the pineapples and putting Ludlow out of business. May 22, 1905; 48711.

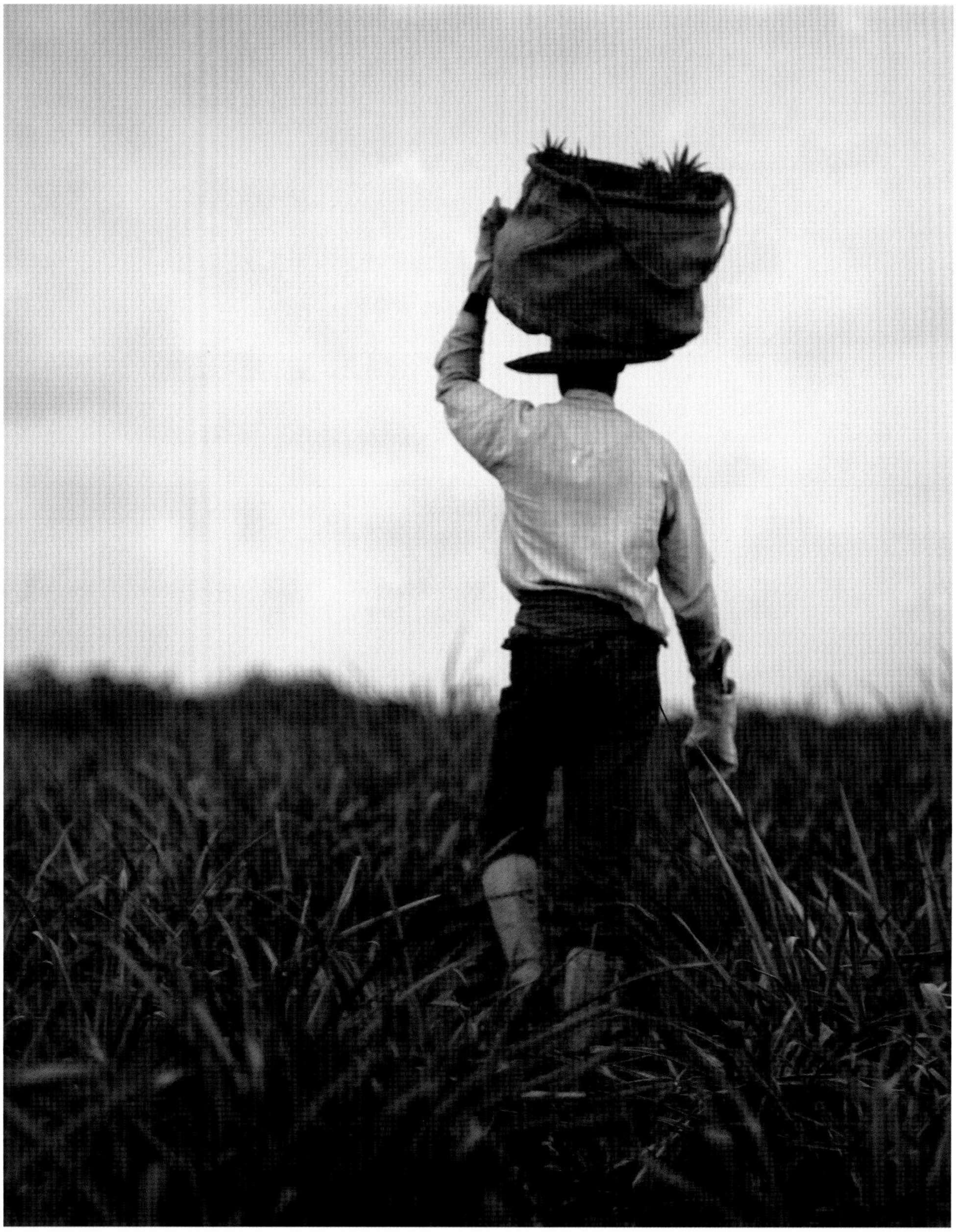

Pineapples were picked by hand . . .
May 22, 1905; 48714.

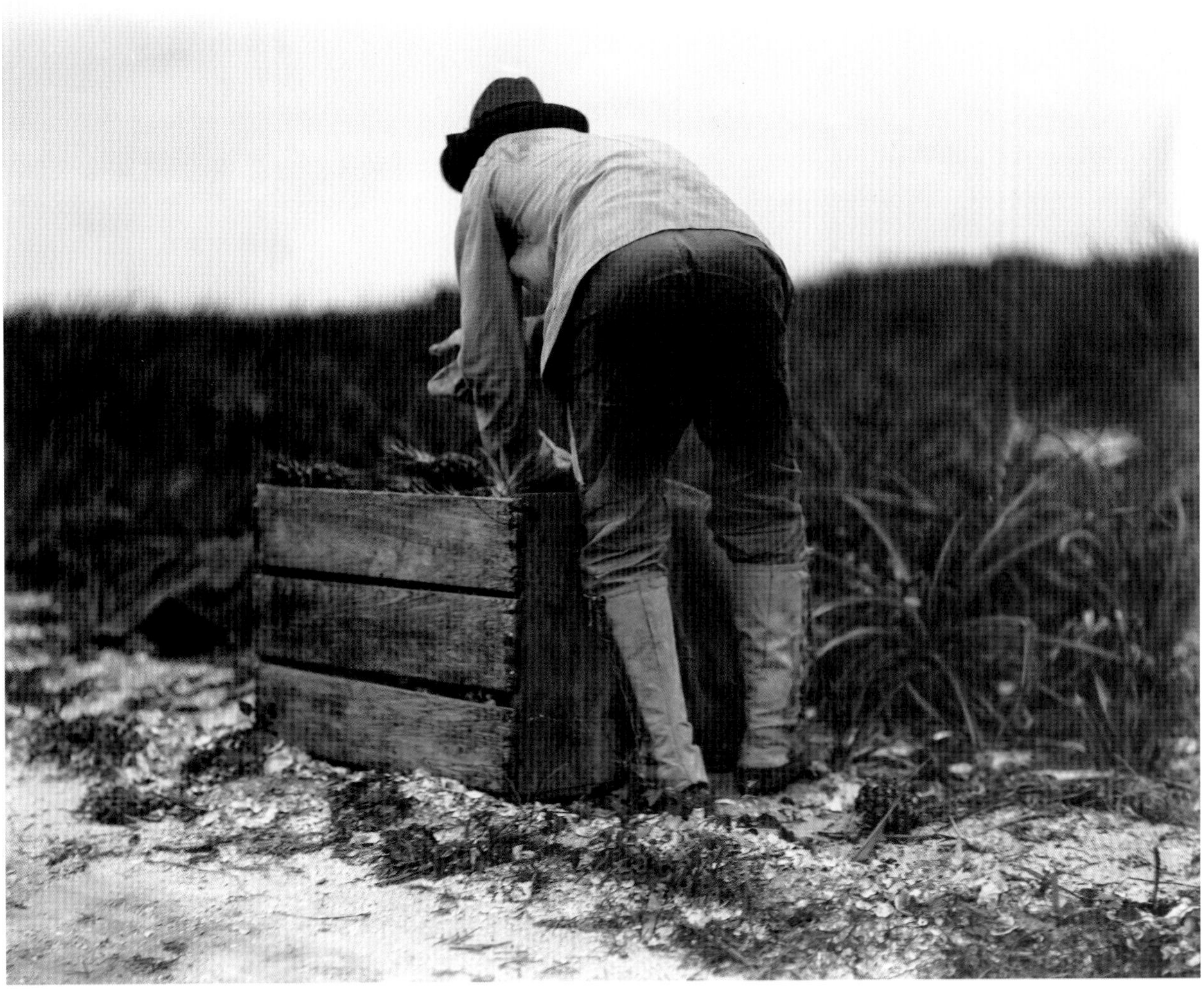

Packed in wooden crates . . .
May 22, 1905; 48716.

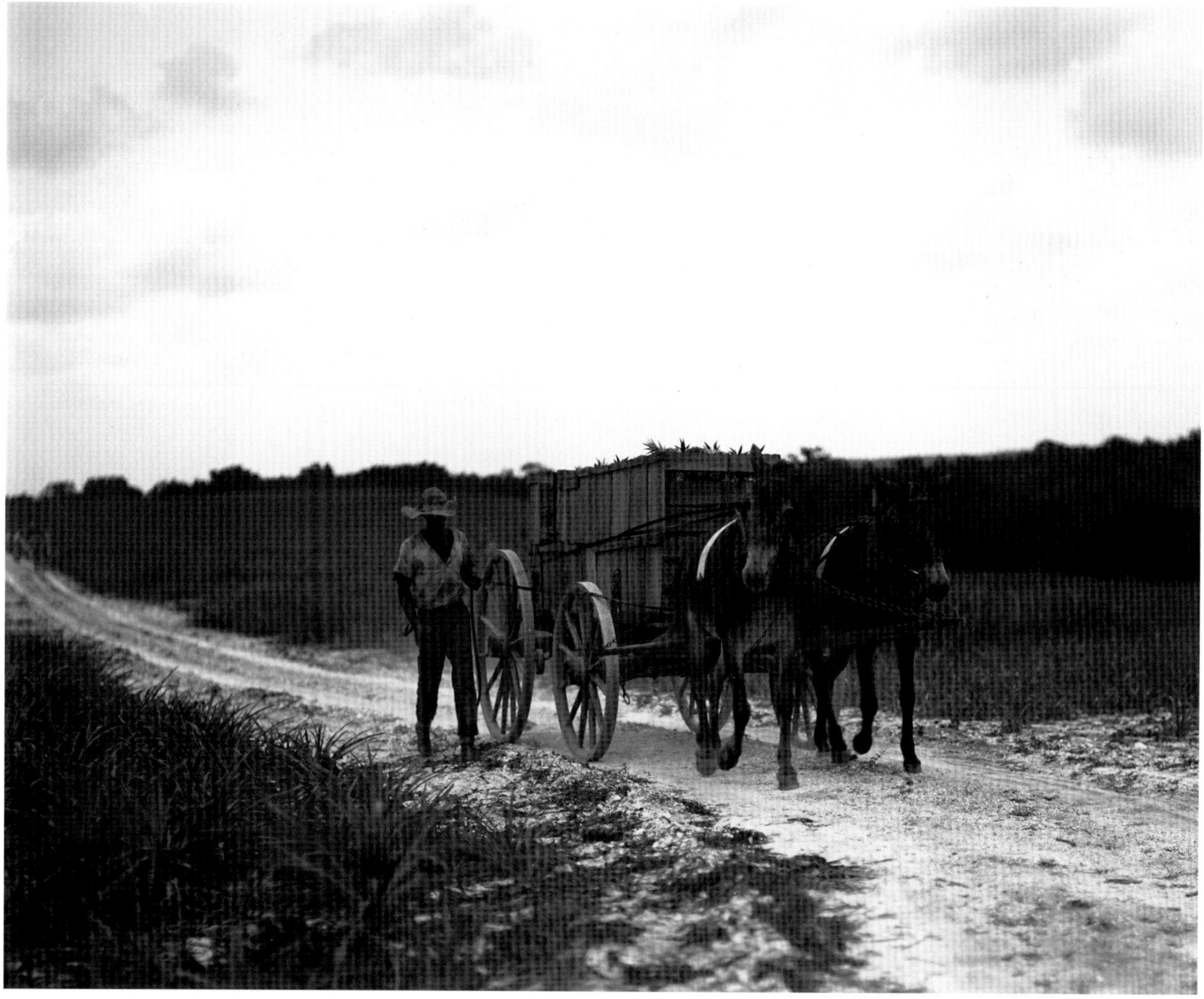

And then transported in mule-drawn wagons to the dock to be shipped off the island. The work was done by African Americans. May 22, 1905; 48719.

Salvaging the *Kitty Horr* (or Not)

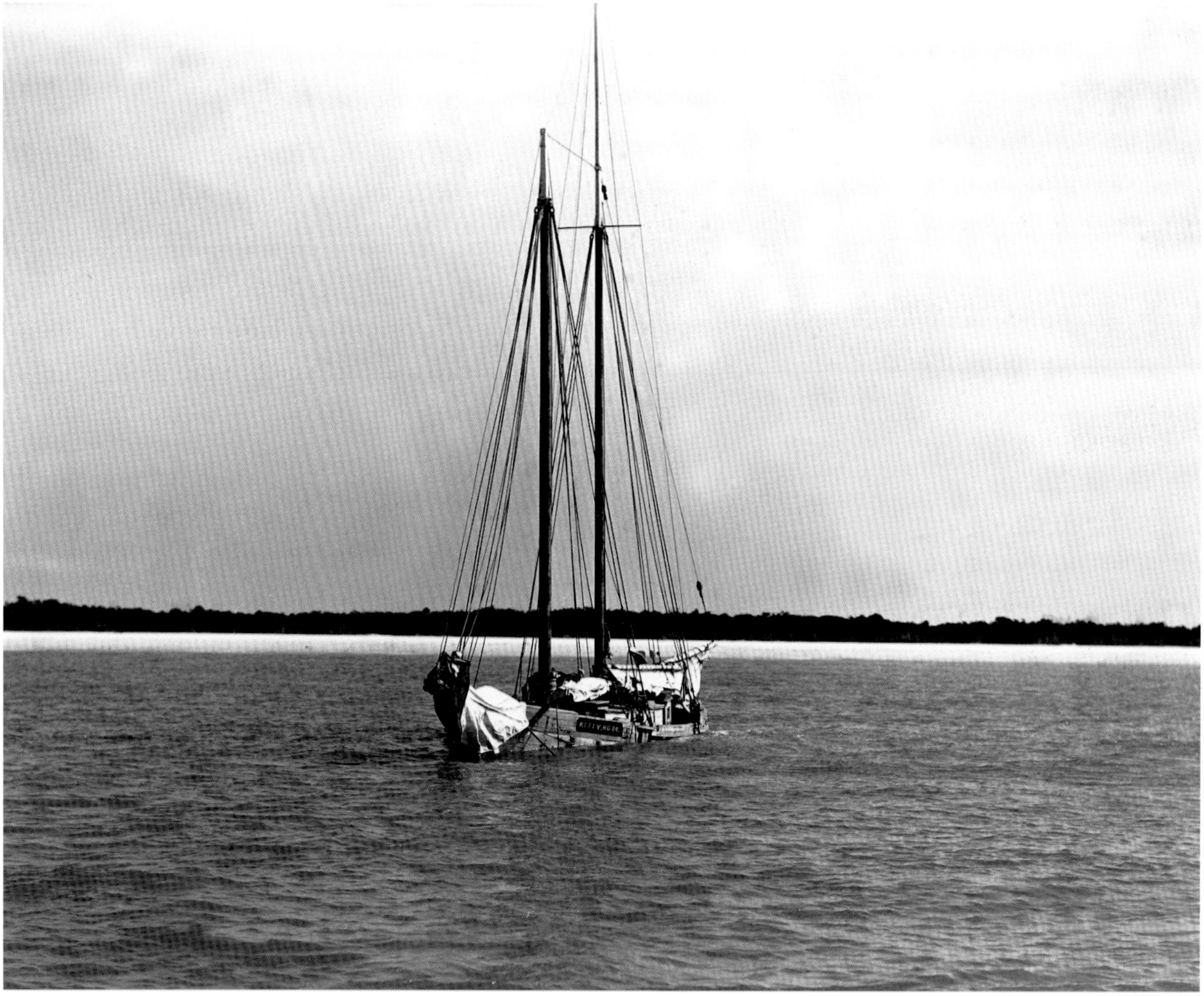

In 1905, the Dimocks accompanied Bill Collier on a voyage aboard Collier's schooner, the *Annie*. A. W. Dimock (in 1906 in "The Wrecker") noted that "'Cap'n Bill,' as even the babies called him, was merchant, shipbuilder and hotel-keeper, the Pooh-Bah of the island which he owned and the bay which bore his name." Rounding a point of Marco Island on the Gulf side, the Dimocks and Collier spied a recently wrecked and abandoned schooner "lying stranded with decks awash." Collier immediately saw it as a financial opportunity. November 15, 1904; 48462.

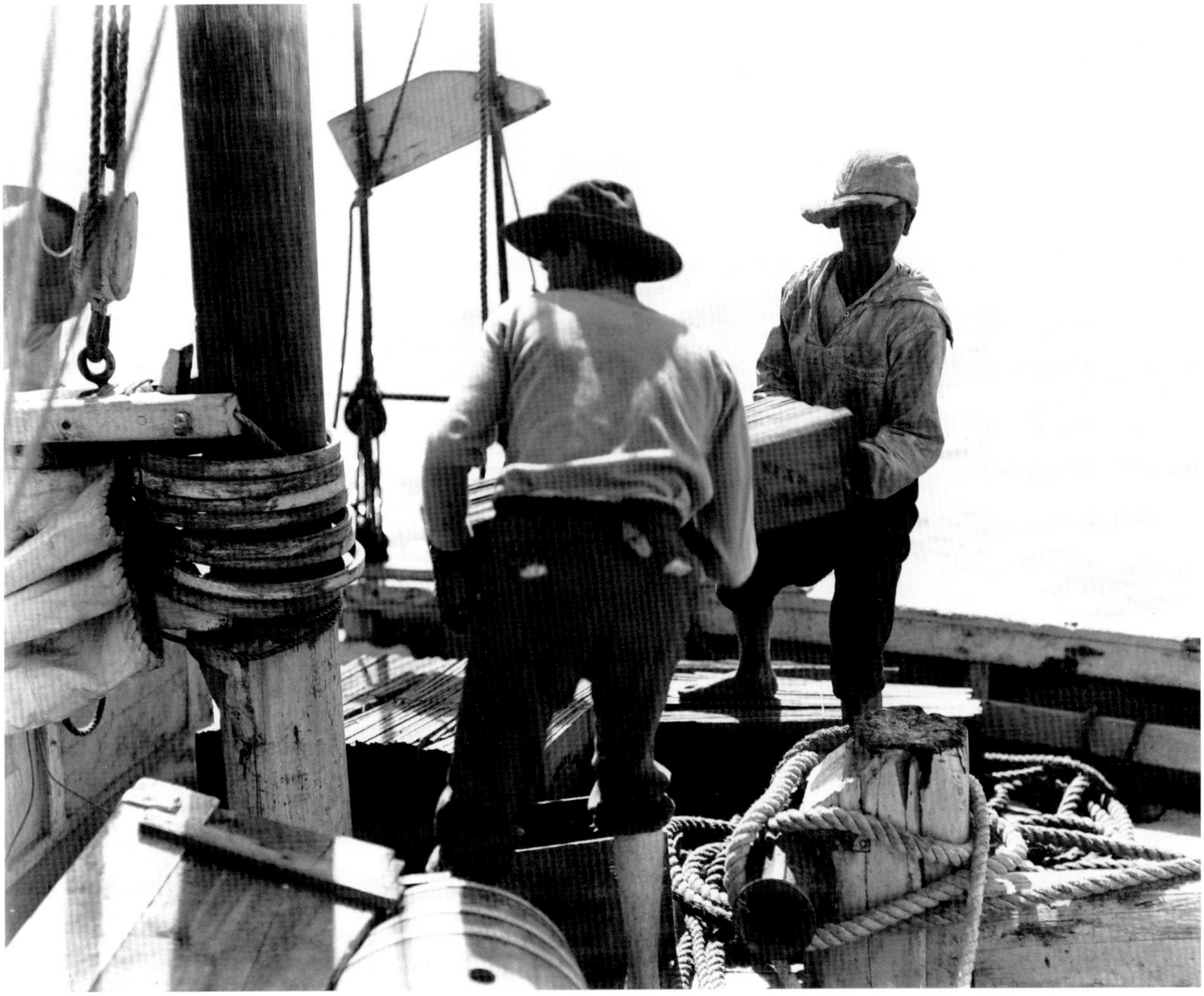

The wrecked boat was the *Kitty Horr*, a 41½-foot schooner registered in Key West. Likely it belonged to John Foley Horr of Horrs Island (just south of Marco Island), who maintained business interests in Key West. The schooner may have been named for Horr's mother, Katherine (Kitty) Horr, or another relative. According to A. W. Dimock, Collier, noting that "the wrecker's motto is 'Get there first,' and we are first," picked up the *Kitty Horr*'s crew, who had swum ashore, and with them and his own crew set about salvaging the schooner's cargo, a load of wooden shingles stowed in the hull. By rights, the cargo was now his. November 15, 1904; 48463.

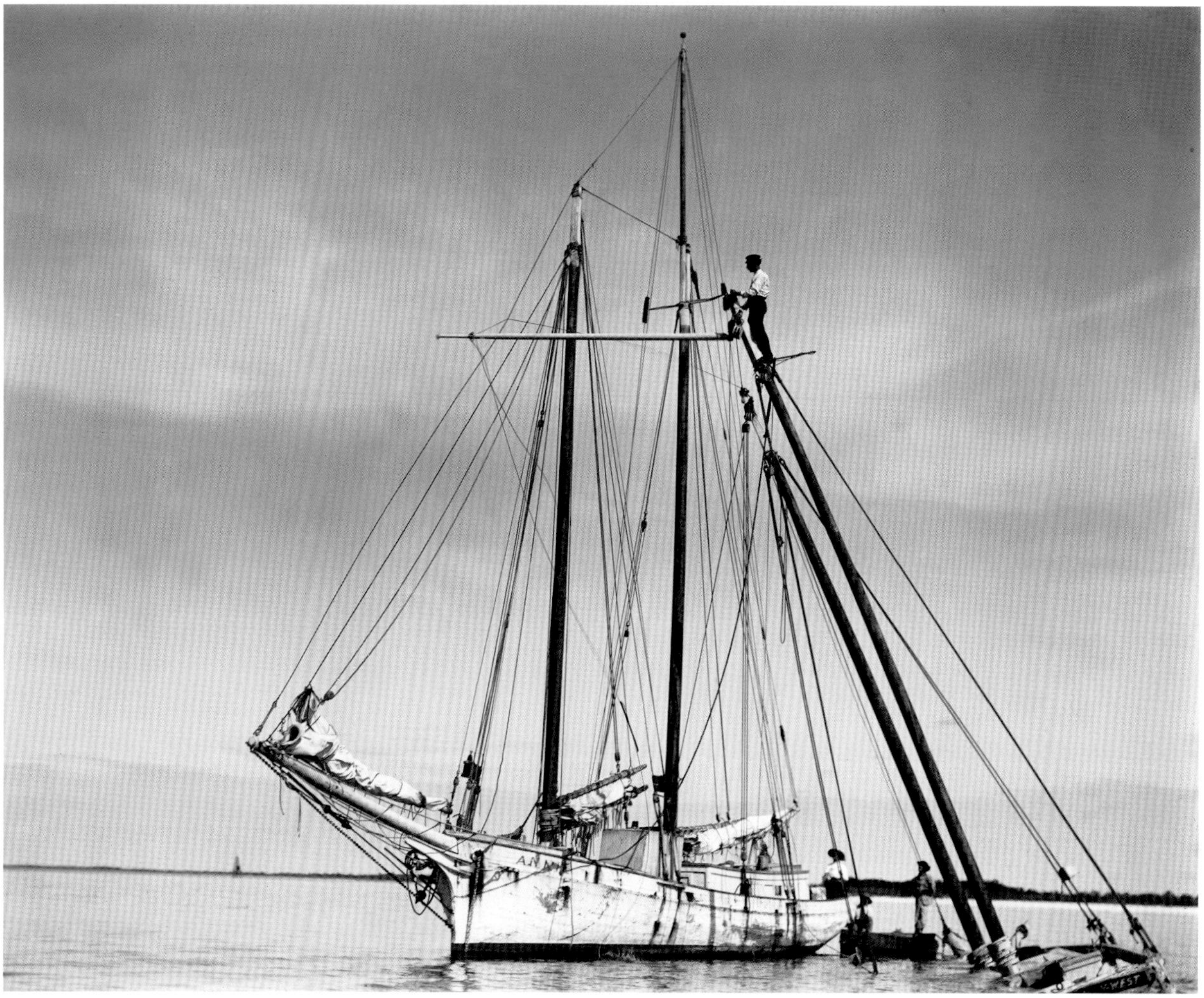

Nine days later, Collier and the Dimocks returned to the wreck to salvage it. The first order of business was to tip the vessel on its side so that the hull could be examined for the damage that had led to its sinking. Regarding salvaging the schooner, Collier explained: "Wrecking is a lottery. You work harder to get a dollar without earning it than you would to earn five legitimately. I've made a little stake . . . [on the cargo], but shall probably waste the most of it trying to get that old tub afloat. I know I ought to let it alone but I shall go down there and strain and bruise my own good boats and waste time and money until I pull the old wreck to pieces or until a nor'wester breaks it up." November 24, 1904; 48503.

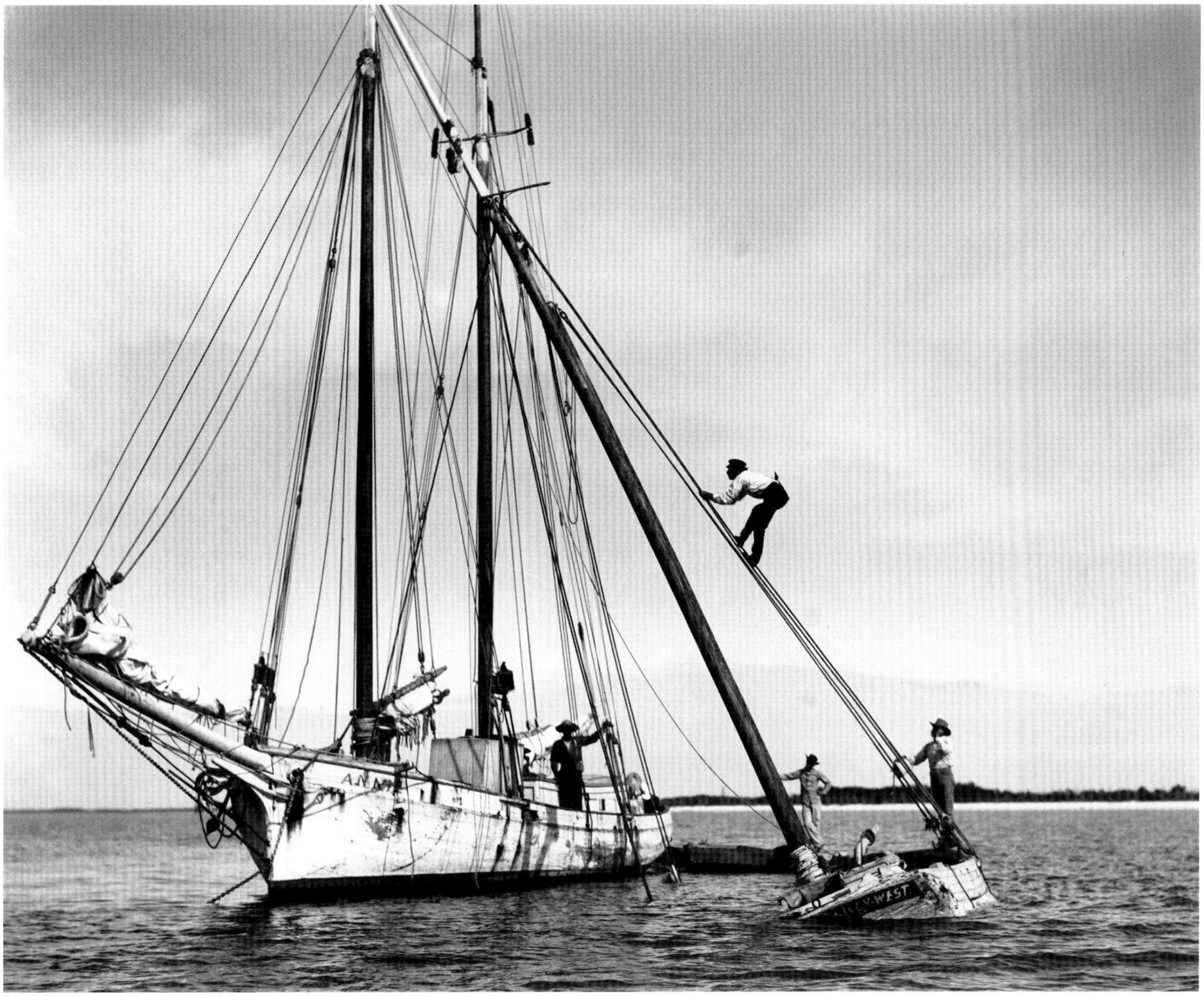

The plan was to attach the top of the schooner's masts to pulleys atop a mast on Collier's boat and then wench the *Kitty Horr*'s masts down, tipping the boat. The initial effort failed when one of the *Kitty Horr*'s masts got tangled in the rigging of Collier's schooner. A crew man with a hatchet was dispatched to solve the problem. November 24, 1905; 48474.

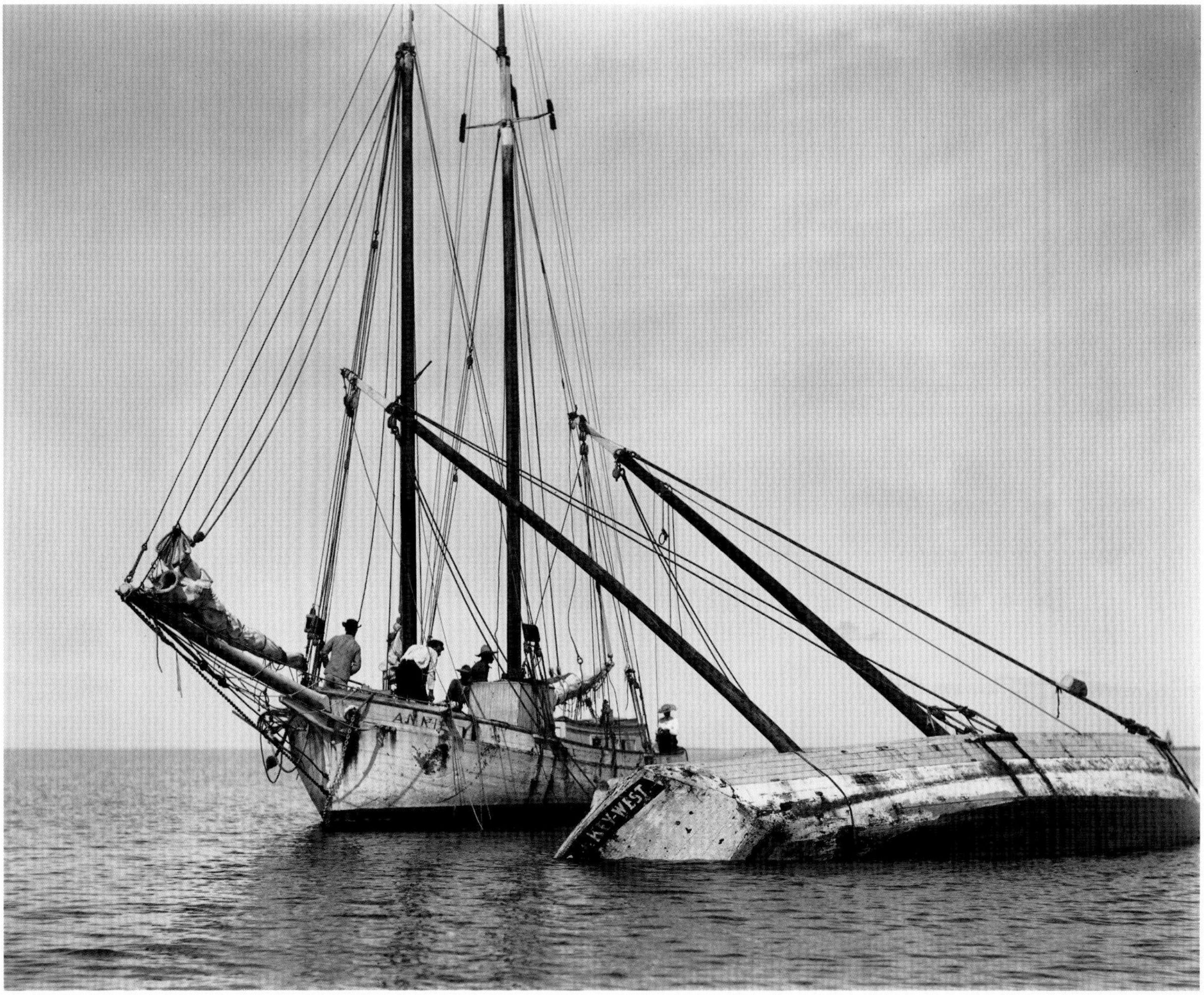

After the mast was freed, the *Kitty Horr* was successfully laid on her side in the water next to the *Annie*. The two schooners, according to records of United States merchant vessels, were much the same size (the *Annie* had been built in 1870 in Key West). November 24, 1904; 48475.

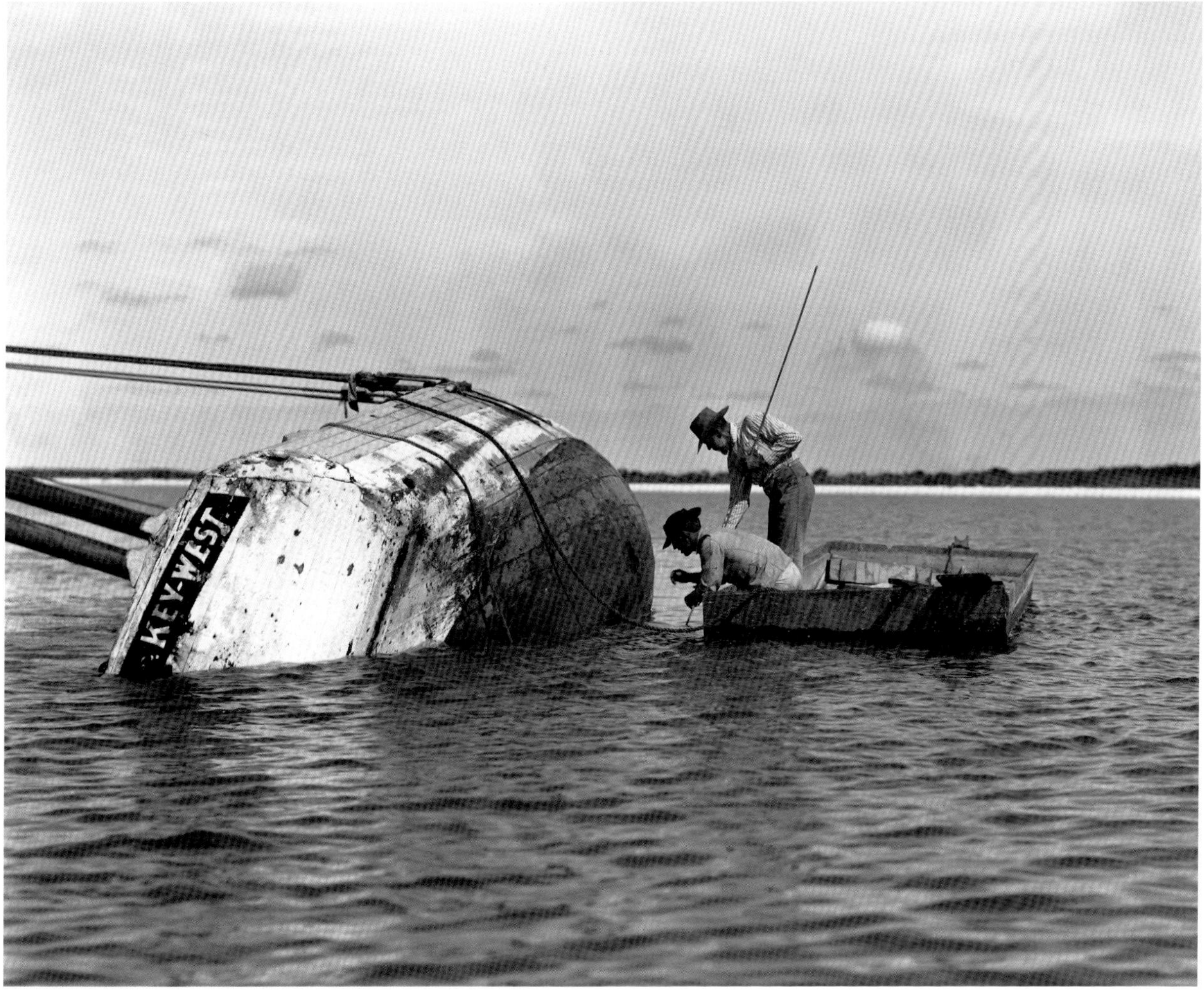

The hull of the *Kitty Horr* was found to have several holes in it. Patches were applied, and then the boat was tipped upright in the water. Collier's men began to bail out the schooner with buckets and pumps, intending to refloat it. November 24, 1904; 48476.

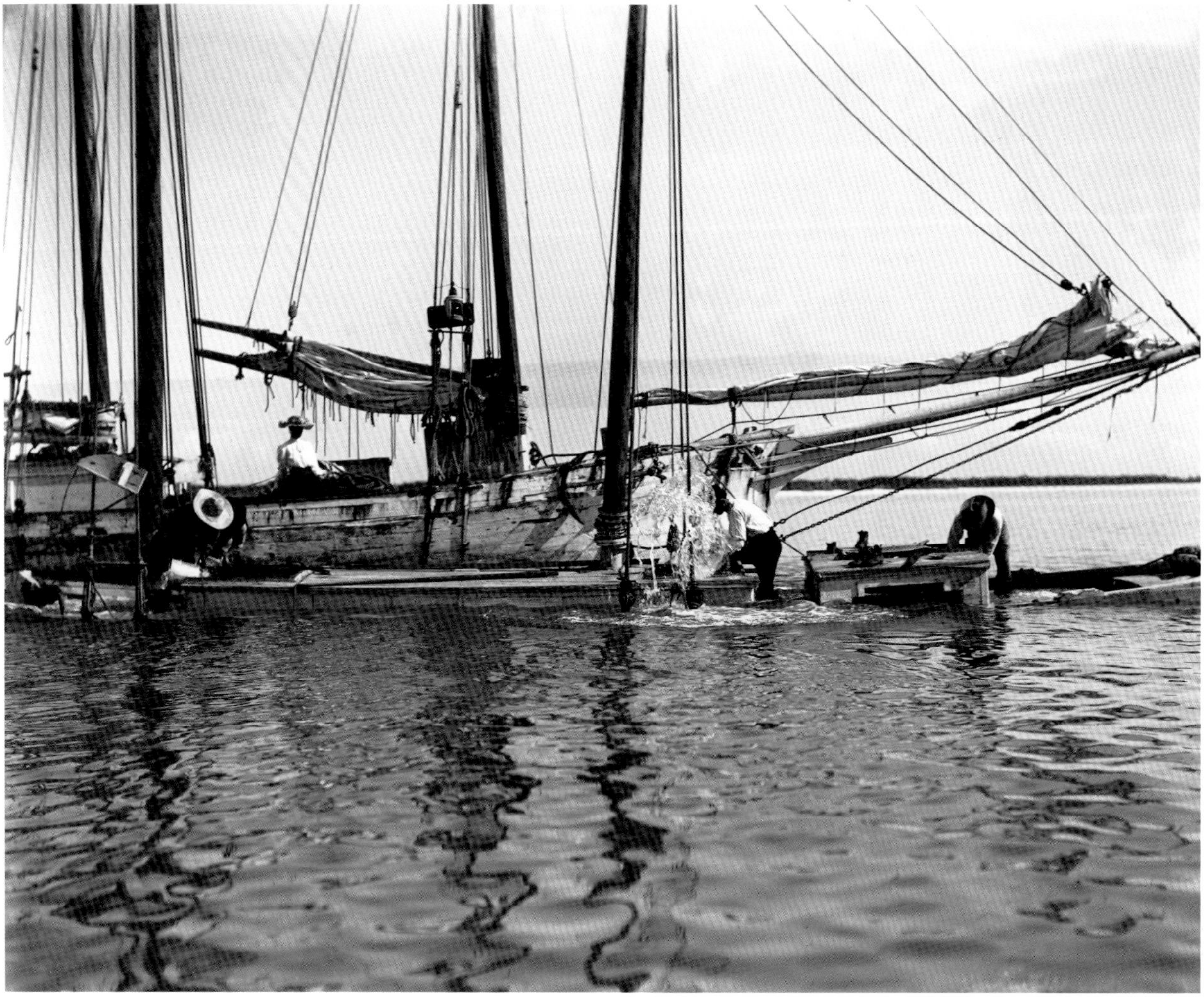

The pumps and bailing, however, could not keep up with the Gulf waters that held the *Kitty Horr*. The attempt to refloat her was abandoned. November 24, 1904; 48477.

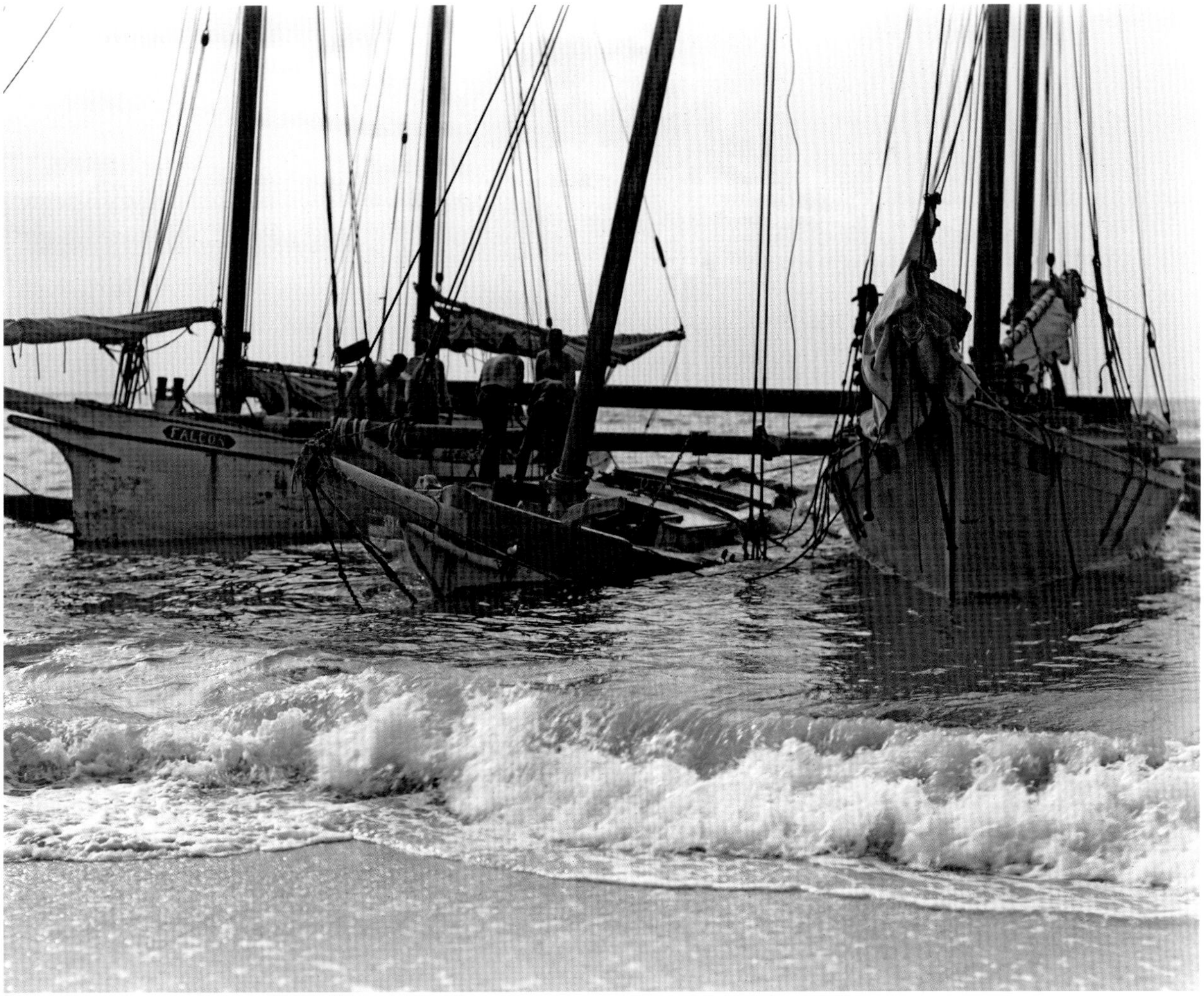

Collier decided to take another tack. As A.W. Dimock described it: "For a few days [actually, it was nearly three weeks] the wind was high, the waves washed the wreck close to the beach and work upon it was impossible. As soon as the weather permitted the captain . . . took to the wreck two schooners [one was the *Falcon*], provided with heavy spars and chains. A schooner was placed on each side of the wreck, and chains around its bow and stern made fast to spars laid across the three boats. Long levers, aided by tackle, turned the spars and winding up the chains lifted the wreck and depressed the other schooners. The arrangement was called a Spanish windlass and proved about as effective as a Spanish battleship. The schooners were bruised and strained, levers and chains broken and time and again the partly lifted wreck went to the bottom." The *Kitty Horr* apparently never was refloated. Merchant vessel records officially list the schooner as "stranded" on November 15, 1904, the day Collier and the Dimocks first saw her. December 13, 1904; 48501.

Pine Island Sound and Charlotte Harbor

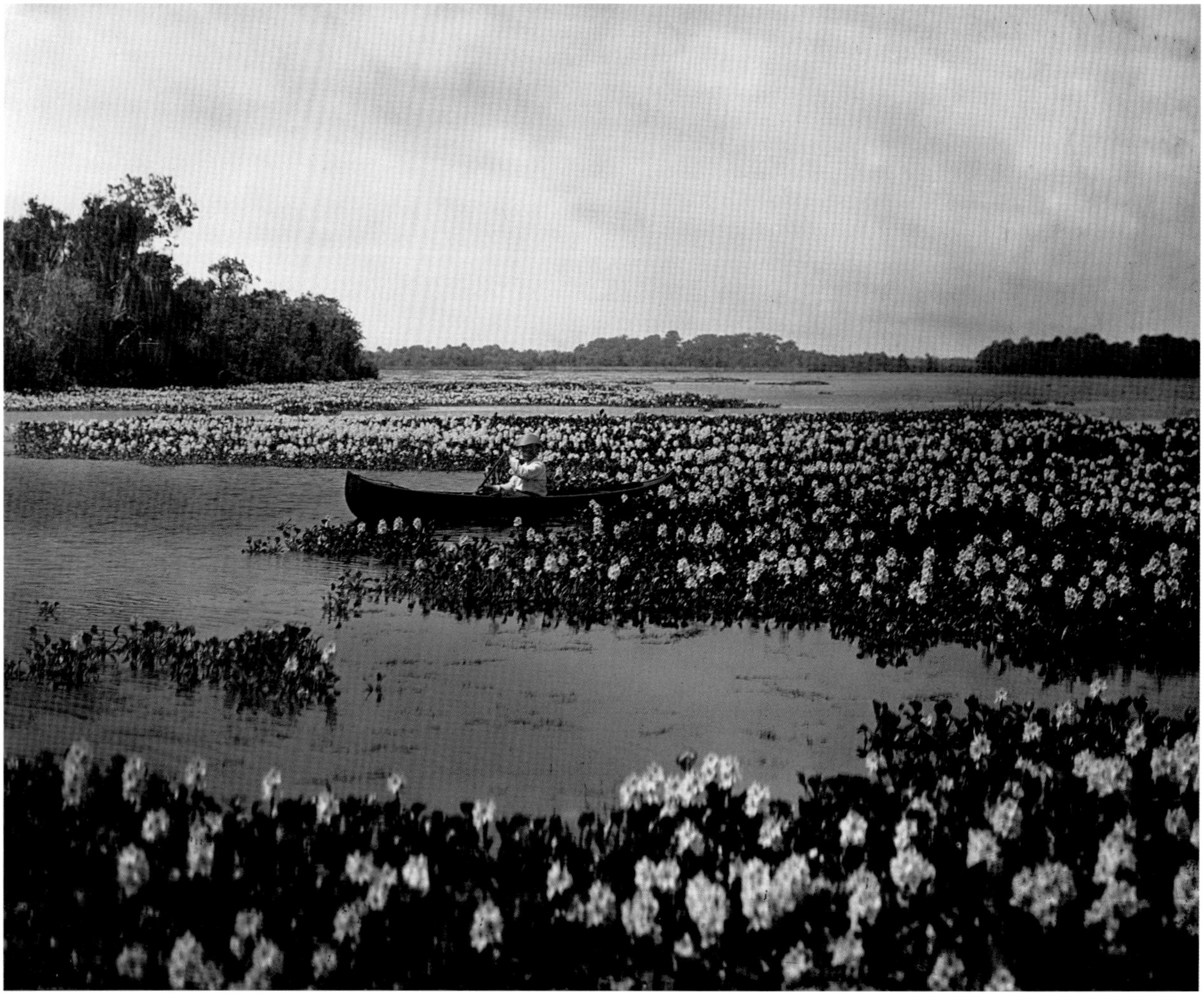

In the *Irene* and the smaller boats carried on her deck, the Dimocks explored, fished, and photographed the Caloosahatchee River and the waters of Charlotte Harbor, Gasparilla Sound, Pine Island Sound, and San Carlos Bay. They described the Caloosahatchee River as a "river of flowers" because of the water hyacinths that nearly filled it from side to side. May 19, 1907; 48411.

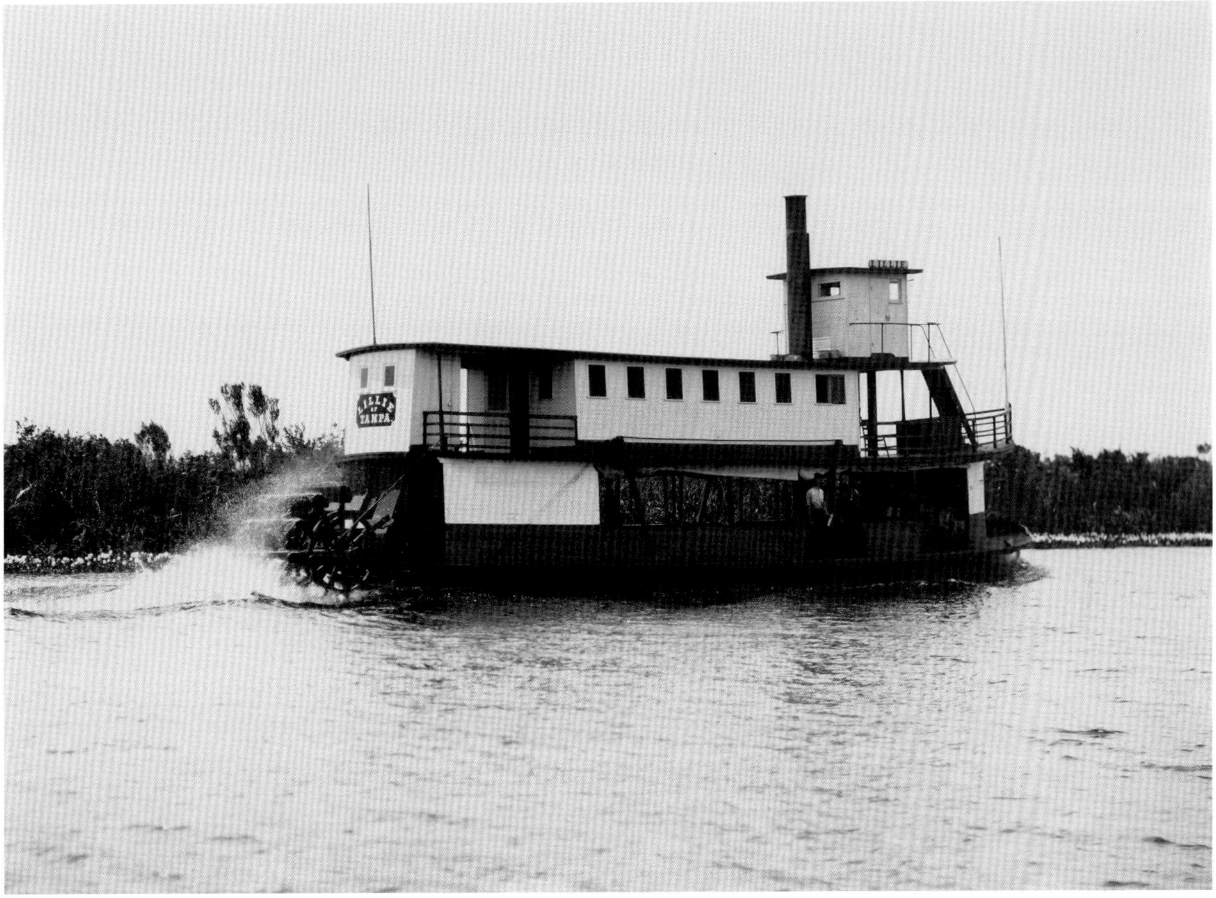

The paddle-wheel steamship *Lillie* out of Tampa on the Caloosahatchee River, probably on the way to Fort Myers. Sixty feet long and drawing only 2.8 feet, the *Lillie* was well suited to southwest Florida waterways. The steamship was built in Kissimmee in 1900. May 18, 1907; 48491.

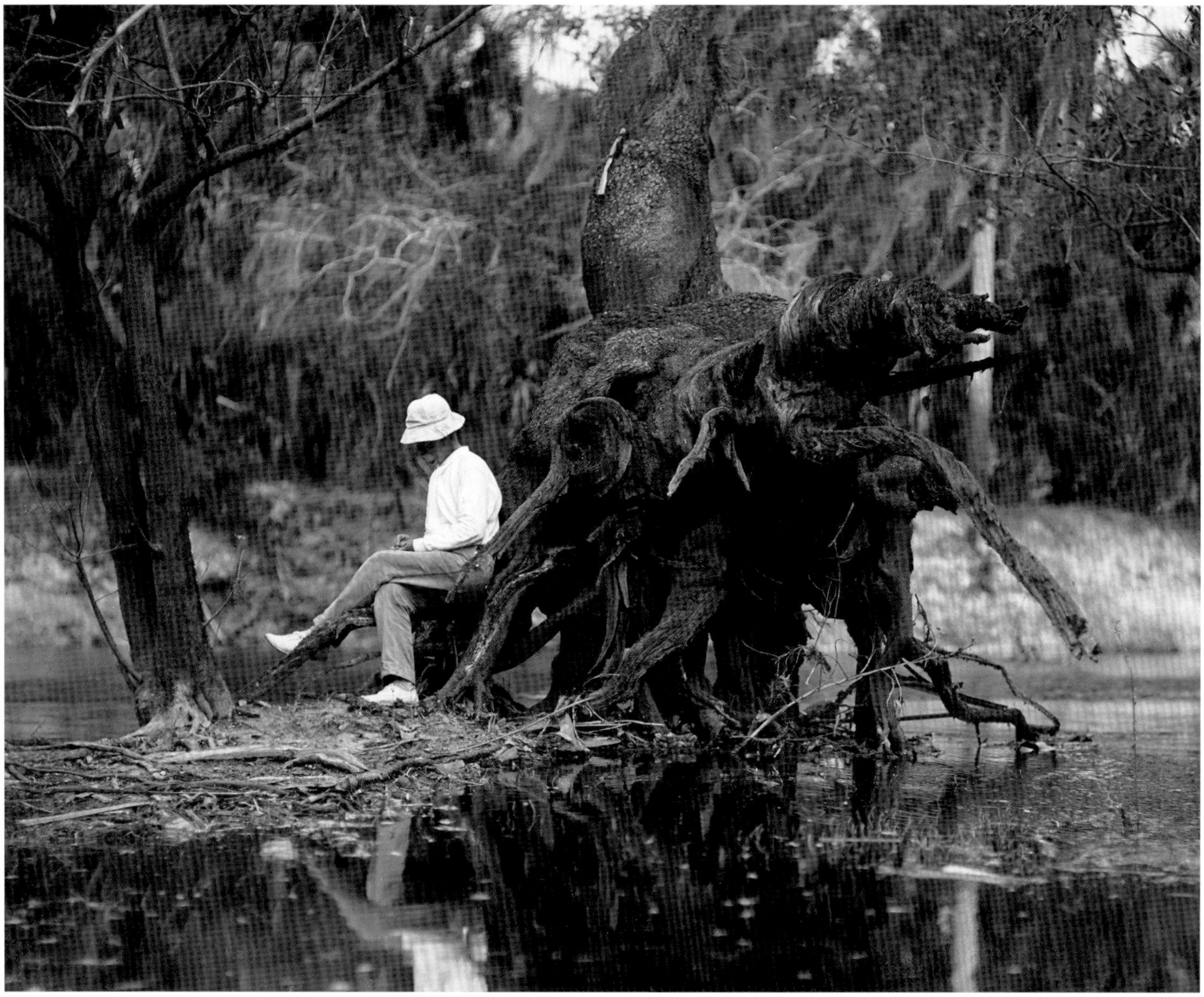

In "An Overlooked River in Florida" (1907), A. W. Dimock wrote that the Myakka River featured "trunks of great live oaks, three feet in thickness, projecting horizontally from the banks broke up into half a dozen octopus arms, each larger than the body of a man, that writhed in the dim light like monster serpents, sometimes so twining with others across the stream as to close the river to craft with spars." September 23, 1906; 48403.

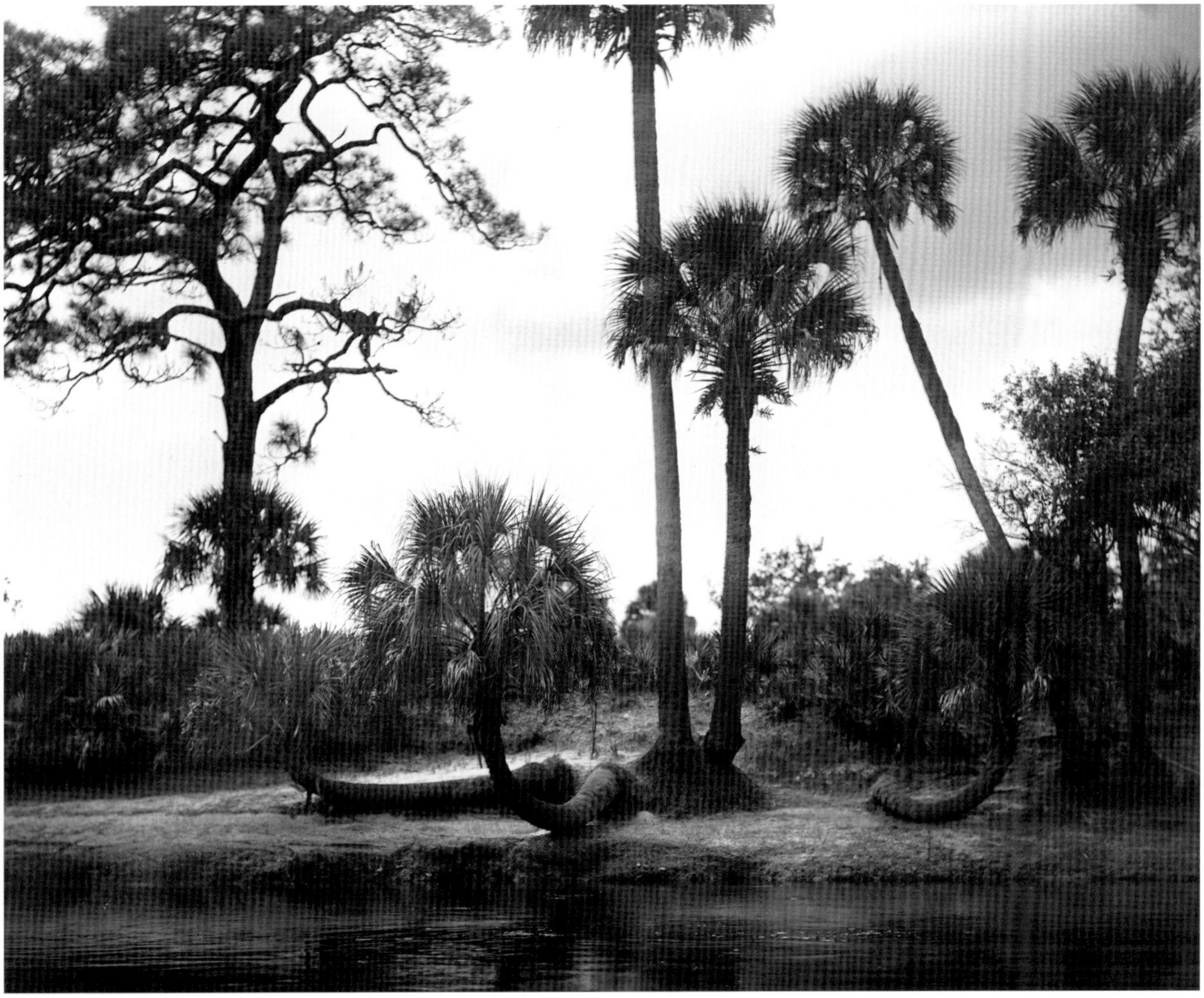

The Dimocks found that the Myakka River (they spelled it "Miakka") had "a current of five or six miles an hour, but it bristled with snags and was defended by sharp pointed rocks. Ends of palmetto logs, held fast to the bottom by their roots, bobbed up and down in the current, sometimes visible but more often hidden." It was a navigational nightmare. After traveling on the river, they sat "watching the wonderful clouds massed in the west and colored by the declining sun and rejoiced in the rest and peace that had followed a strenuous day." September 23, 1906; 48402.

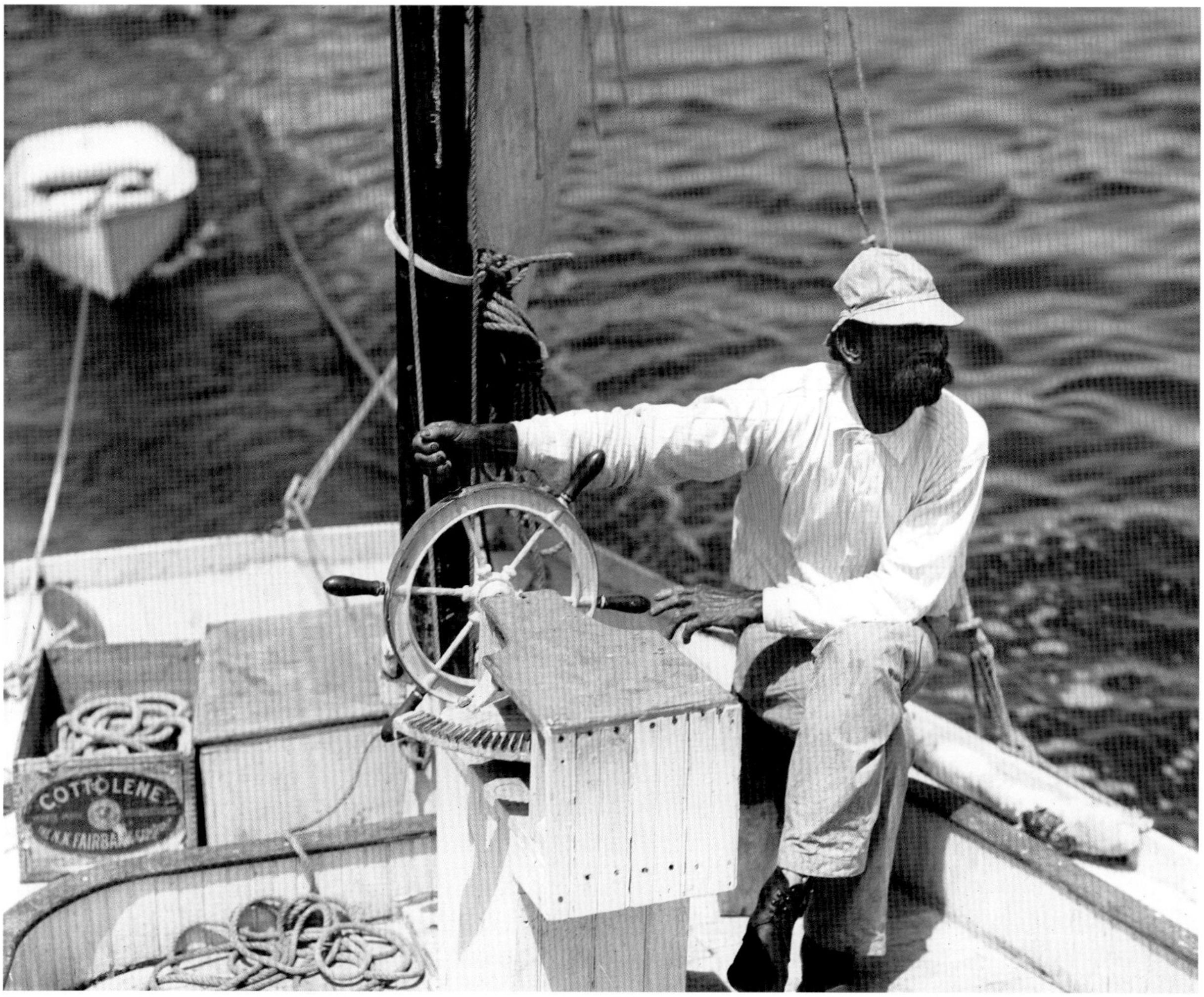

"O. B.," one the *Irene*'s hired hands, at the wheel in Charlotte Harbor.
June 24, 1905; 48484.

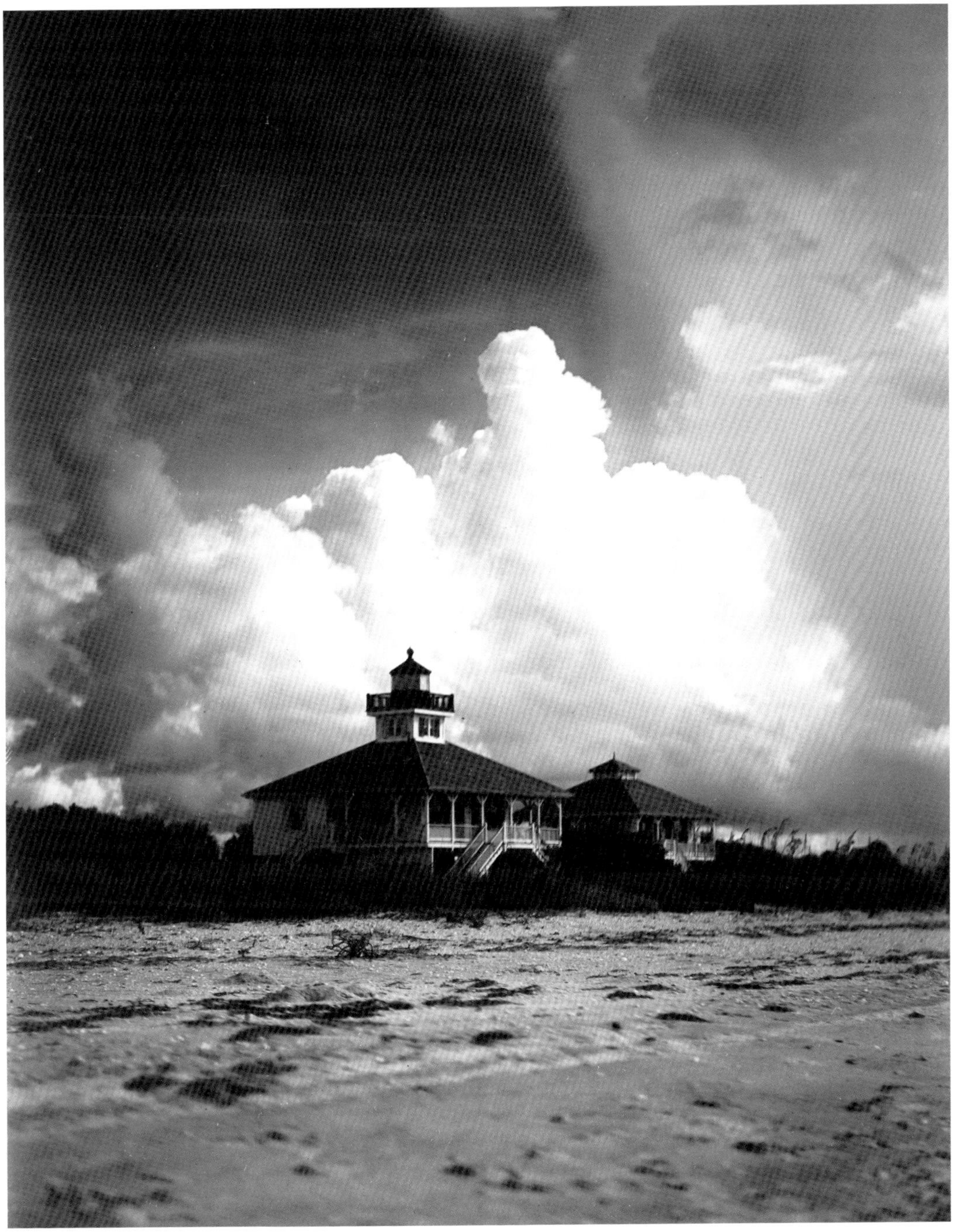

"Lighthouse at Boca Grande." Built in 1890 on the south end of Gasparilla Island, the restored lighthouse today is in Gasparilla Island State Park and is open to the public. The assistant lighthouse keeper's house is on the right. July 31, 1908; 48527.

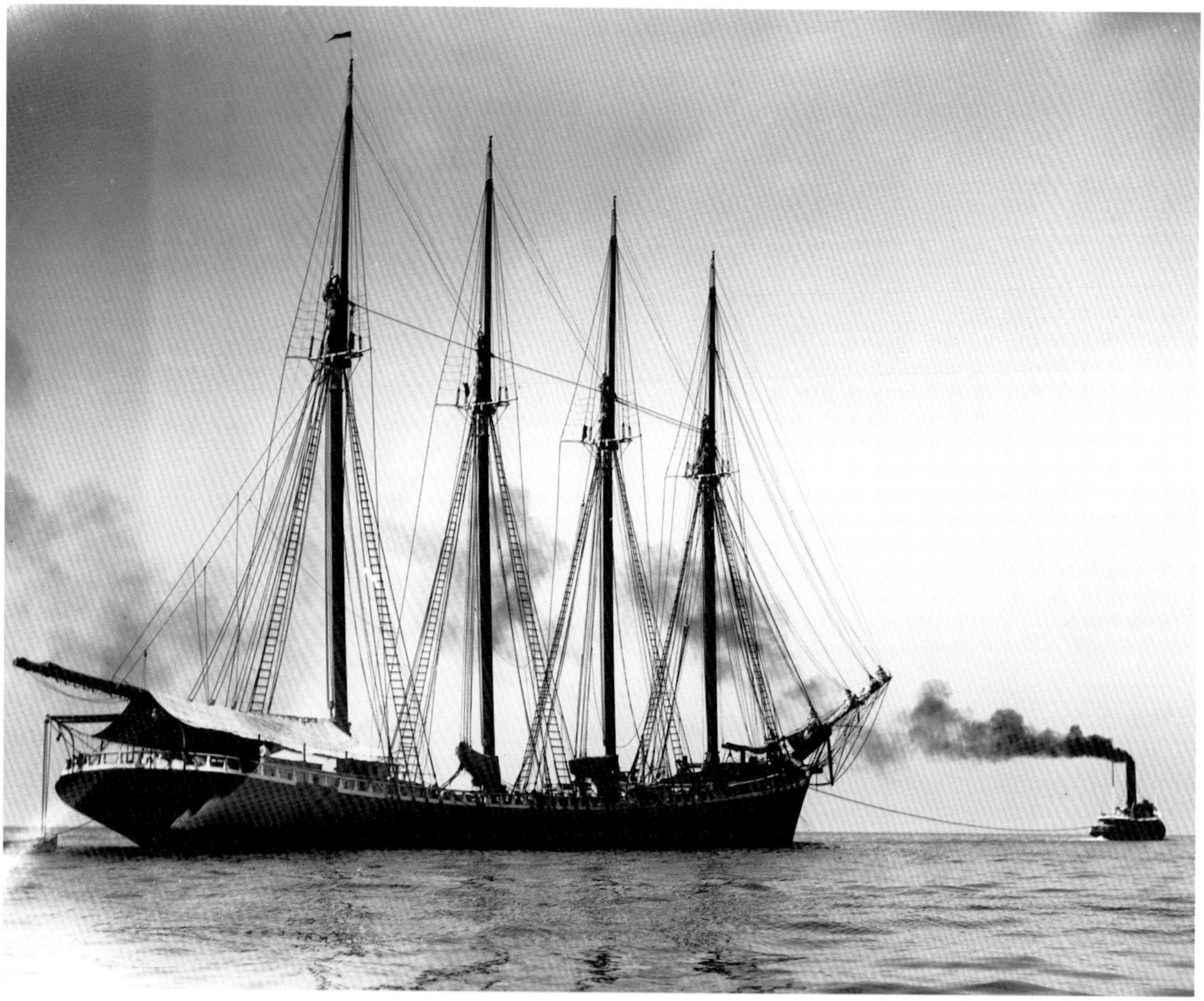

Prior to the building of the railroad to Boca Grande in 1907, phosphate mined out of the Peace River was barged to the port and then loaded on ships, like this phosphate schooner being towed by a tug after leaving Boca Grande. July 7, 1907; 48500.

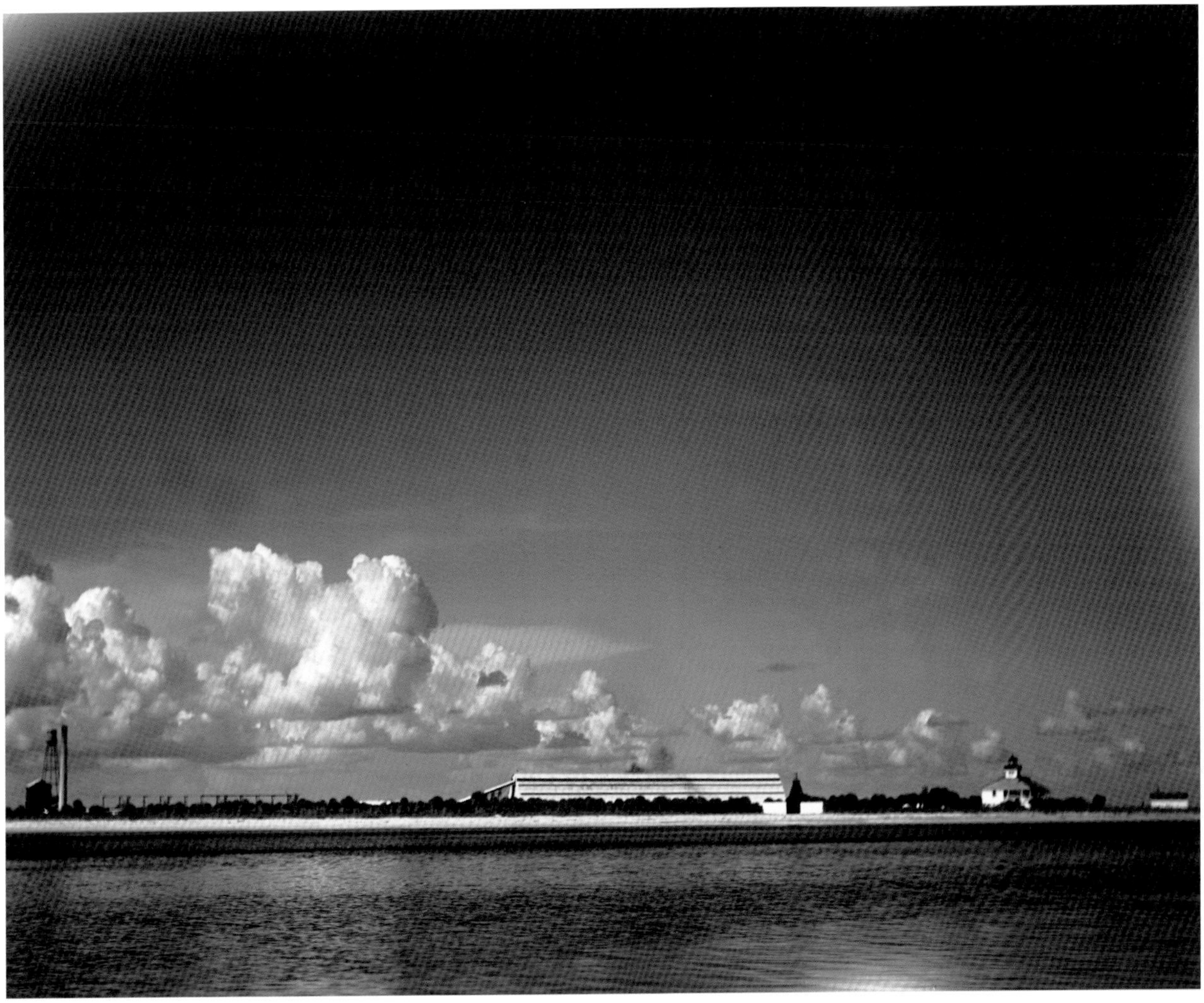

The Boca Grande lighthouse and a phosphate storage "shed" on Gasparilla Island. The assistant keeper's house is behind the lighthouse. By the time this photograph was taken, phosphate mined from the Peace River was brought by rail to the storage facility on the island and then shipped out. September 9, 1913; 49316.

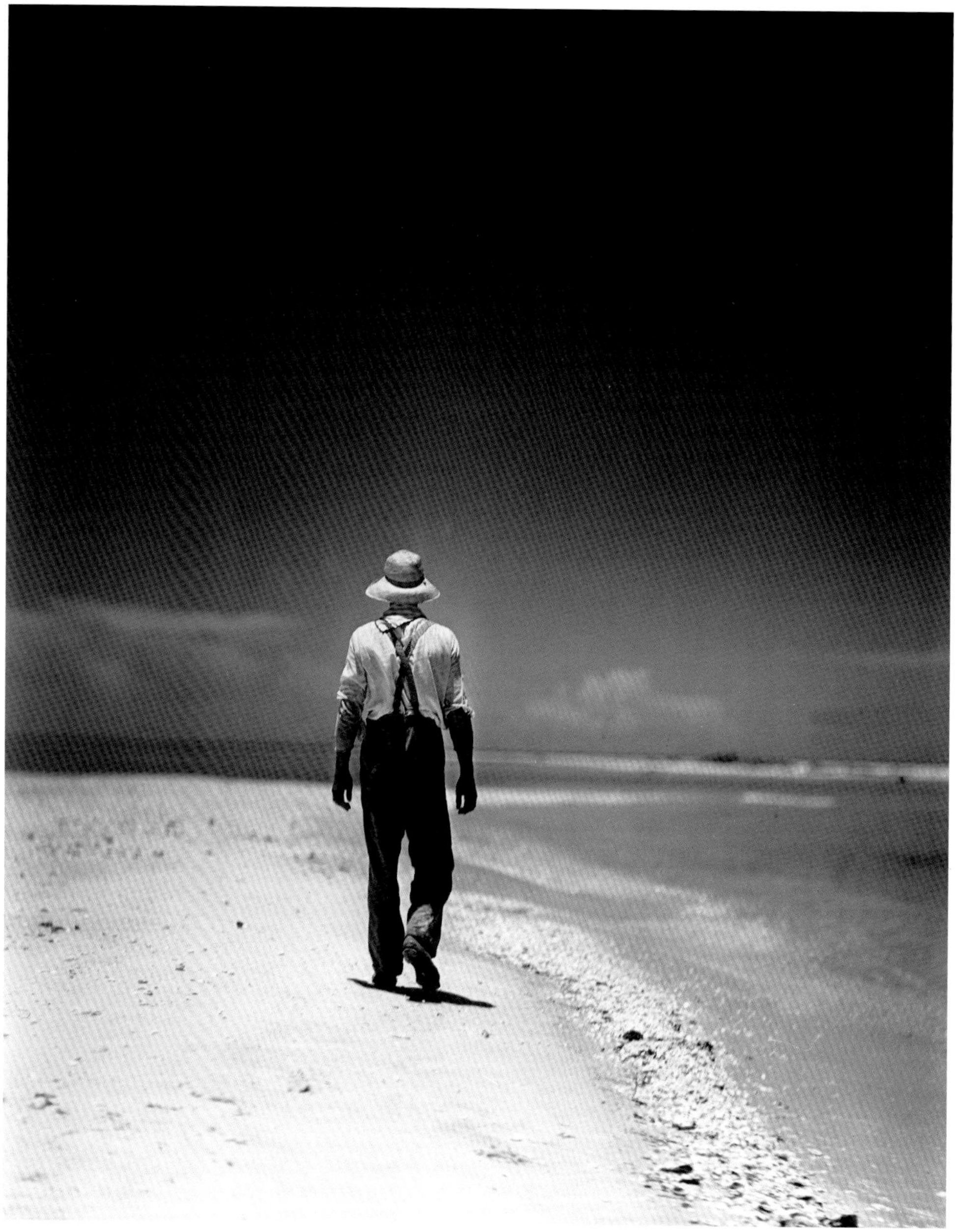

According to Julian Dimock, this photograph, titled "Dode on the Beach," was taken at Gasparilla Pass. It may actually be Boca Grande Pass. In *The Book of the Tarpon*, A. W. Dimock used this photo to represent the "Bee Man" of La Costa Island (Cayo Costa), described as a barefoot, bearded hermit who raised bees and lived in "a shack of a cabin" next to a "tumble-down dock." A. W. also wrote that they drank metheglyn (spiced mead) with the Bee Man, whose last name was Franklin. July 14, 1908; 48525.

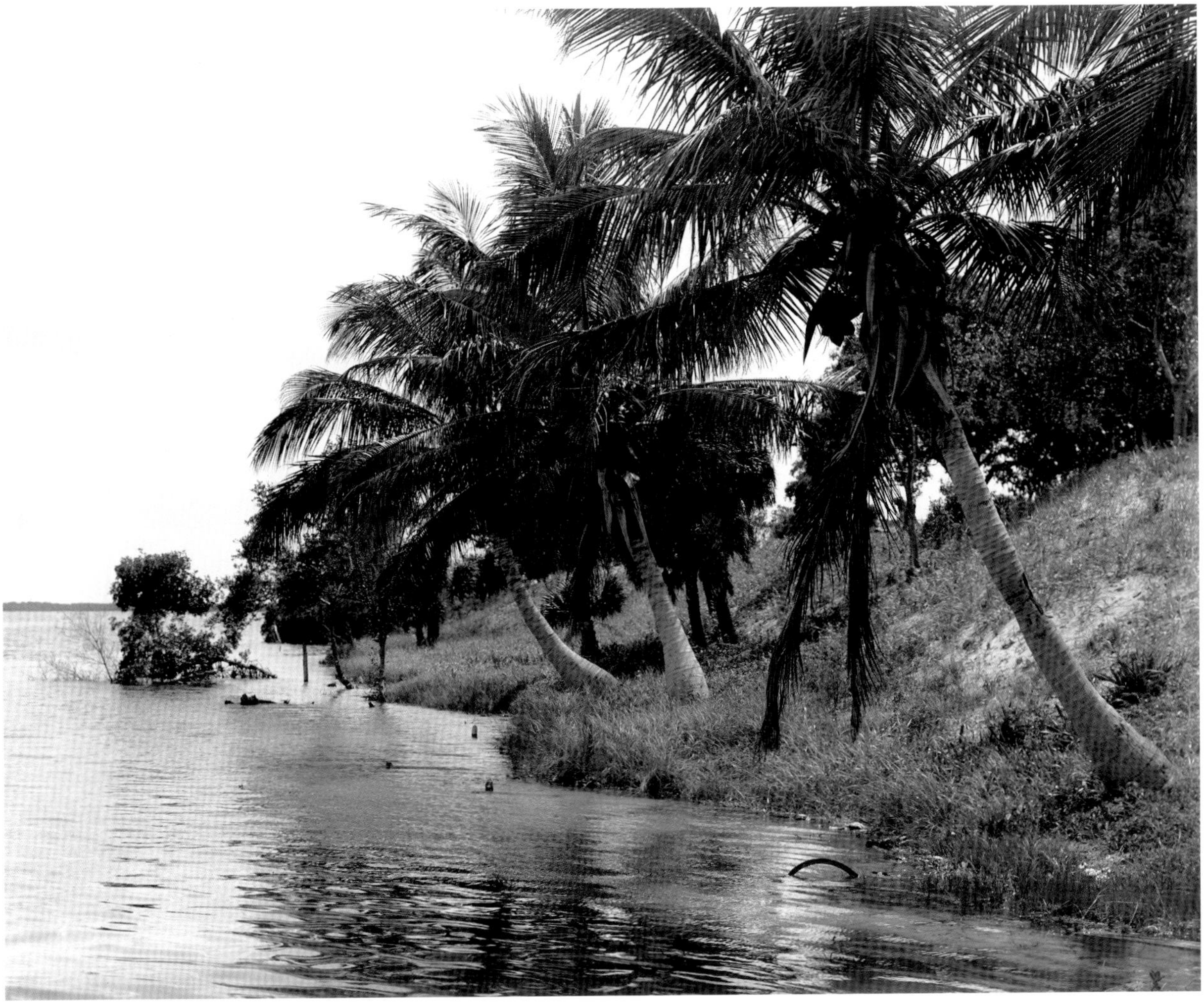

Palm trees on Mondongo Island (Julian spelled it "Mundungo") in Pine Island Sound.
June 6, 1905; 48598.

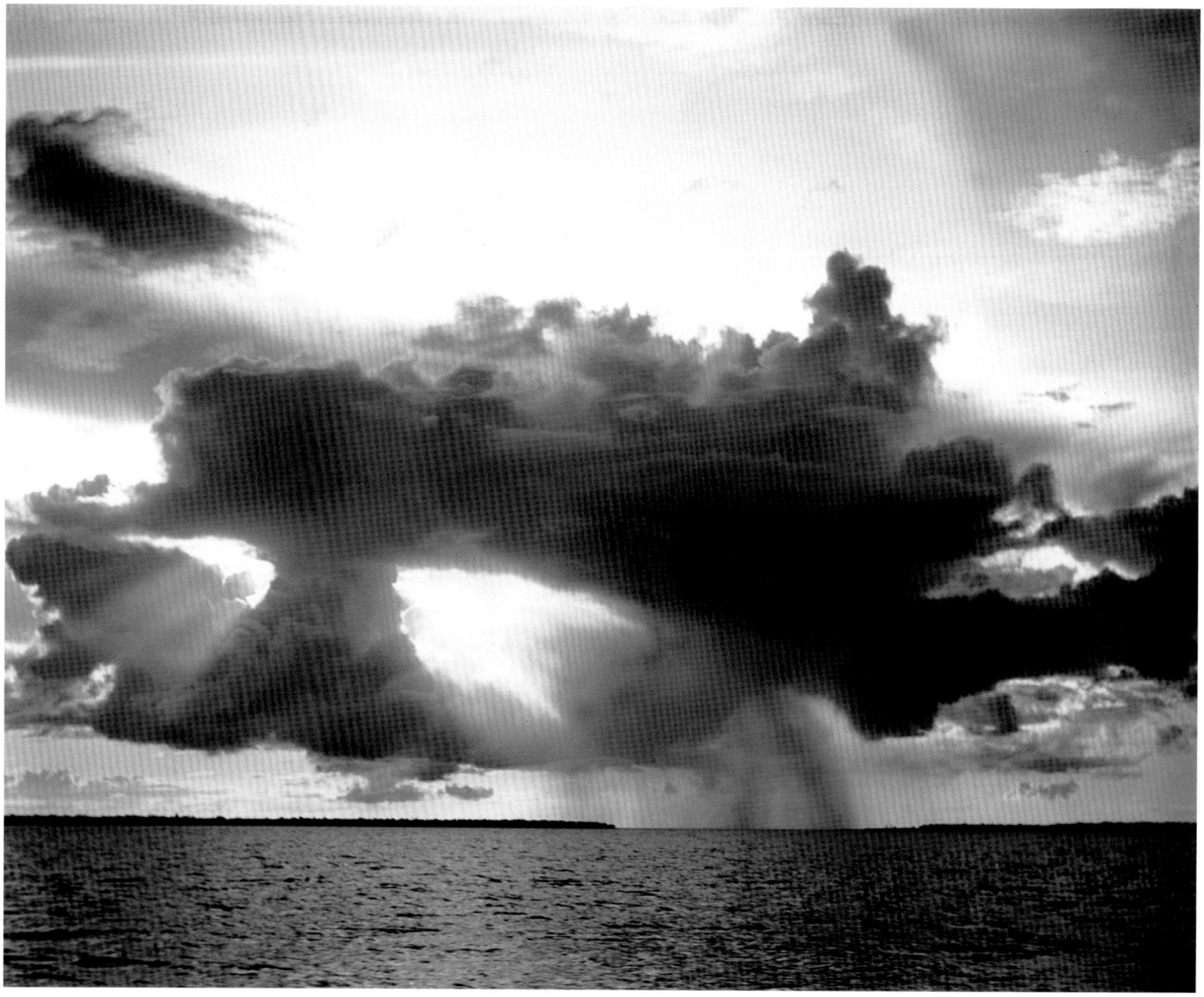

Sunset in back of Captiva Pass.
September 8, 1913; 49324.

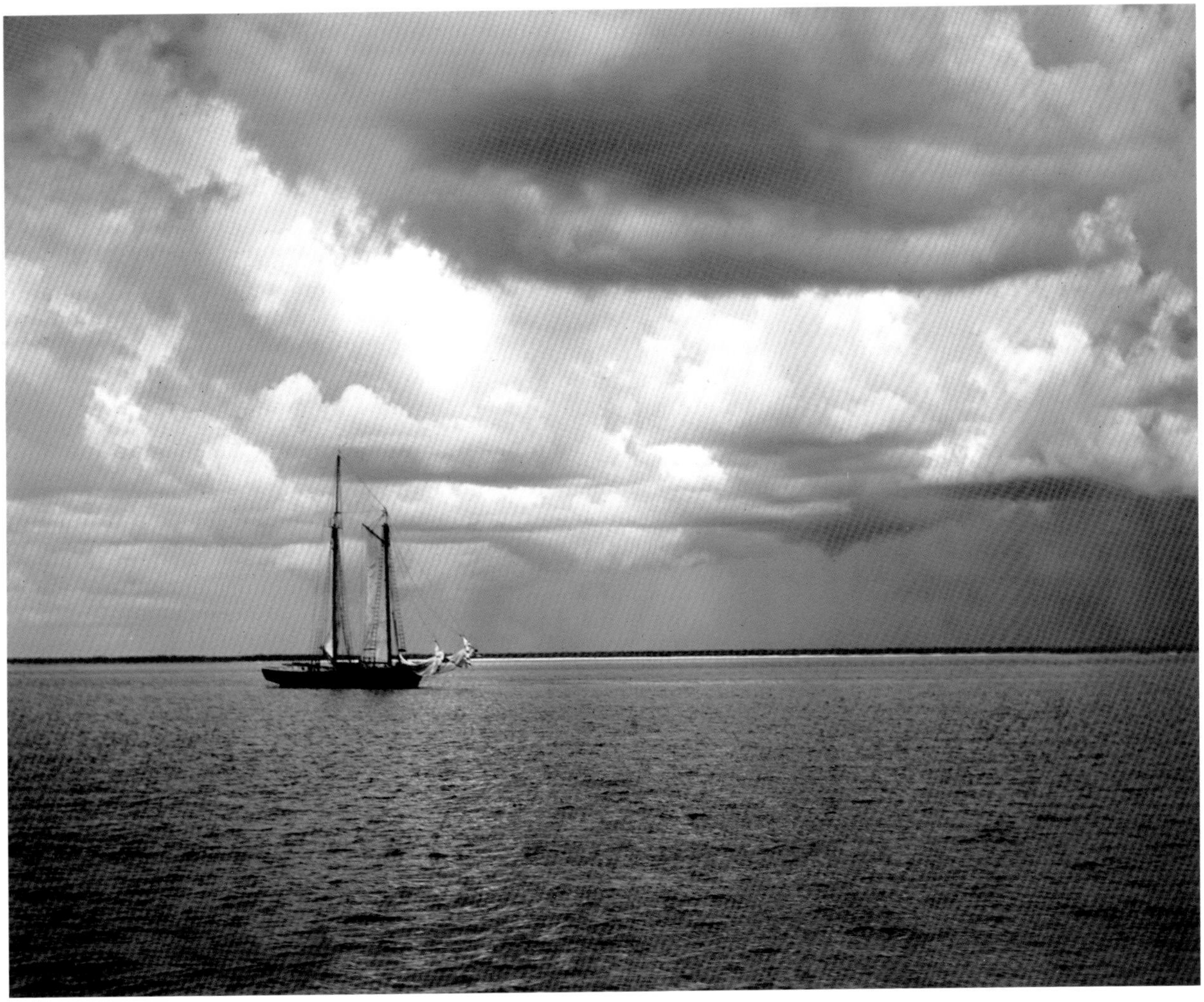

A schooner aground in the shallows, Pine Island Sound.
September 8, 1913; 49320.

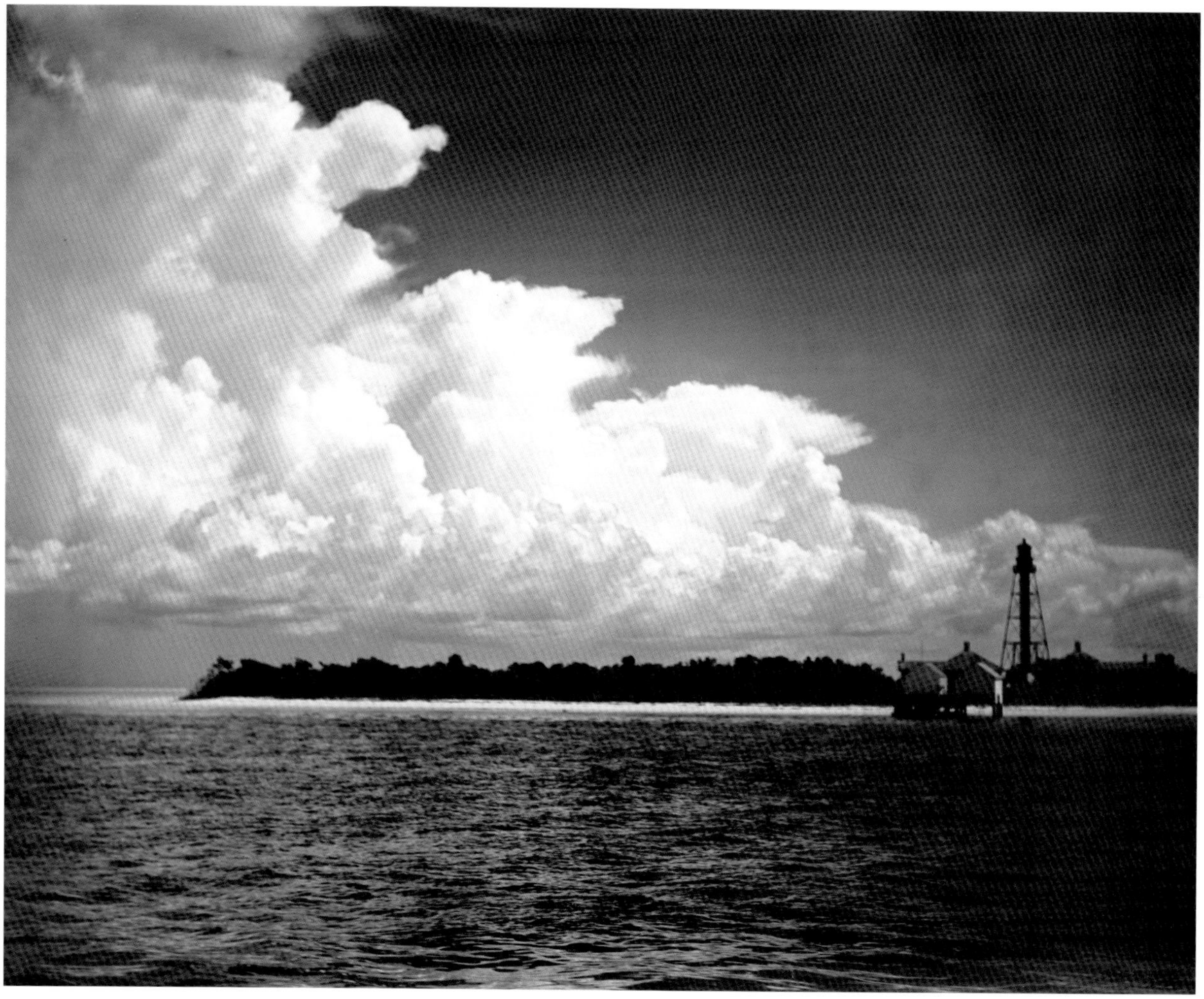

The Sanibel Island light on the eastern tip of Sanibel Island. The light went into operation in 1884. Houses for the keepers can be seen in back of the buildings on the dock. The light remains in use, and the public can visit the grounds. September 8, 1913; 49319.

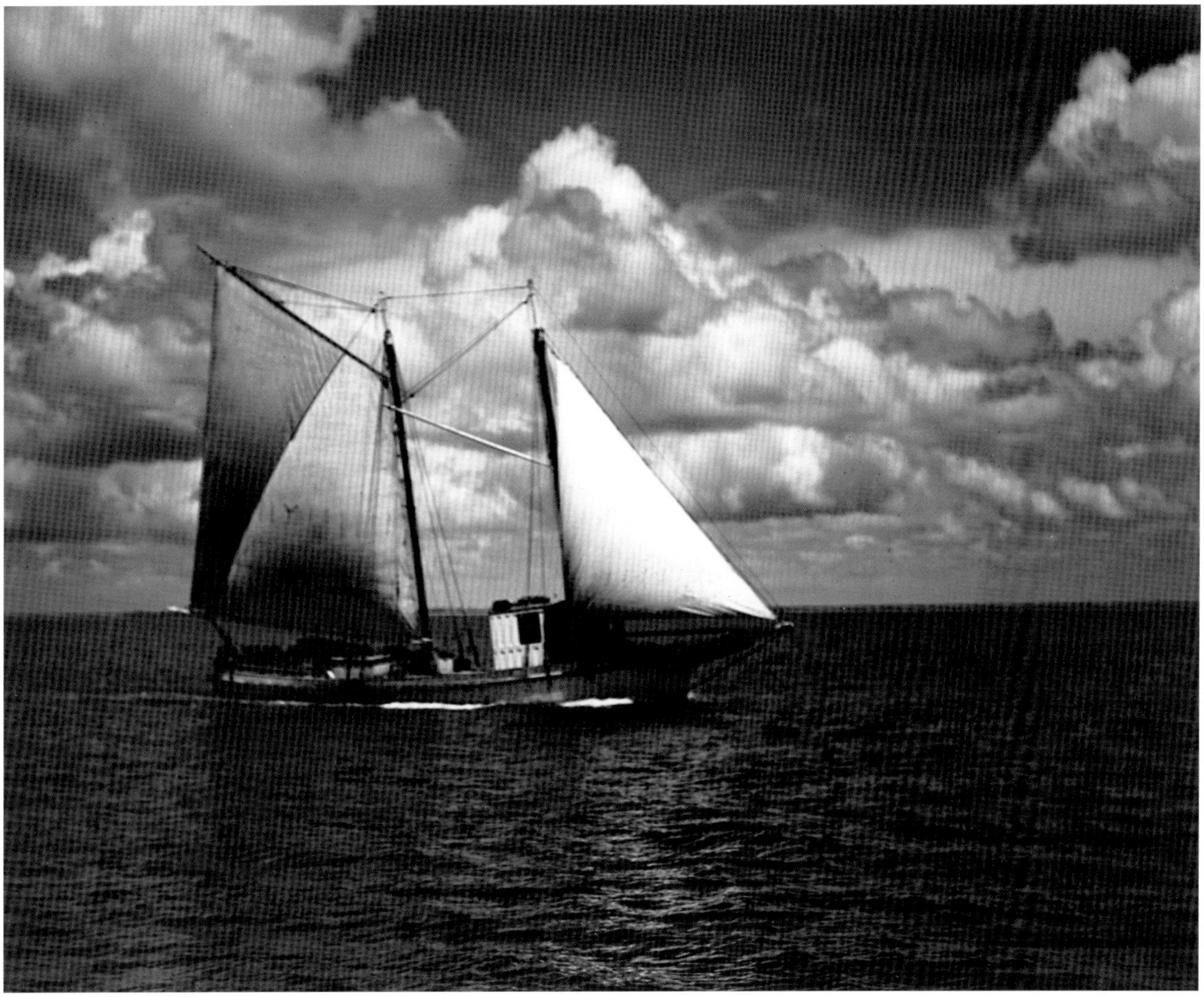

A working schooner off Sanibel Island.
September 8, 1913; 49317.

The Mainland

Boat Landing in the Everglades

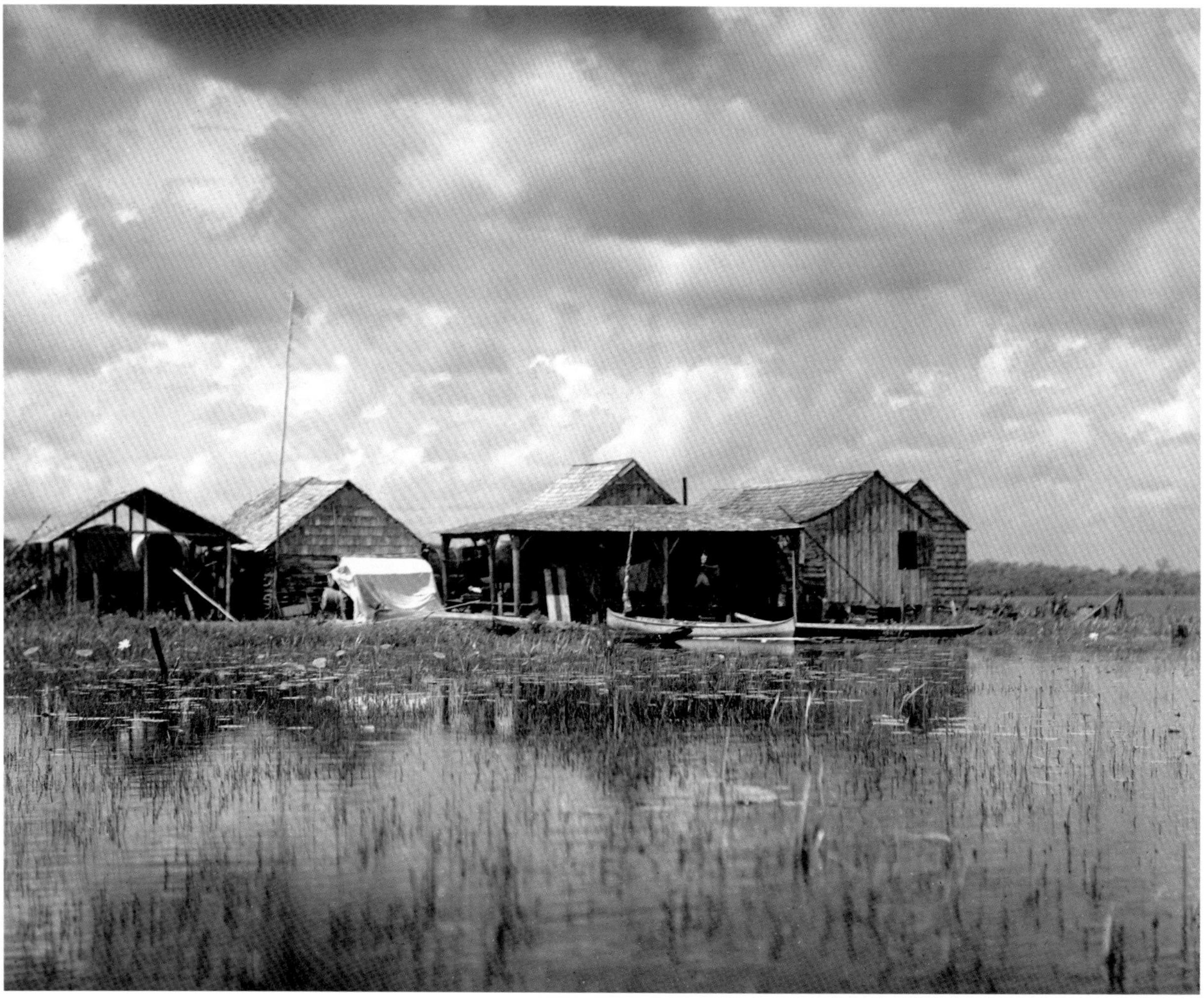

In 1907, the Dimocks visited Brown's Boat Landing, a trading outpost operated by William H. "Bill" Brown and his family in the Everglades. The Dimocks had intended to canoe across the Everglades to Miami, but water levels were too low for their canoes, so they gave up and headed north to Boat Landing, led by their Seminole Indian guide. Bill Brown had dug a canal through which Seminoles could pole their canoes to reach his store, hence its name. The site of Brown's Boat Landing today is north of I-75 on the Seminole Indian Big Cypress Reservation about 35 miles southeast of Immokalee. August 12, 1907; 48353.

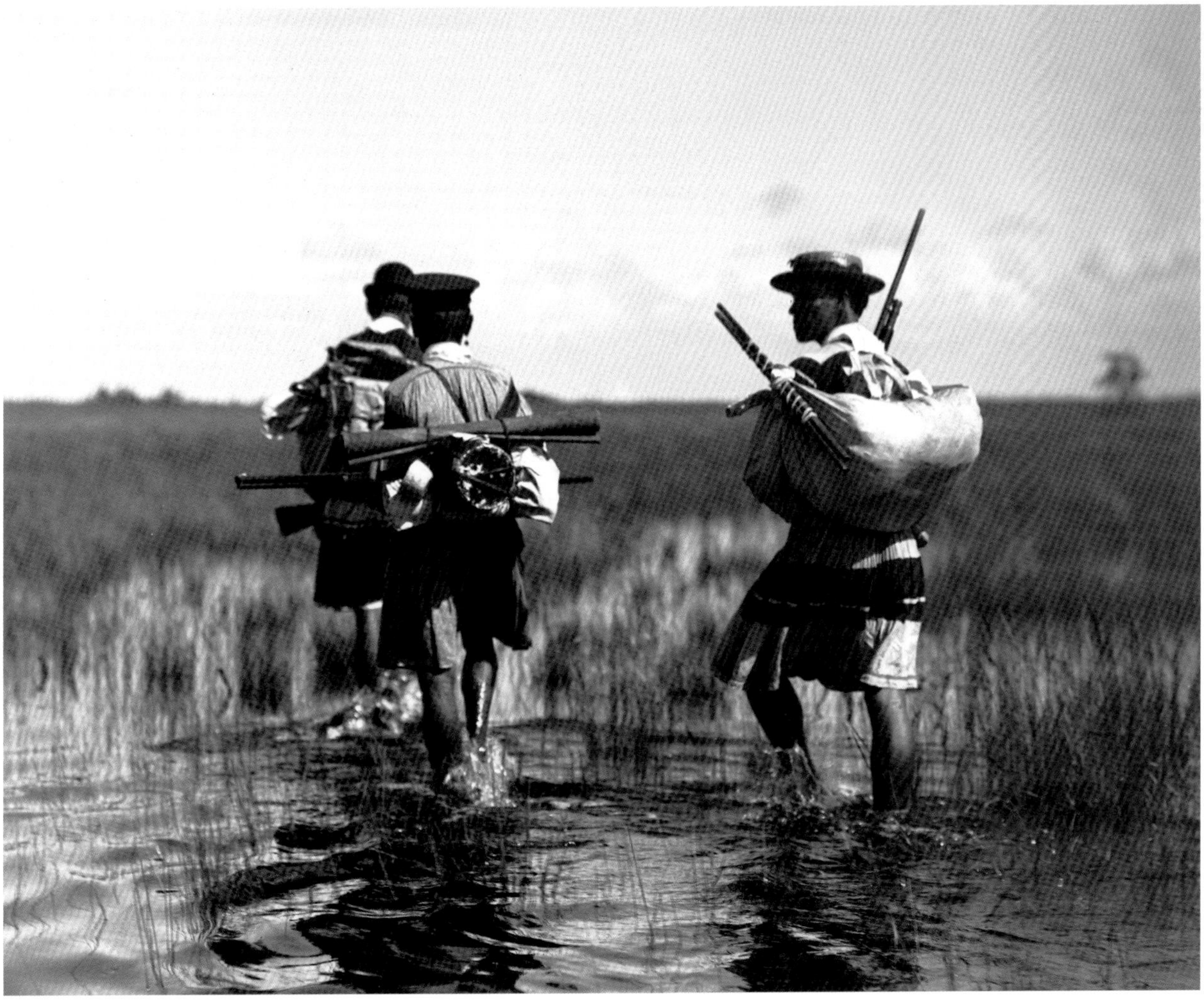

Bill Brown, a native of England, was called Mackillessee (foreigner) by the Seminoles. In 1908, Brown sold his store to the Episcopal Church and moved his family to Immokalee. The Church used the site as a mission, but continued to run the store where Seminole families came to obtain goods. These three Seminole men are on their way home after shopping. August 18, 1910; 48135.

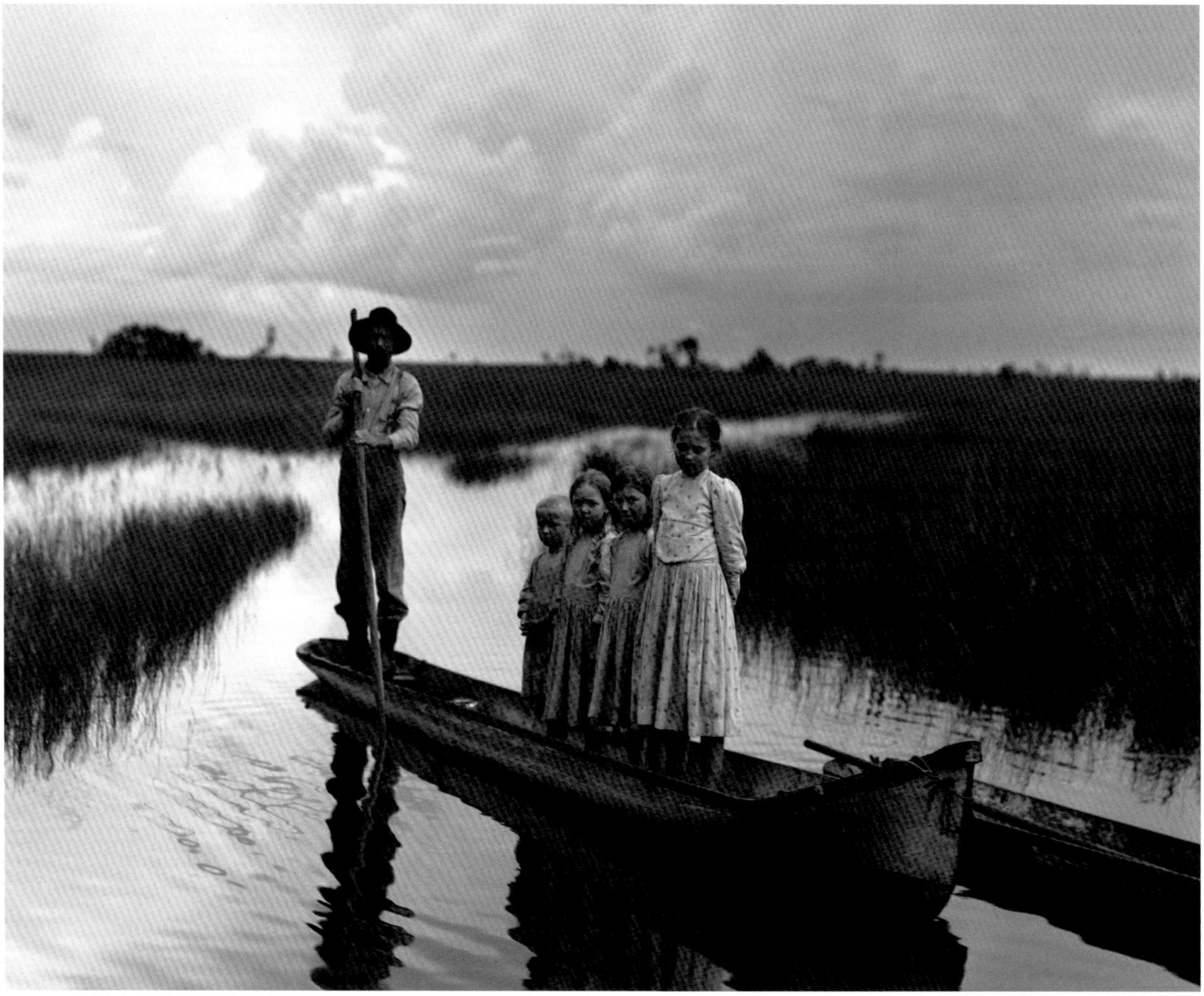

In 1910, Julian Dimock was again at the store, now called Godden's Landing, this time as photographer for the American Museum of Natural History's expedition to the Seminole Indians led by Alanson Skinner. Before the expedition left the landing to canoe east across the Everglades to Miami, Julian took photographs of Seminole Indians and local non-Indians. According to the 1910 U.S. census, William H. Crawford, portrayed here with his family, was a thirty-two-year-old farmworker who was widowed and raising three children (Jannie, Mary, and Buster; the fourth child may have been a friend). The family probably lived at the mission or nearby. August 17, 1910; 48218.

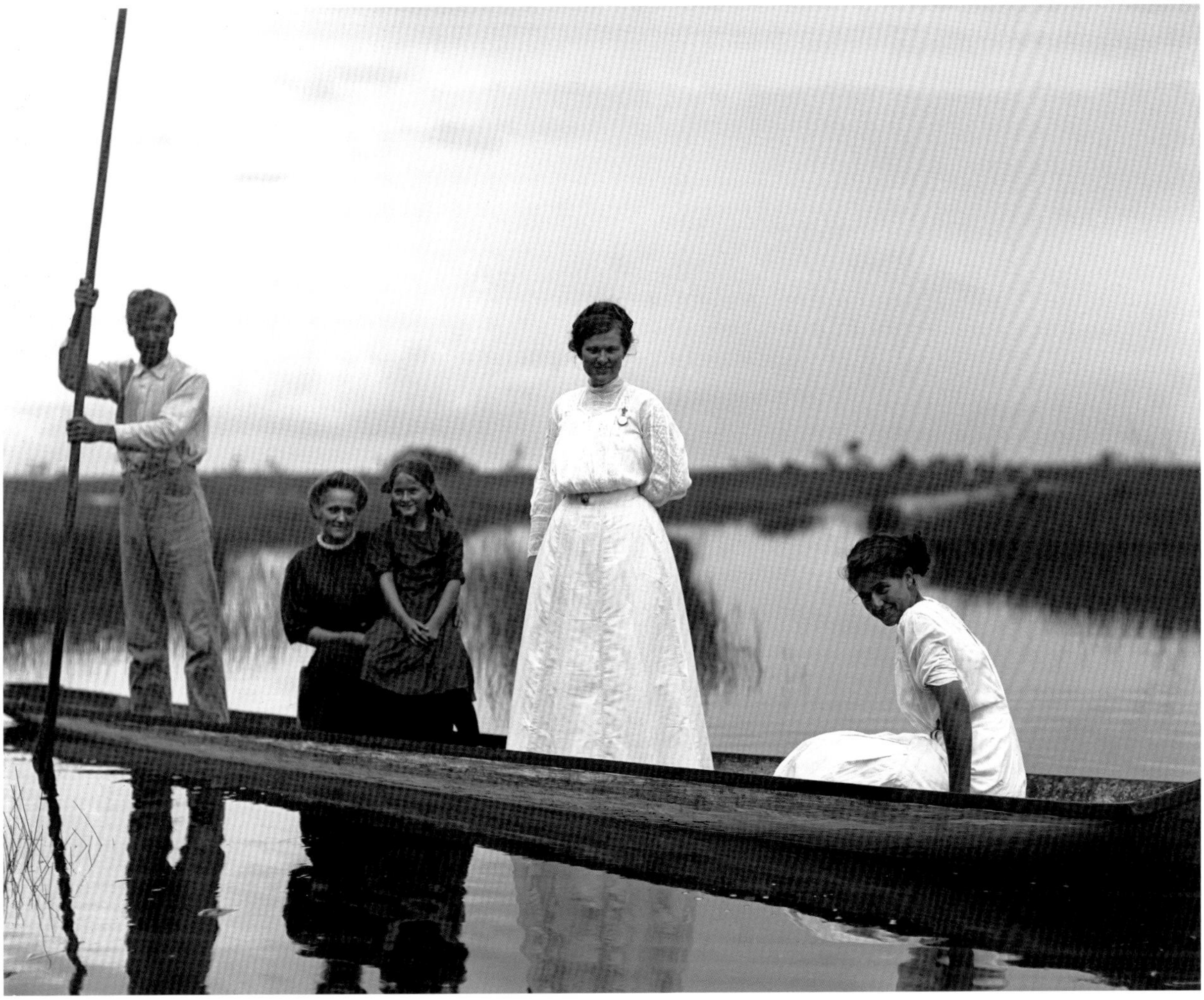

Mr. and Mrs. R. W. Cox and child; Ethel and Wilhelmina Kern. Robert Cox (age 42) and his wife, Alice (age 46), appear in the 1910 U.S. census, as does the young girl (listed as stepdaughter). Alice Cox was a schoolteacher, possibly at an Episcopal mission school near the landing. In the same census, Wilhelmina Kern (17) also is identified as a teacher. Ethel may be her 19-year-old sister visiting from Philadelphia, where, according to the census, a person with that name lived with her grandparents and worked as a stenographer. August 17, 1910; 49309.

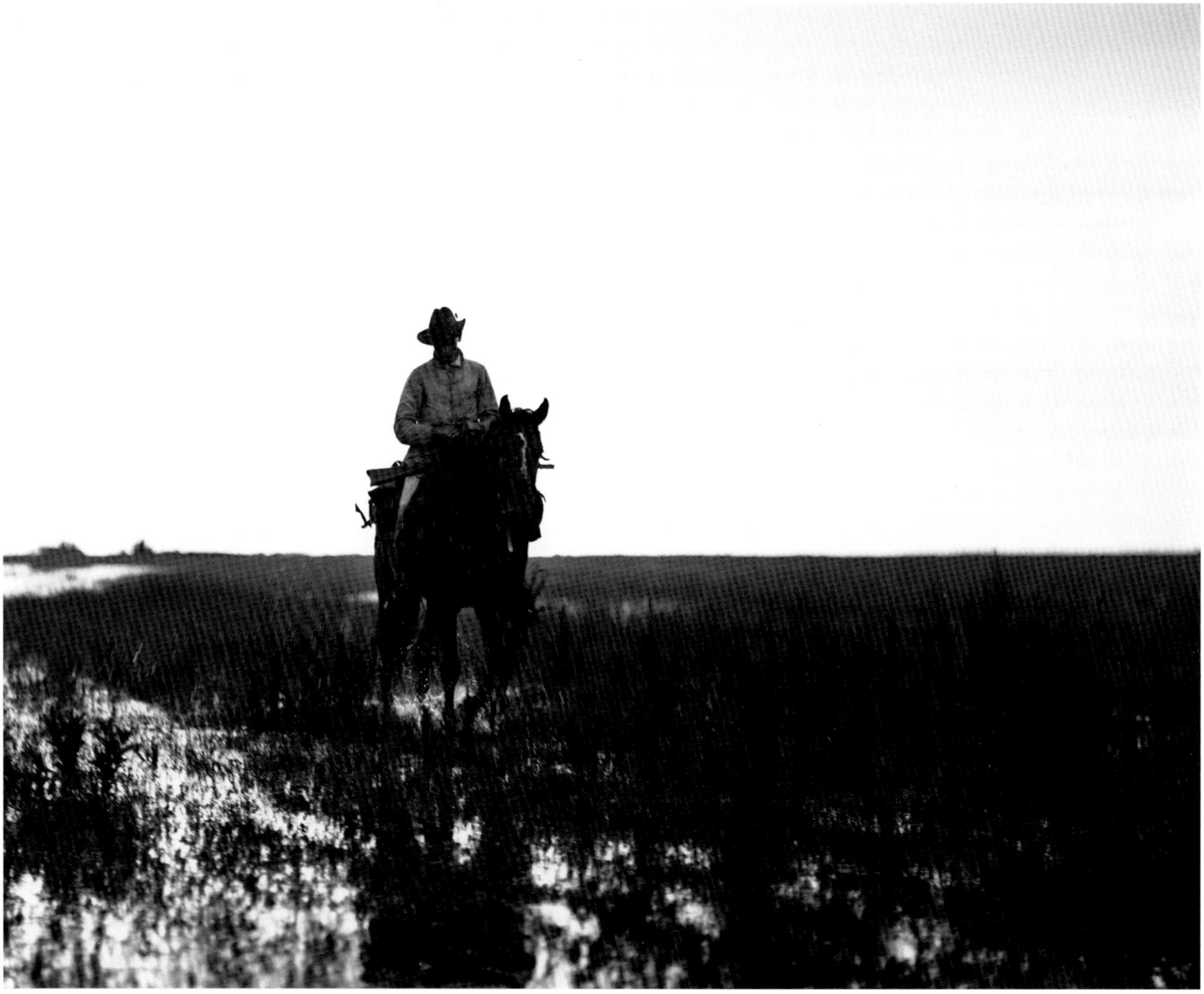

Mail was delivered to Boat Landing by horse, an Everglades Pony Express.
August 17, 1910; 49311.

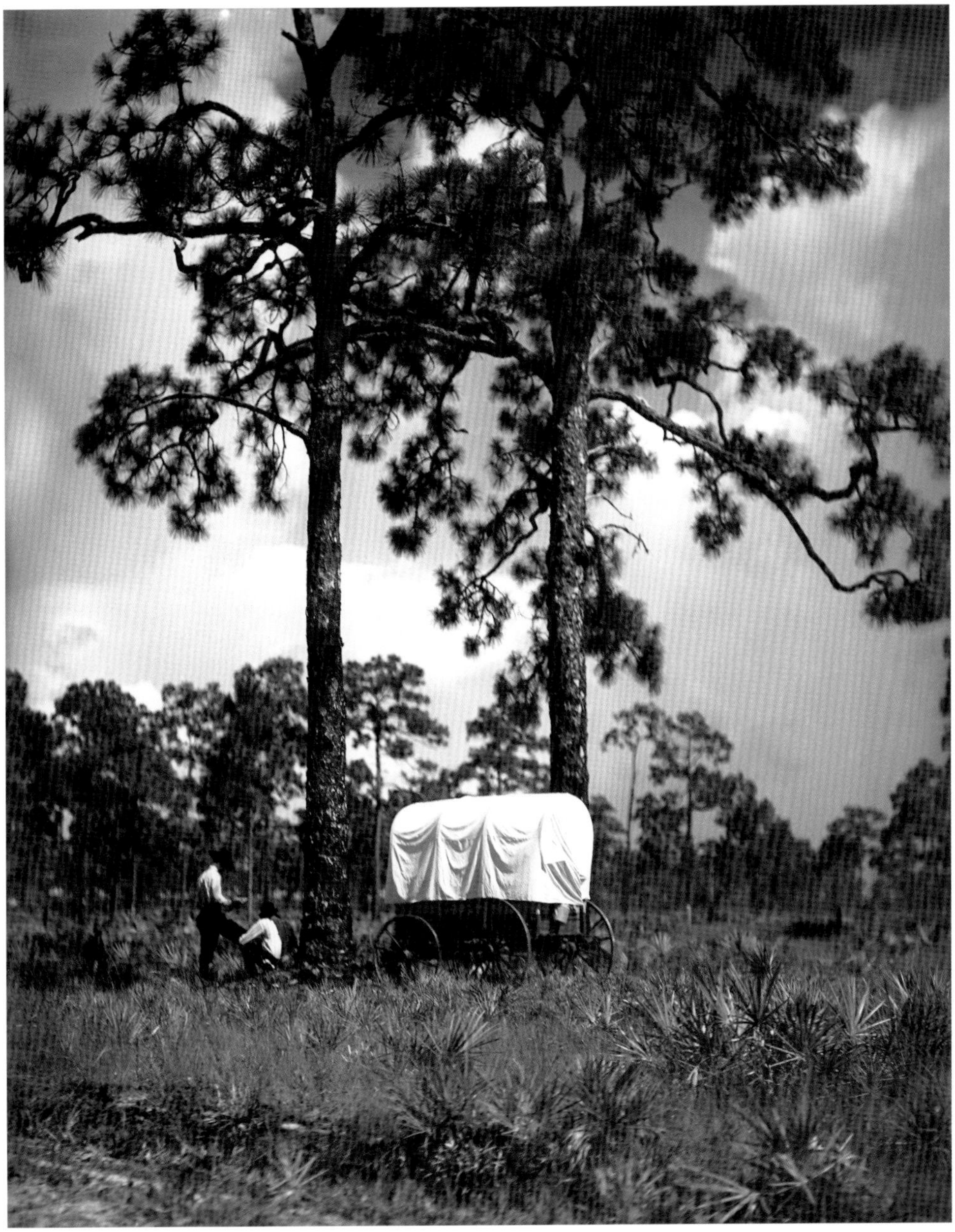

From Fort Myers, one could reach Boat Landing from the north via a journey of several days across higher, drier ground than one encountered traveling from the south or west through the Everglades or Big Cypress Swamp. In 1910, the American Museum expedition used a covered wagon drawn by four oxen to make the trip from Fort Myers to Boat Landing. August 9, 1910; 49366.

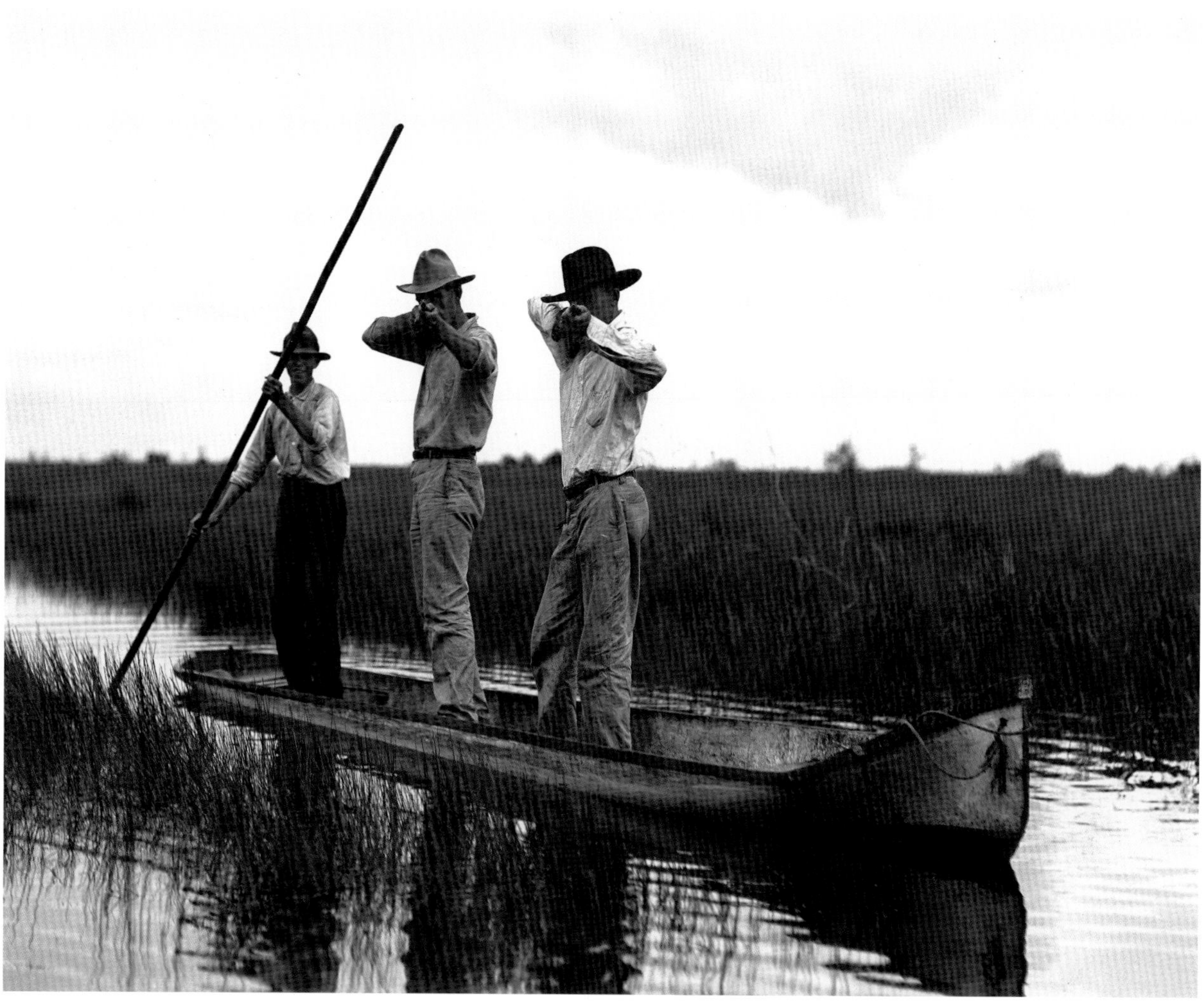

At the landing, Frank Brown, the son of Bill Brown (*right*), and two other men have a bit of fun with the "camera-man," as A. W. Dimock referred to Julian. The canoe the men are standing in was likely made by Seminole Indians. August 17, 1910: 49310.

Deep Lake Plantation

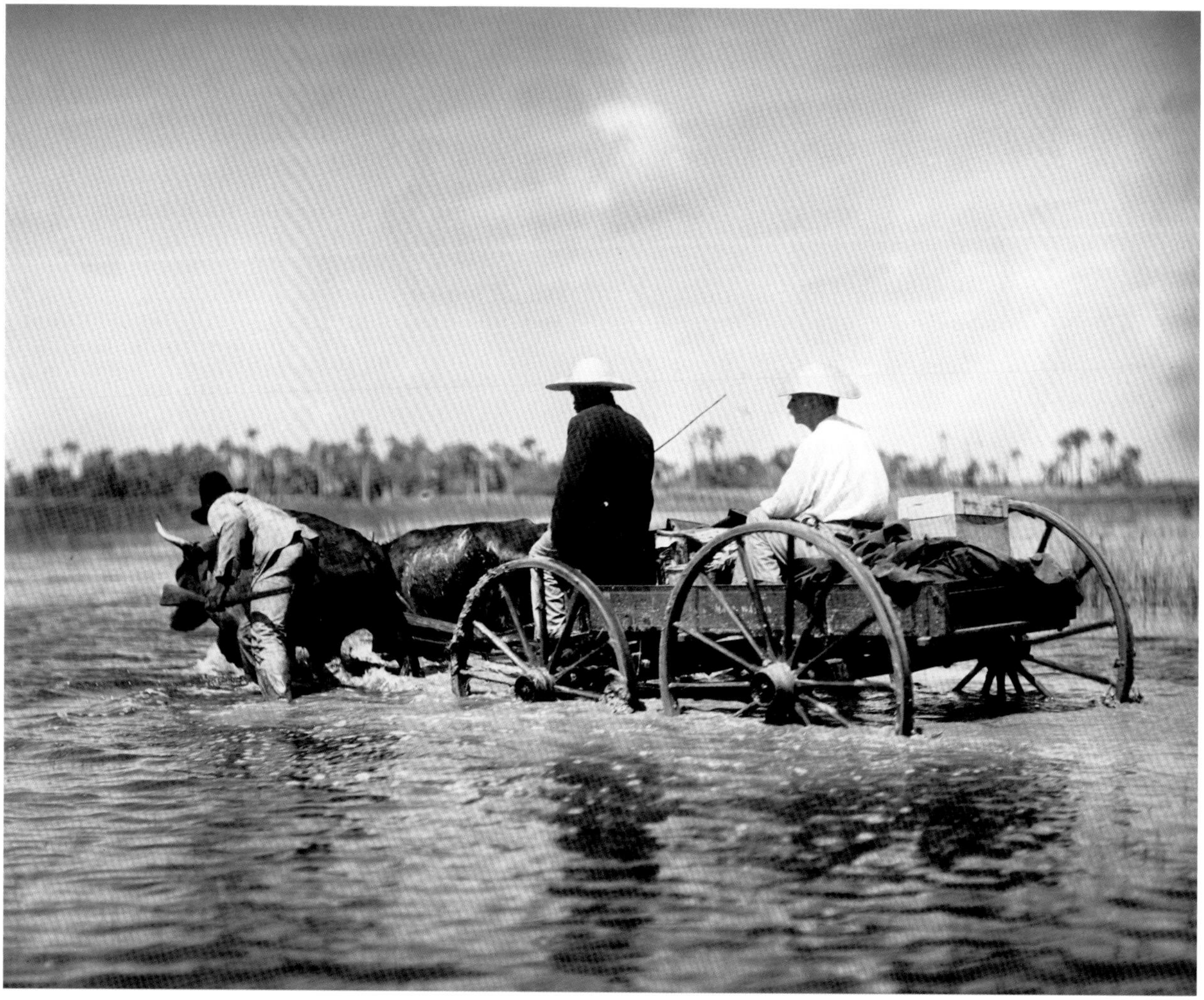

On two occasions (a nine-day trip in mid-January 1905 and a four-day one in late spring 1907), the Dimocks traveled to Deep Lake Plantation, located north of Everglades City and well east of Marco Island on the mainland. A. W. (in "A Southern Industrial Experiment") wrote that it took eight hours on a sometimes wet trail to reach the Plantation. Today the location is in the western portion of the Big Cypress National Preserve. June 2, 1907; 48571.

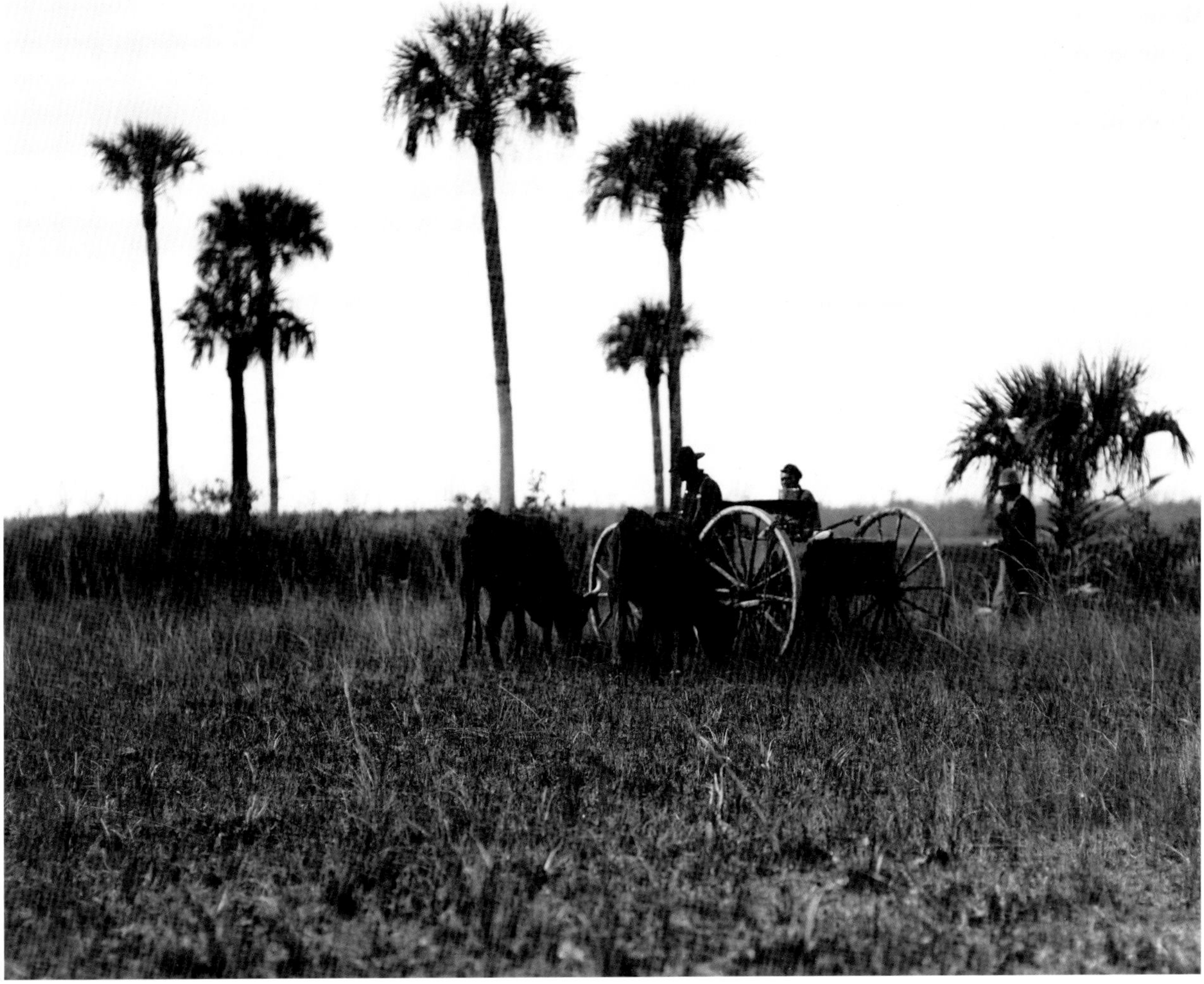

Portions of the trail to Deep Lake Plantation crossed what A. W. described in 1905 as "a prairie level as the sea threaded with strands of cypress" ("A Southern Industrial Experiment"). Along the route, the oxen were allowed to graze while the Dimocks and their guides also had their lunch. A. W. characterized the oxen as "small, active creatures capable of scrambling like cats out of mudholes [*sic*] in which larger animals would be hopelessly stalled." January 18, 1905; 48562.

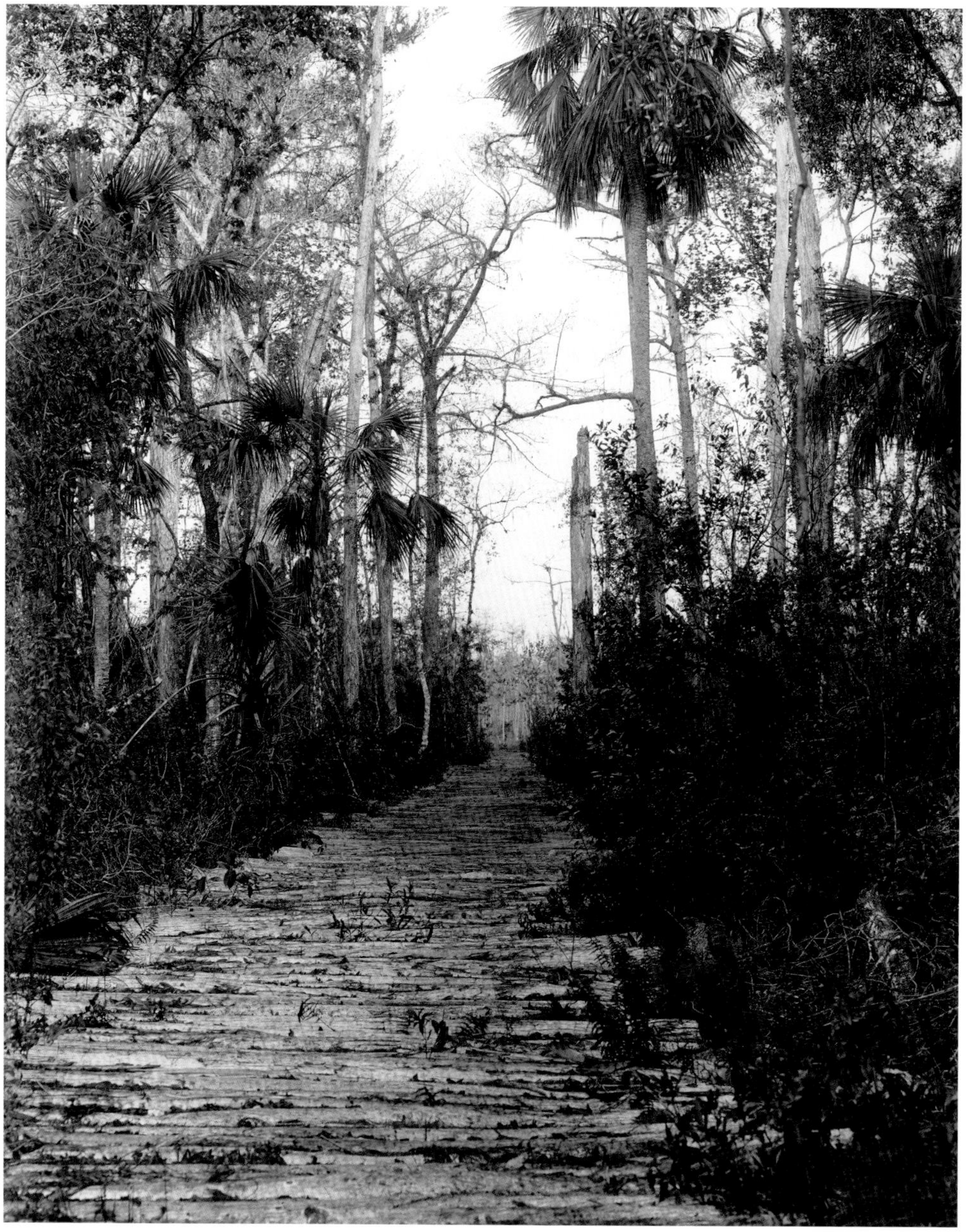

Near Deep Lake Plantation, the trail was "paved" with logs, making a corduroy road. According to A. W., the plantation owners (Walter Langford of Fort Myers and John M. Roach of the Chicago Street Railway Company) had bought 300 acres, clearing two-thirds of the area to plant twelve thousand grapefruit trees. January 12, 1905; 48543.

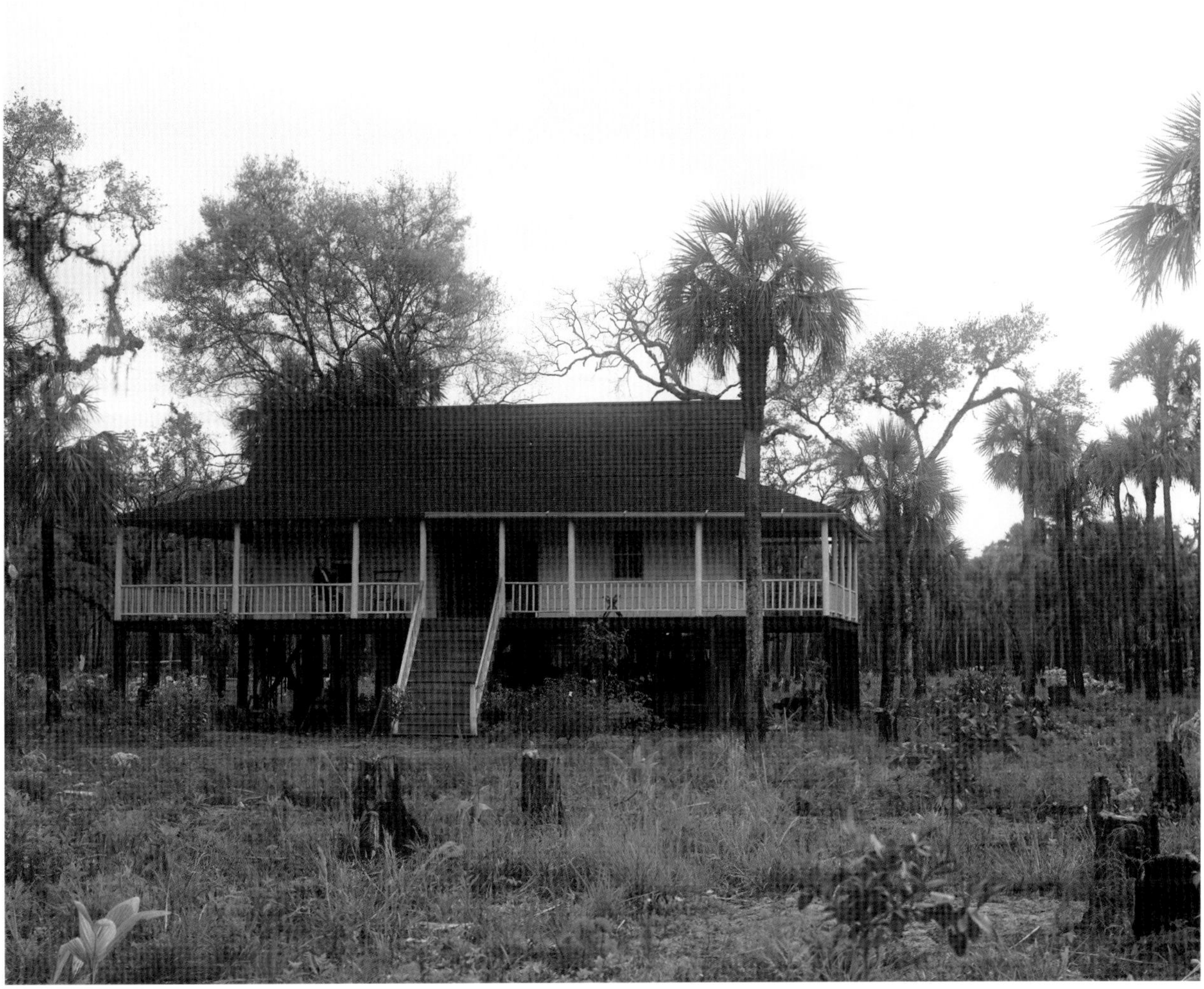

The surprisingly modern-looking house at Deep Lake Plantation "was built upon stilts . . . from trees that grew on its site, out of which timbers were hewed, rafters formed, and shingles split by the axe of the pioneer. . . . Within the boundaries of the [grapefruit] grove are a few low-lying primeval tangles of tree and vine, called heads, of present interest to moccasins, alligators, and wading birds, awaiting redemption through drainage, the promise of which secured to the Governor of the State the office which he now holds. The deep lake from which the plantation takes its name is about five hundred feet in diameter, with a maximum depth of one hundred and thirty feet, or about twice that of the average 'bottomless lake' of Florida fiction." The governor, of course, was Napoleon Bonaparte Broward whose agenda was to drain the Everglades for agricultural farmland. January 13, 1905; 48553.

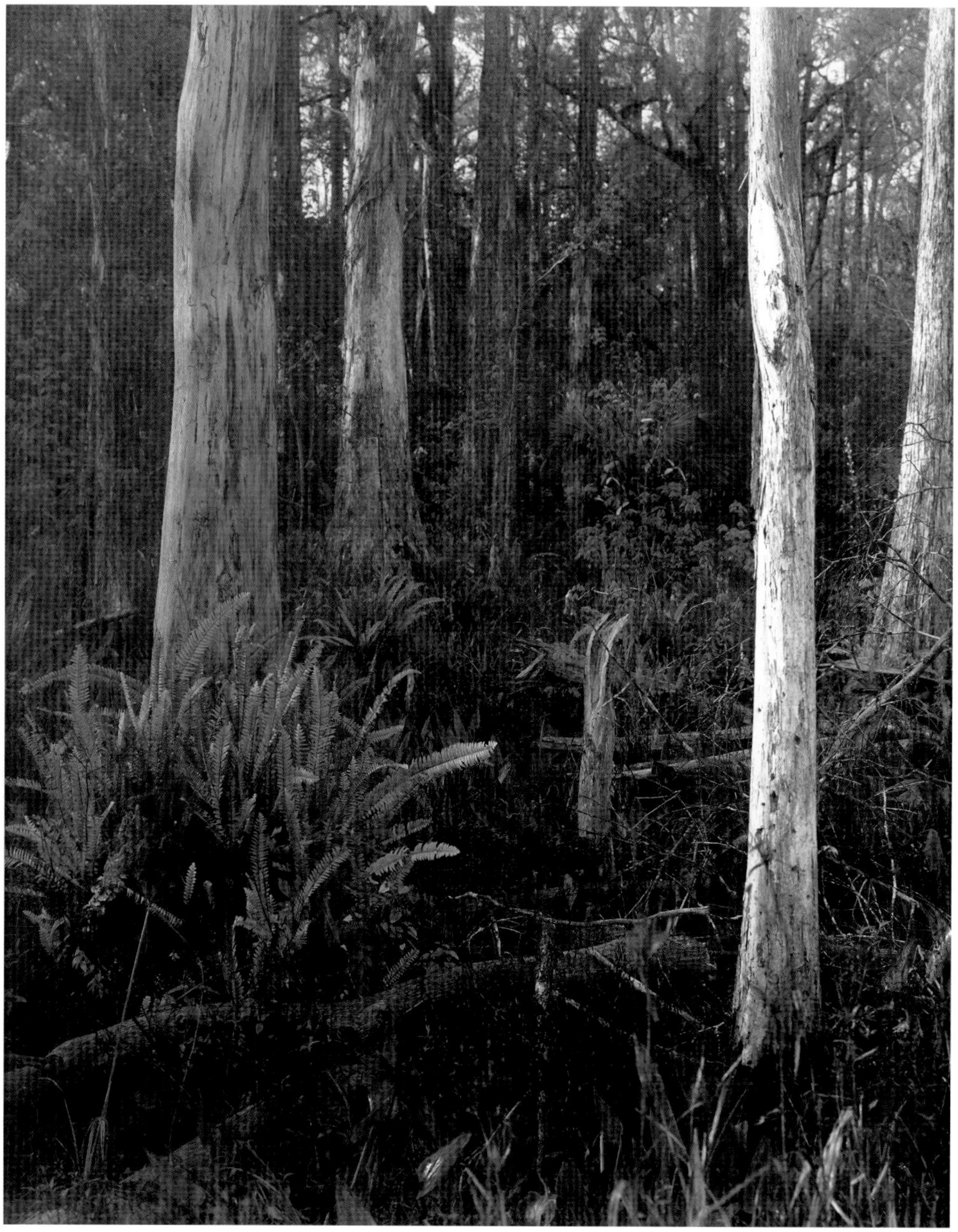

In his 1905 article "A Southern Industrial Experiment," A. W. Dimock wrote about what "the imaginative maps of Florida call the Big Cypress Swamp," and its "islands containing hundreds of acres of rich hummock-lands densely covered with forests of palm and pine; live and water oak; bays, red, white, and sweet; wild guava, fig, and other choice trees, with vines and flowers growing in tropical profusion. Within the swamp proper, much of which is dry half the year [are] . . . forests of cypress, with individual trees containing five thousand feet of lumber." January 12, 1905; 48557.

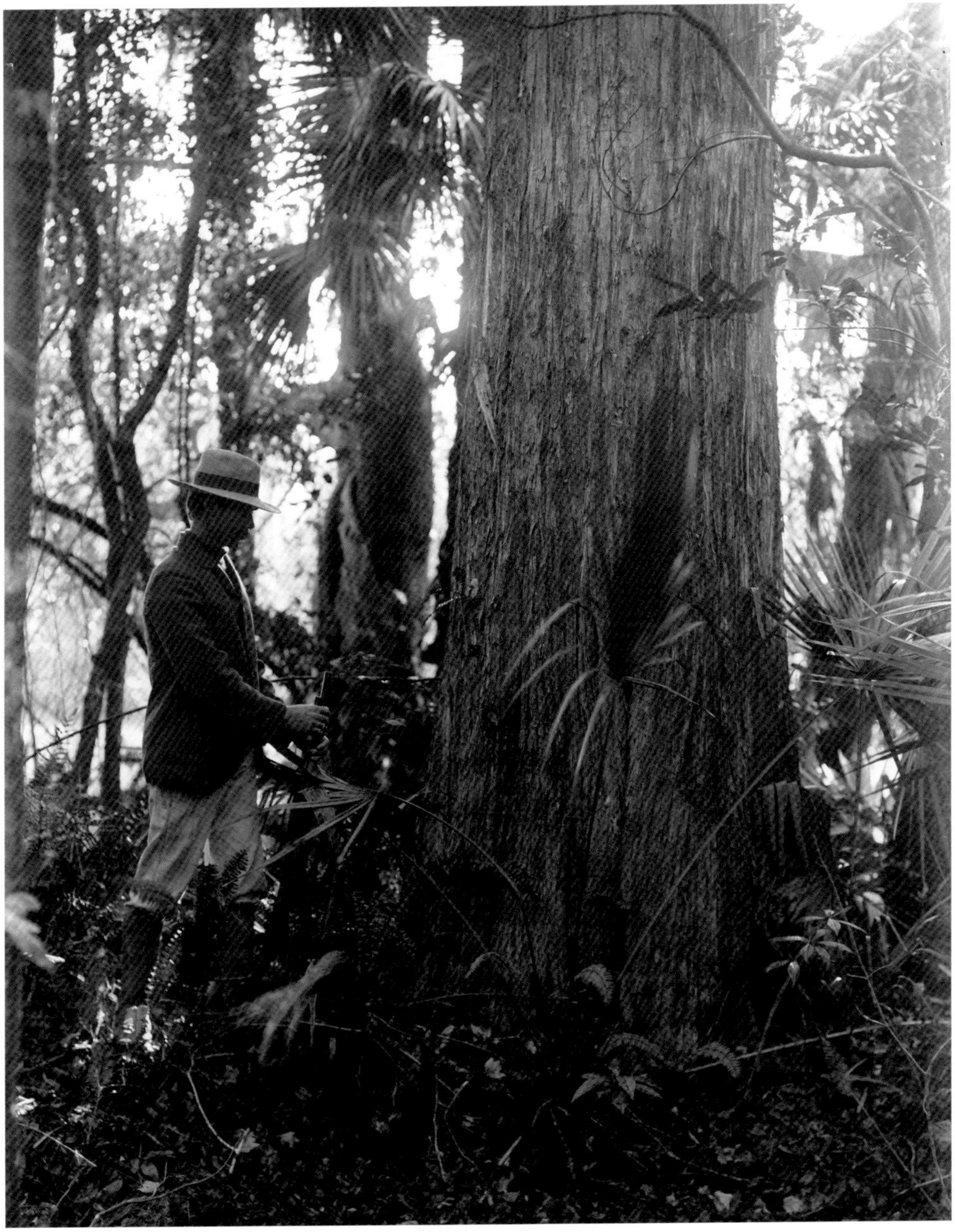

Mr. T. J. Ward next to one of the many cypress trees on the 300 acres of land that comprised the plantation. Ward may have been the plantation manager. January 17, 1905; 48559.

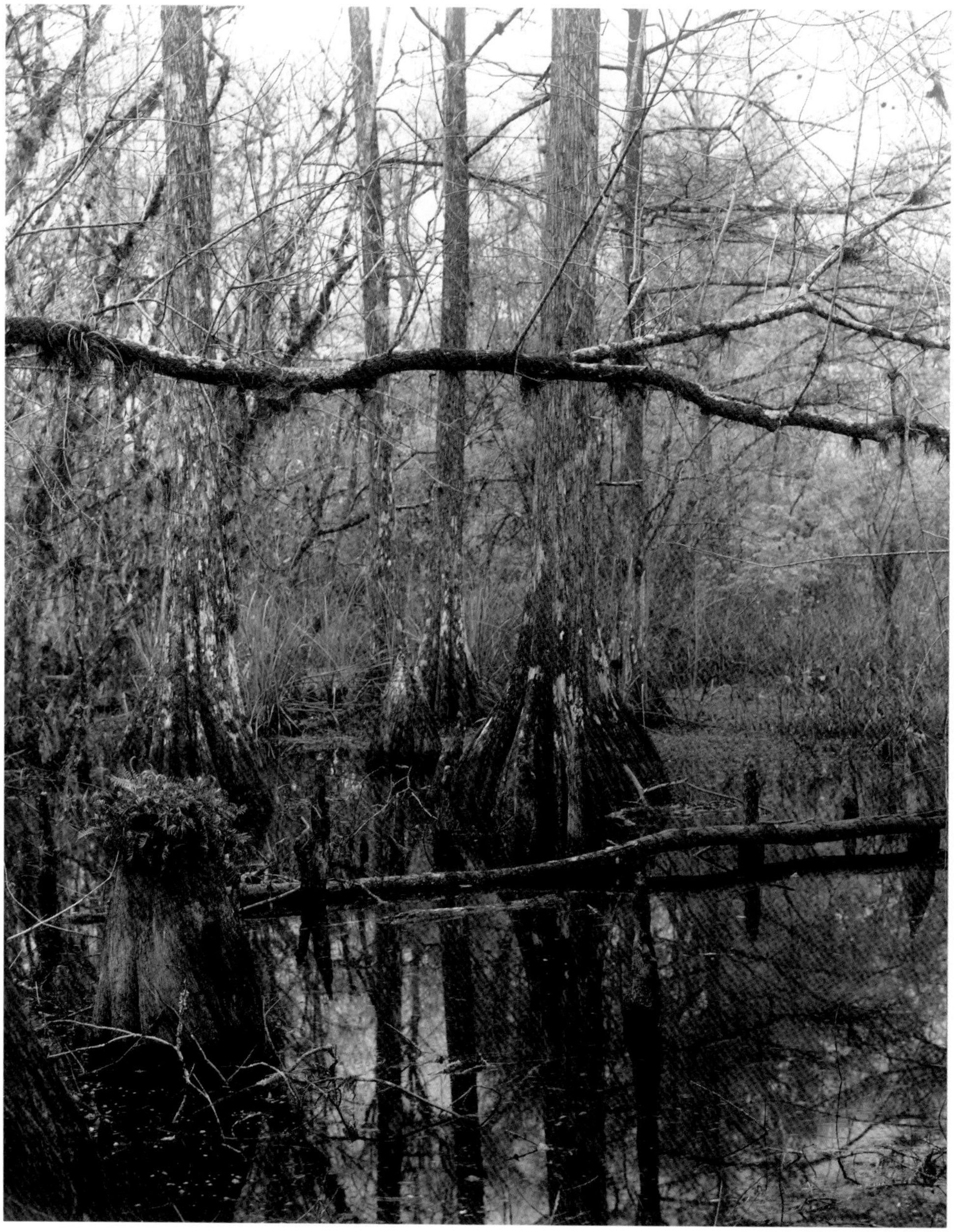

Deep Lake Plantation was on one of the tracts of dry land (hammocks or hummocks) found within the Big Cypress Swamp. A. W. Dimock described the plantation's setting: "A cypress swamp surrounds it like the moat of an ancient castle, and the corduroyed entrance is a floating drawbridge." January 15, 1905; 48558.

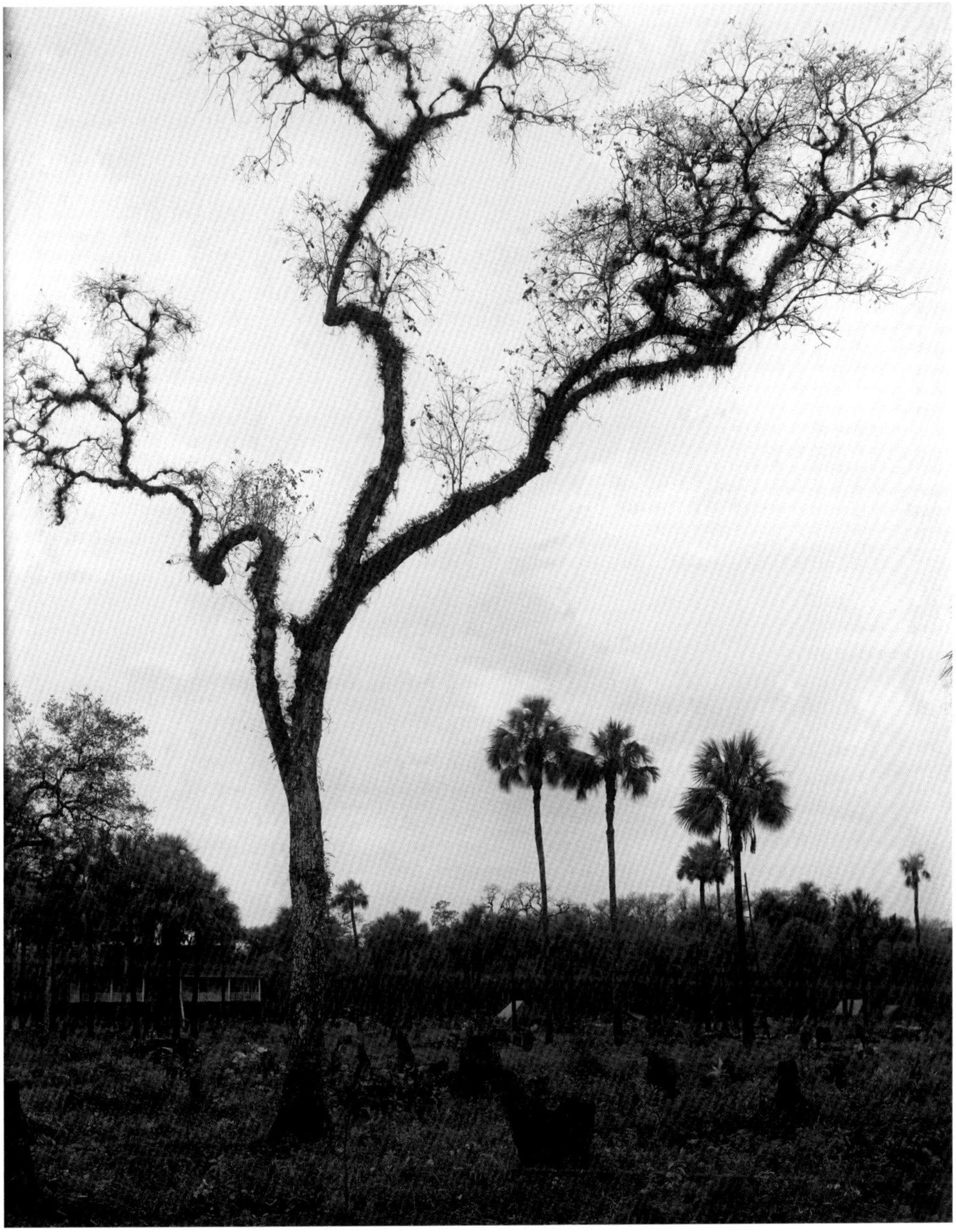

Clearing the land to plant grapefruit trees and put in gardens was no easy task. The live oaks were girdled (like the one on the left) and allowed to die before being removed. The workers at Deep Lake lived in tents, several of which can be seen in the center and back right. January 15, 1905; 48552.

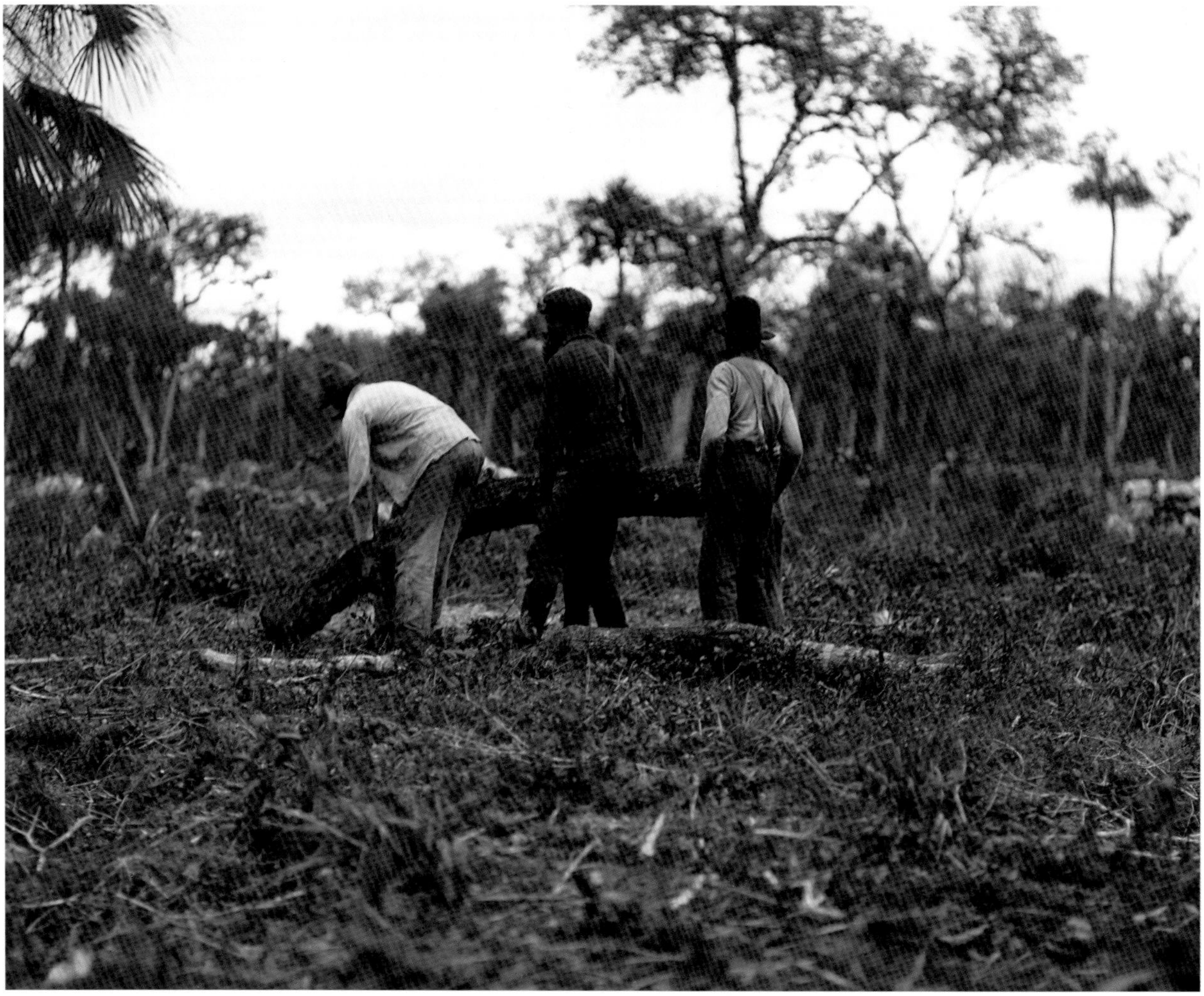

African American men were hired to clear the land while living in the tents pitched on-site. Julian called this photograph "Toting Logs." January 14, 1905; 48551.

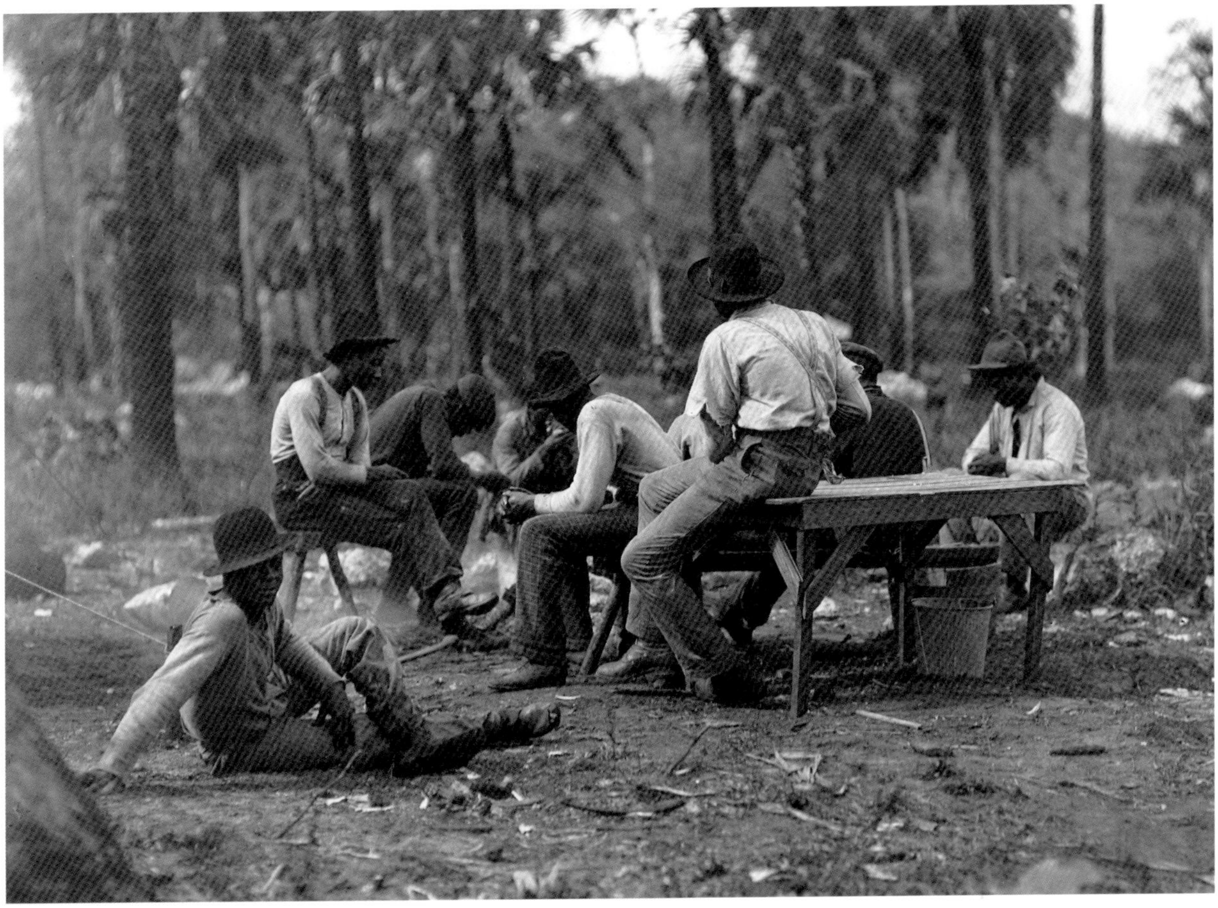

Workers at Deep Lake, photographed here at dinner time, did not have it easy. They lived at the plantation in the middle of a swamp, isolated from the outside world. January 14, 1905; 48561.

Henderson Creek

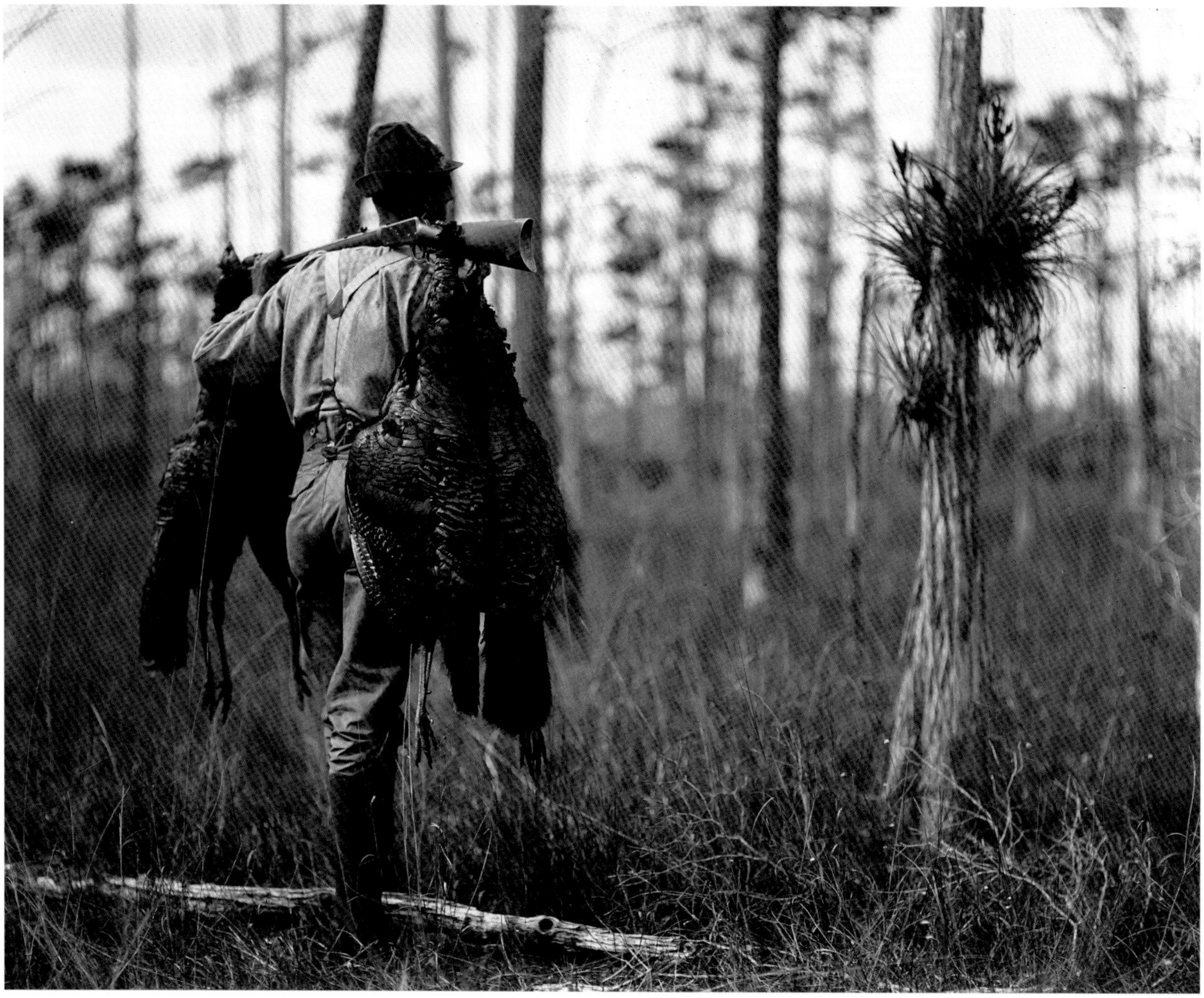

Before they had the *Irene*, the Dimocks were restricted to exploring and photographing Marco Island and the nearby mainland. They apparently also used small craft to traverse the waters adjacent to Marco. At the end of January 1905, they traveled to a small settlement on Henderson Creek (east of Rookery Bay) on the mainland northward from Marco. Over several days, Julian took photographs, including this one of Schwamb, a local resident, with four turkeys he had shot. February 1, 1905; 47659.

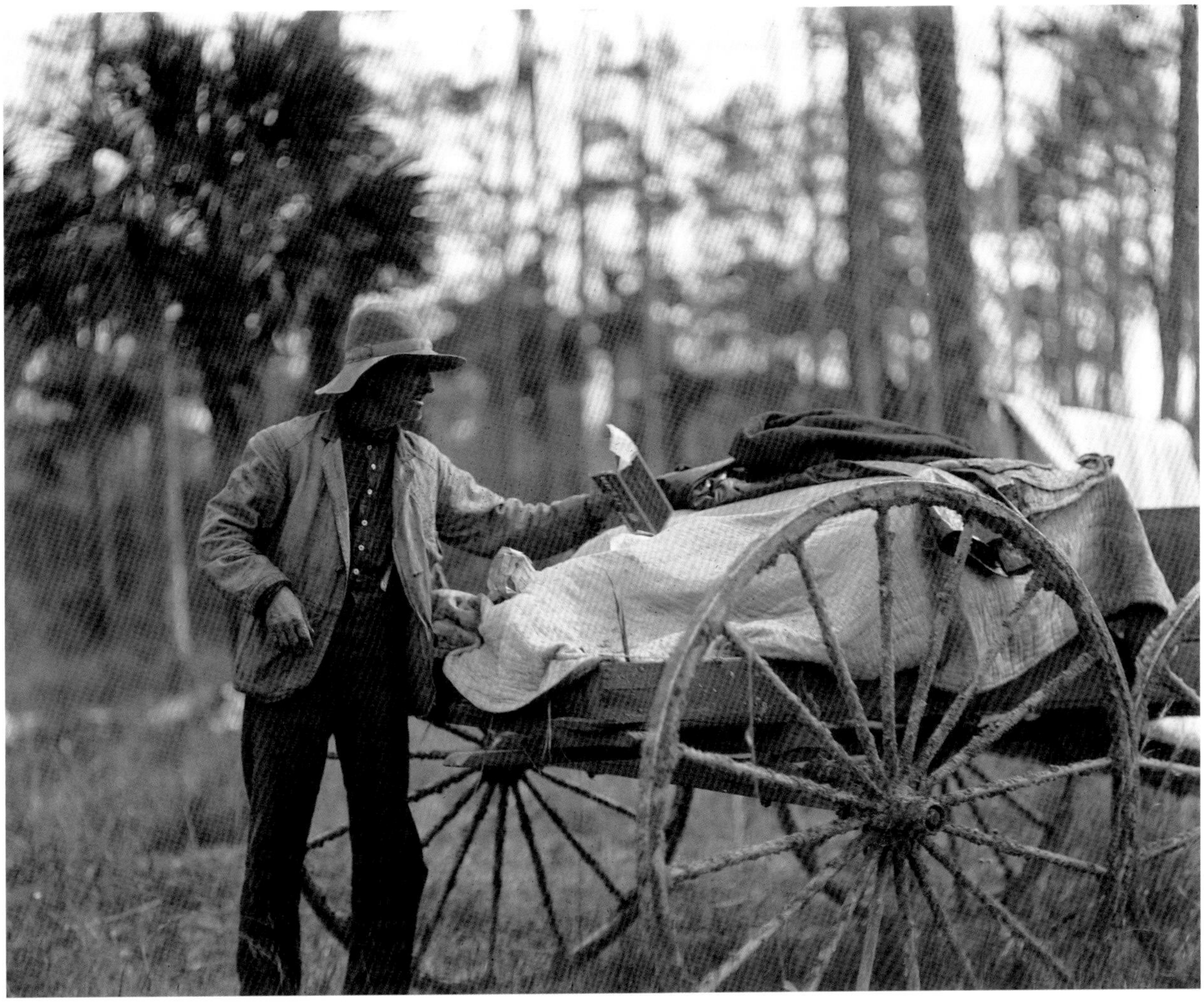

Reese, another Henderson Creek resident, next to a wagon with mud-encrusted wheels and spokes. The wagon was likely drawn by a mule. February 1, 1905; 48592.

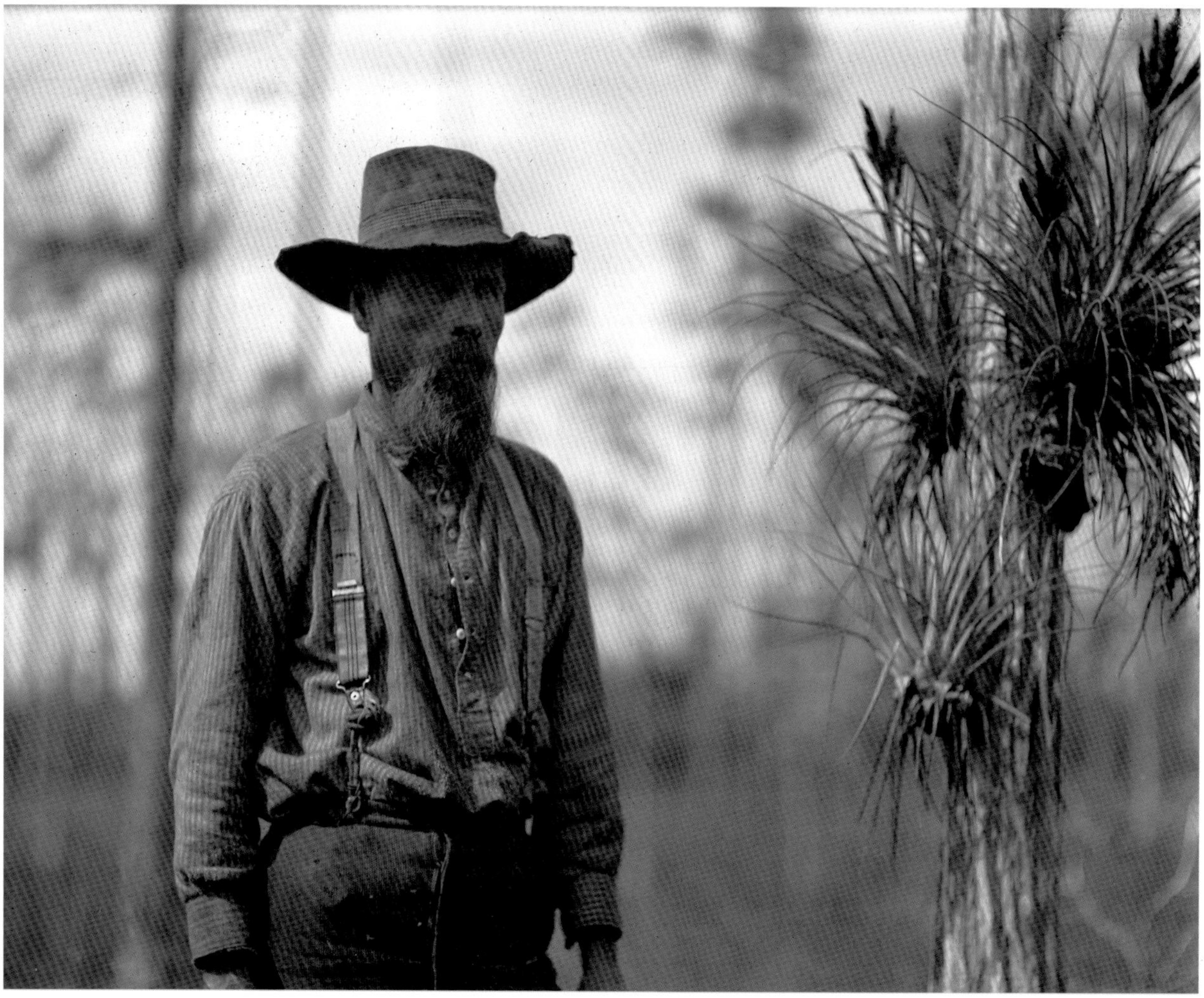

Bill Kirkland, also a resident of Henderson Creek.
February 1, 1905; 48593.

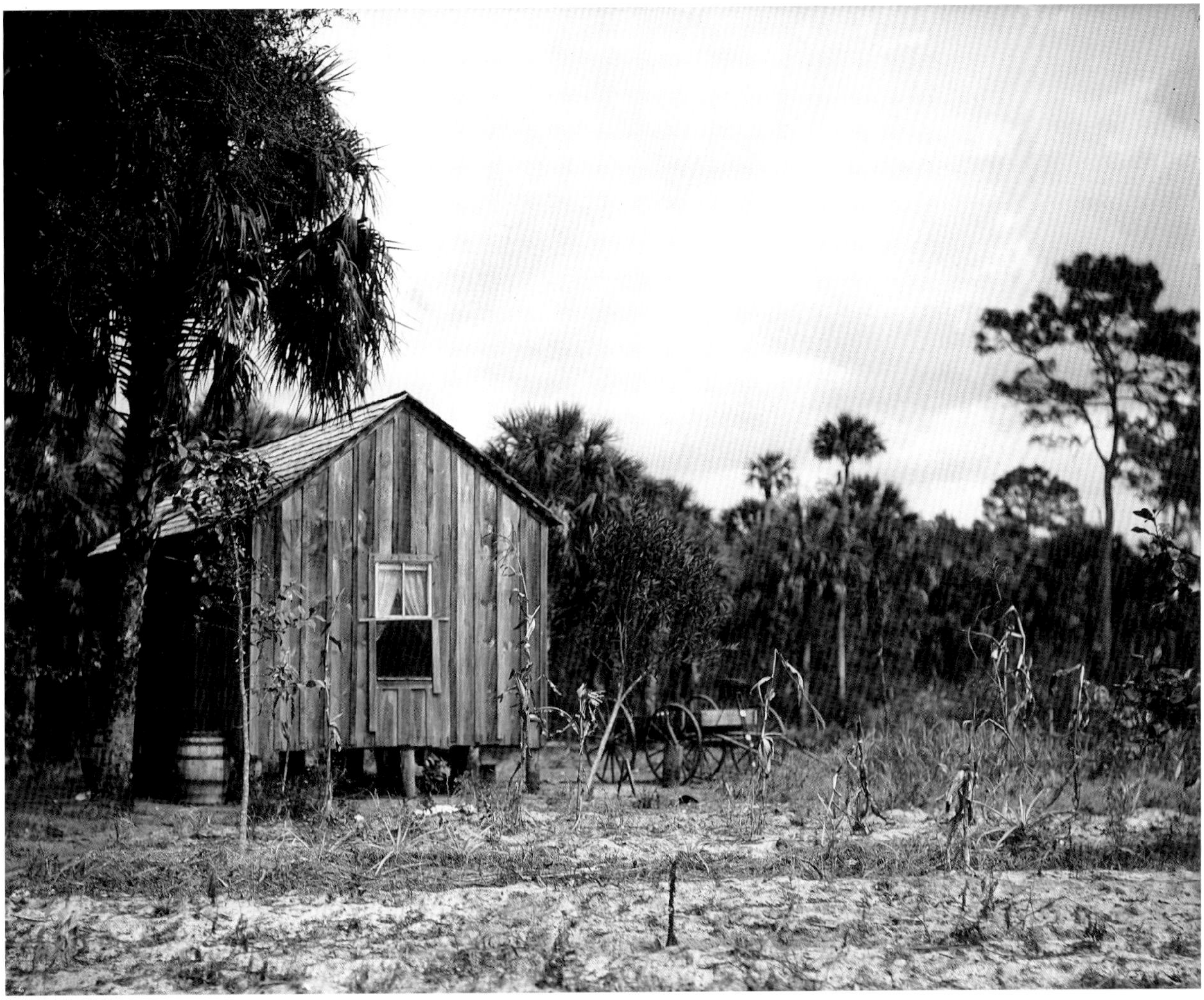

Bill Kirkland's house at Henderson Creek.
February 2, 1905; 48594.

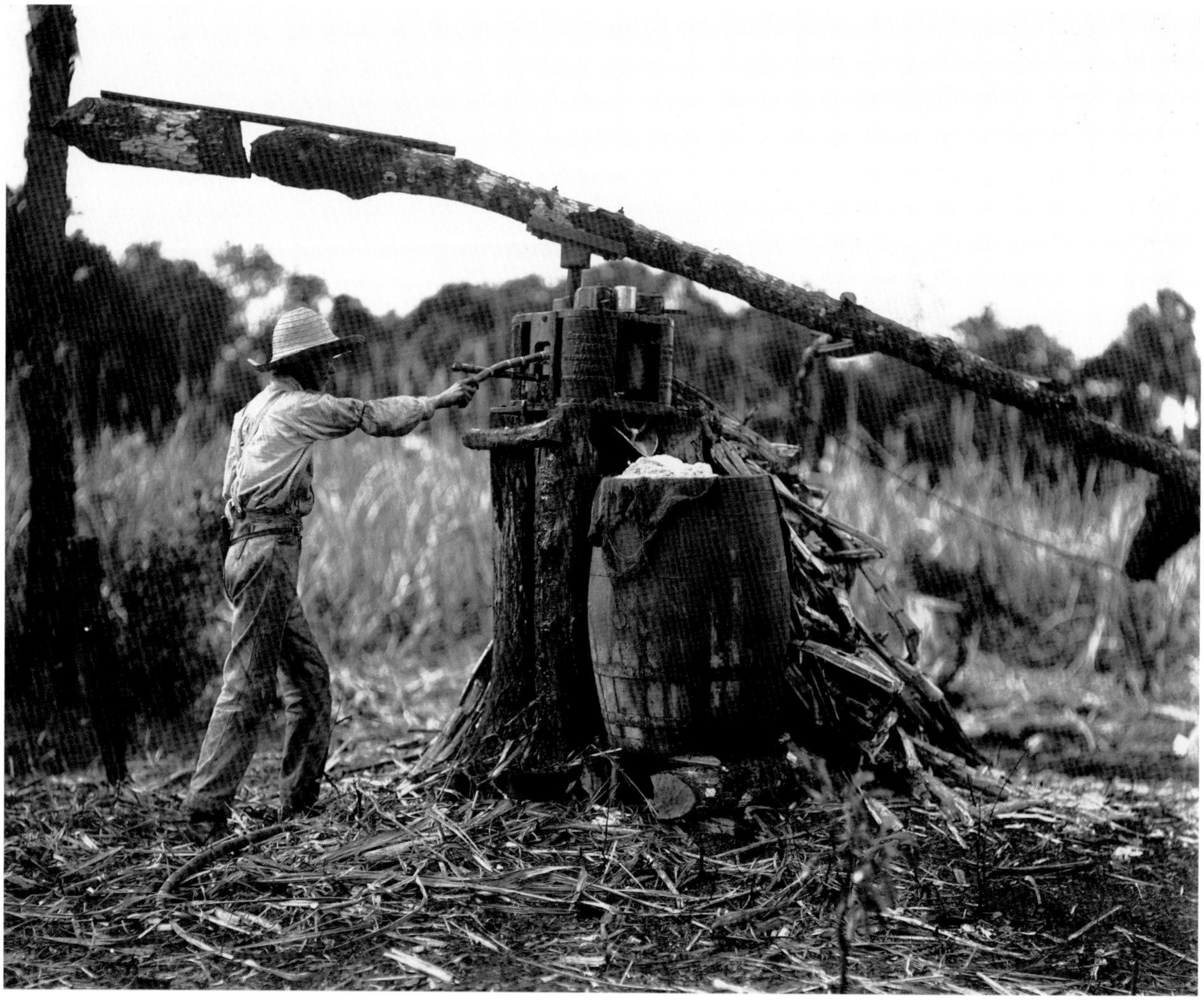

At Henderson Creek, there was a mill used to grind sugarcane to extract the juice used to make syrup. February 2, 1905; 48750.

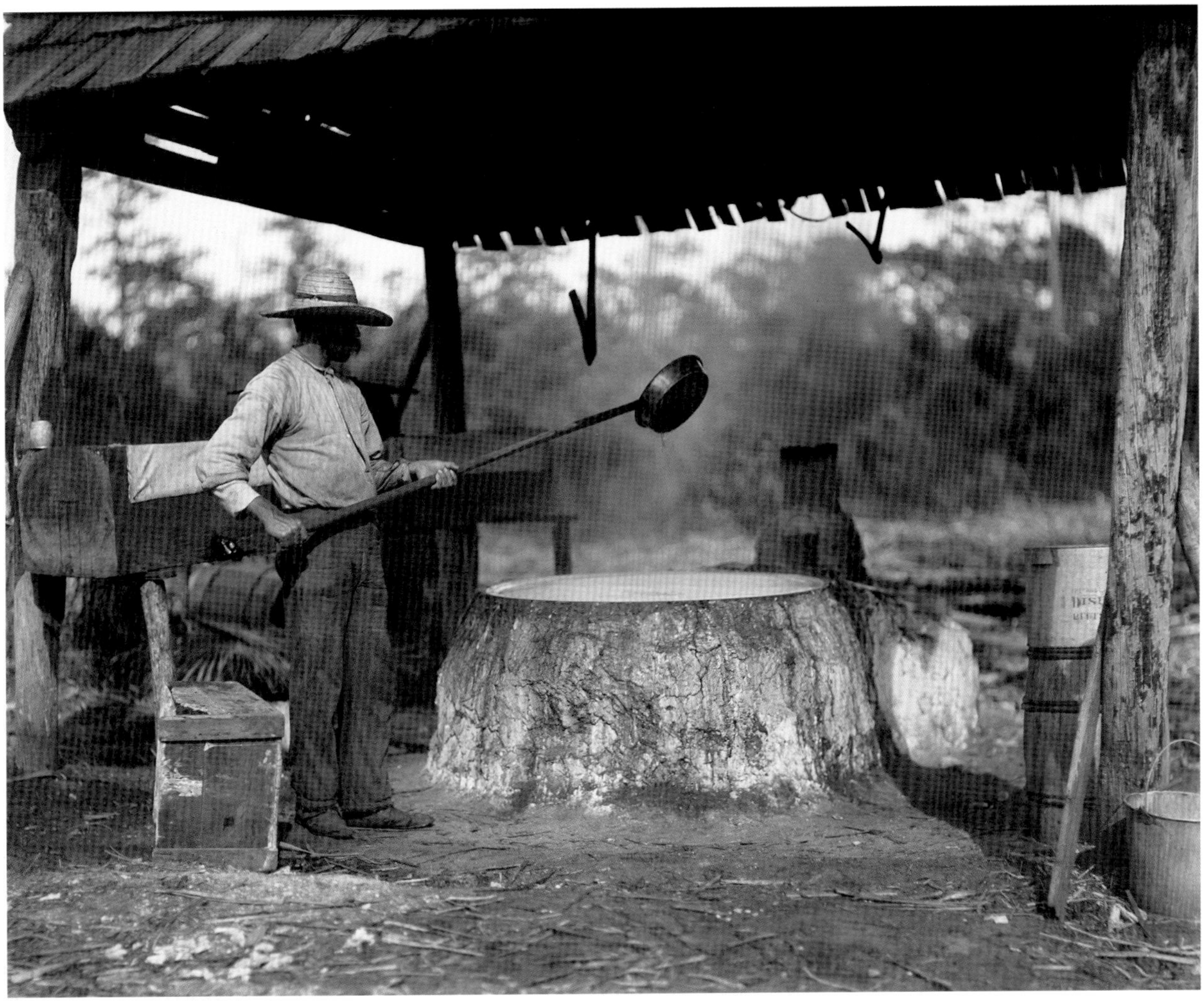

The sugarcane juice was boiled down as a part of the process used to make syrup.
February 2, 1905; 48752.

The Honey Tree

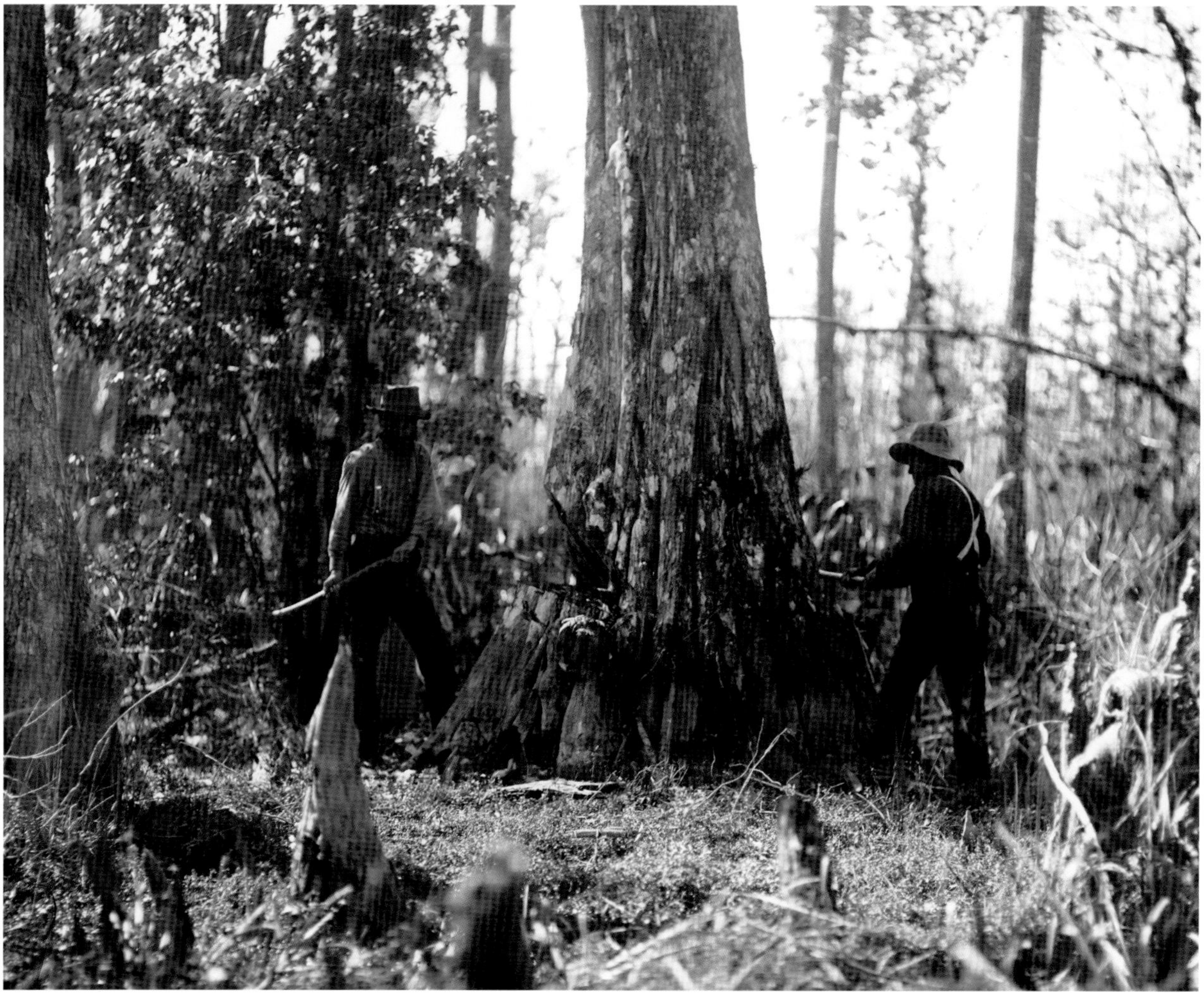

Schwamb and Reese chop down a bee tree said by A. W. (in *Florida Enchantments*) to have been in the Big Cypress Swamp, 23 miles from the Henderson Creek settlement. The Dimocks traveled overland to the tree in a mule-drawn cart. January 29, 1905; 48778.

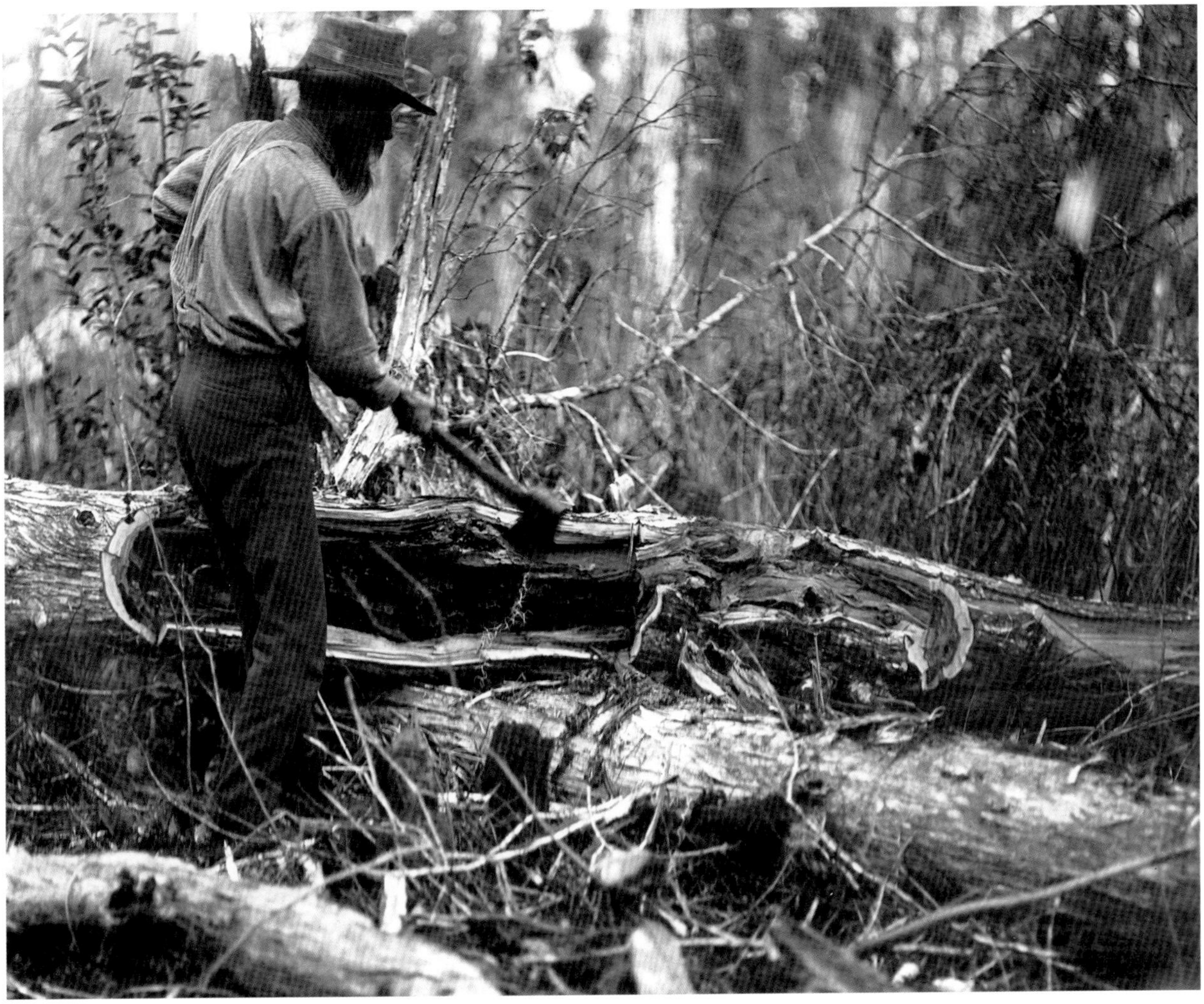

To find the tree, Schwamb and Reese first attracted bees with a honeycomb, then visually plotted the direction the bees took back to their hive. Moving some distance away, the men repeated the exercise, using the second track to help triangulate the location of the bee tree, which was about a quarter mile away. After it was felled, the section of the tree covering the hive was chopped away. January 29, 1905; 48779.

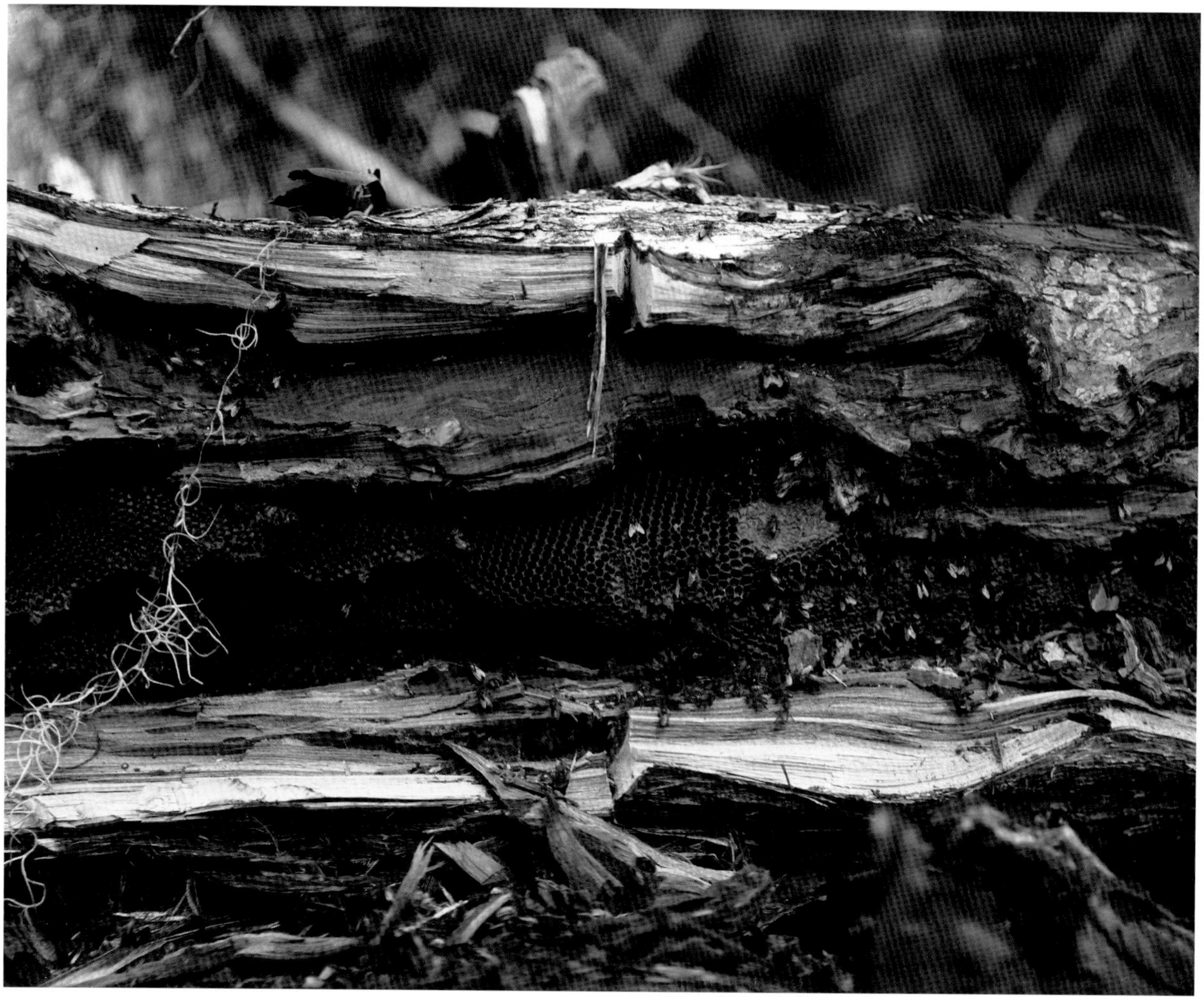

A portion of the honeycomb in the tree hive.
January 29, 1905; 48780.

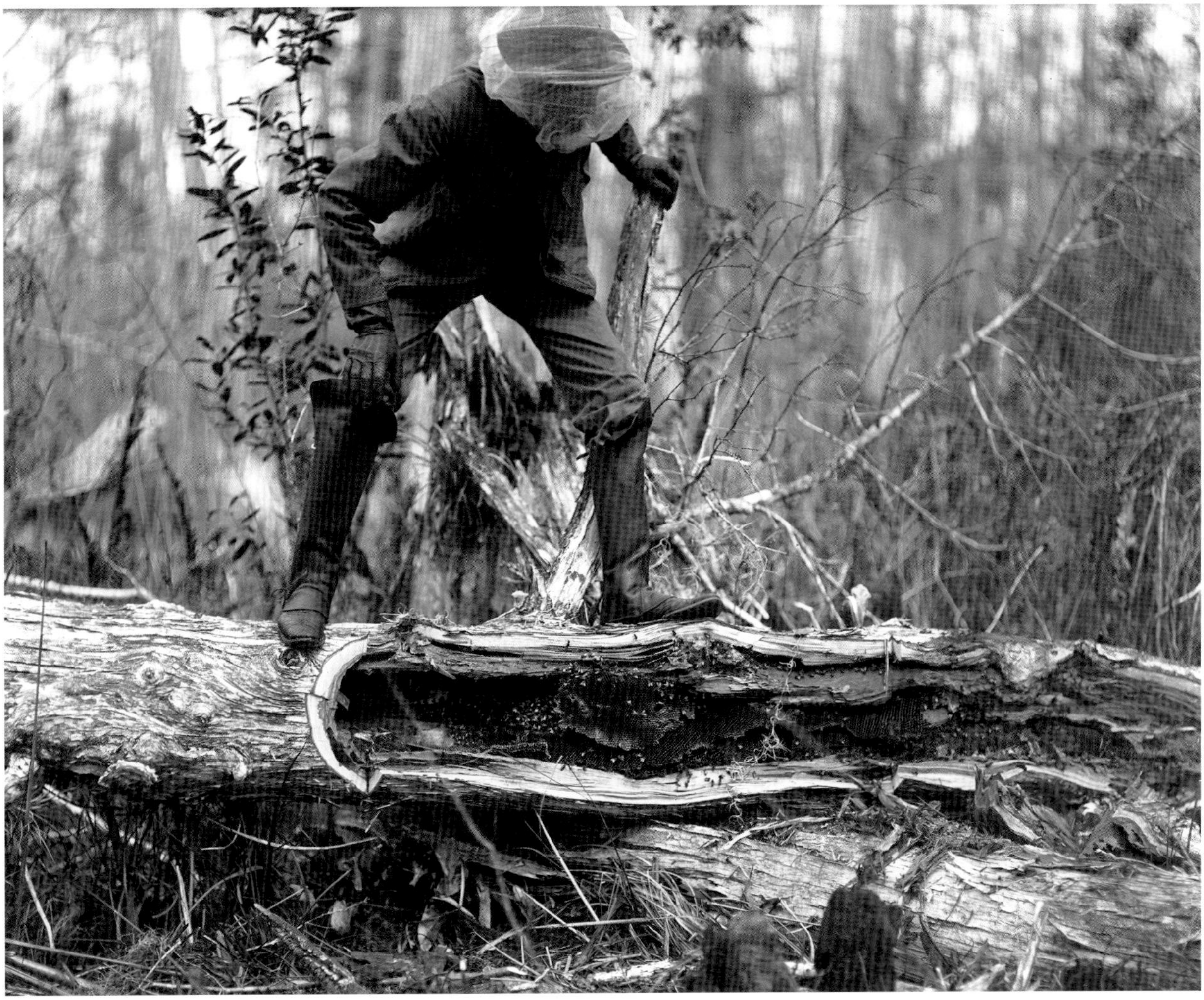

Schwamb, with gloves and netting covering his head, prepares to smoke the bees in order to get to the honey. January 29, 1905; 48790.

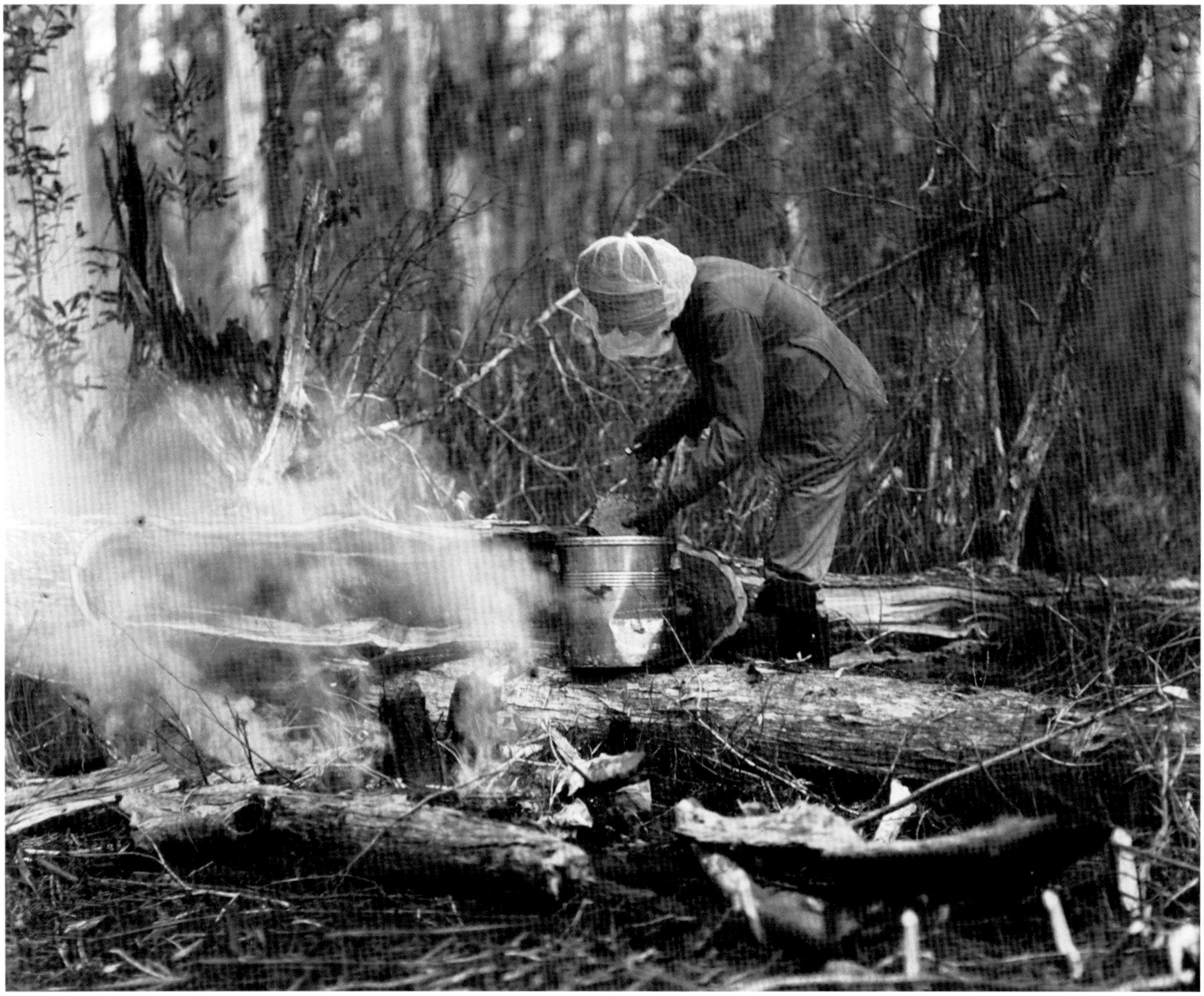

After smoking the bees to quiet them, Schwamb removed what A. W. said was 50 pounds of honeycomb, packing it in pails to take back to Henderson Creek. Some of Julian's photographs of the honey tree were used in a September 1905 article in *Country Calendar* magazine written by Martha McCulloch-Williams, the author of the well-known book *Dishes & Beverages of the Old South* (1913). Her account of the outing to locate the bee tree is quite different from that penned by A. W. Dimock. Neither of the Dimocks is mentioned in her story. January 29, 1905; 48791.

The In-Between

Ten Thousand Islands

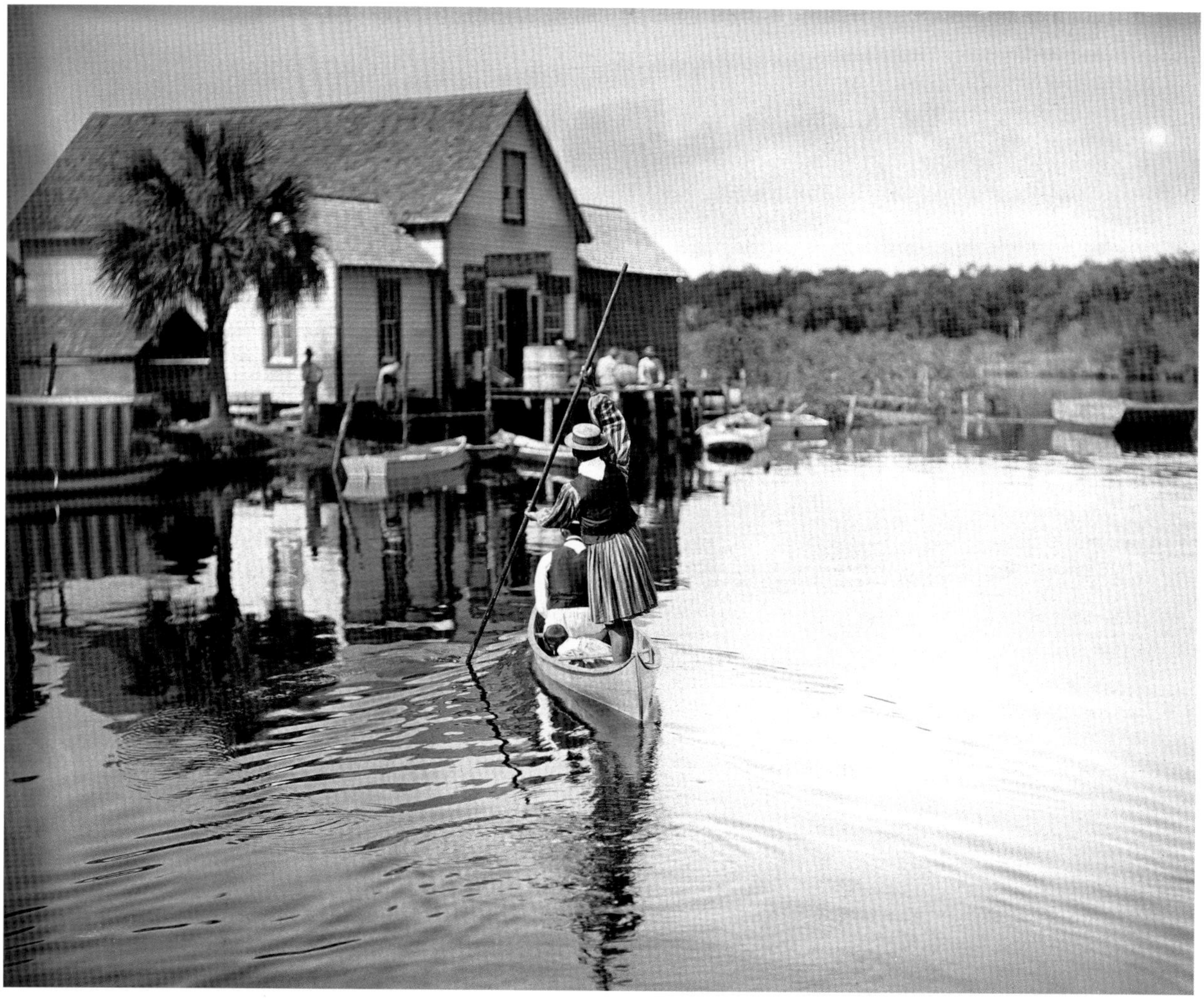

On their travels into the Ten Thousand Islands and the Everglades, the Dimocks often stopped at a store in Everglades City (on Chokoloskee Bay) operated by George W. Storter and his family. A. W. Dimock noted that the store "was the last place on the west coast at which the fisherman can be comfortably housed. If the Storters like your looks you will find yourself in pleasant quarters" (*The Book of the Tarpon*). It was at Storter's store that Julian first photographed Seminole Indians, men and their families who had come to shop and trade. The two Seminole men photographed here are in the Dimocks' canoe. May 16, 1906; 48123.

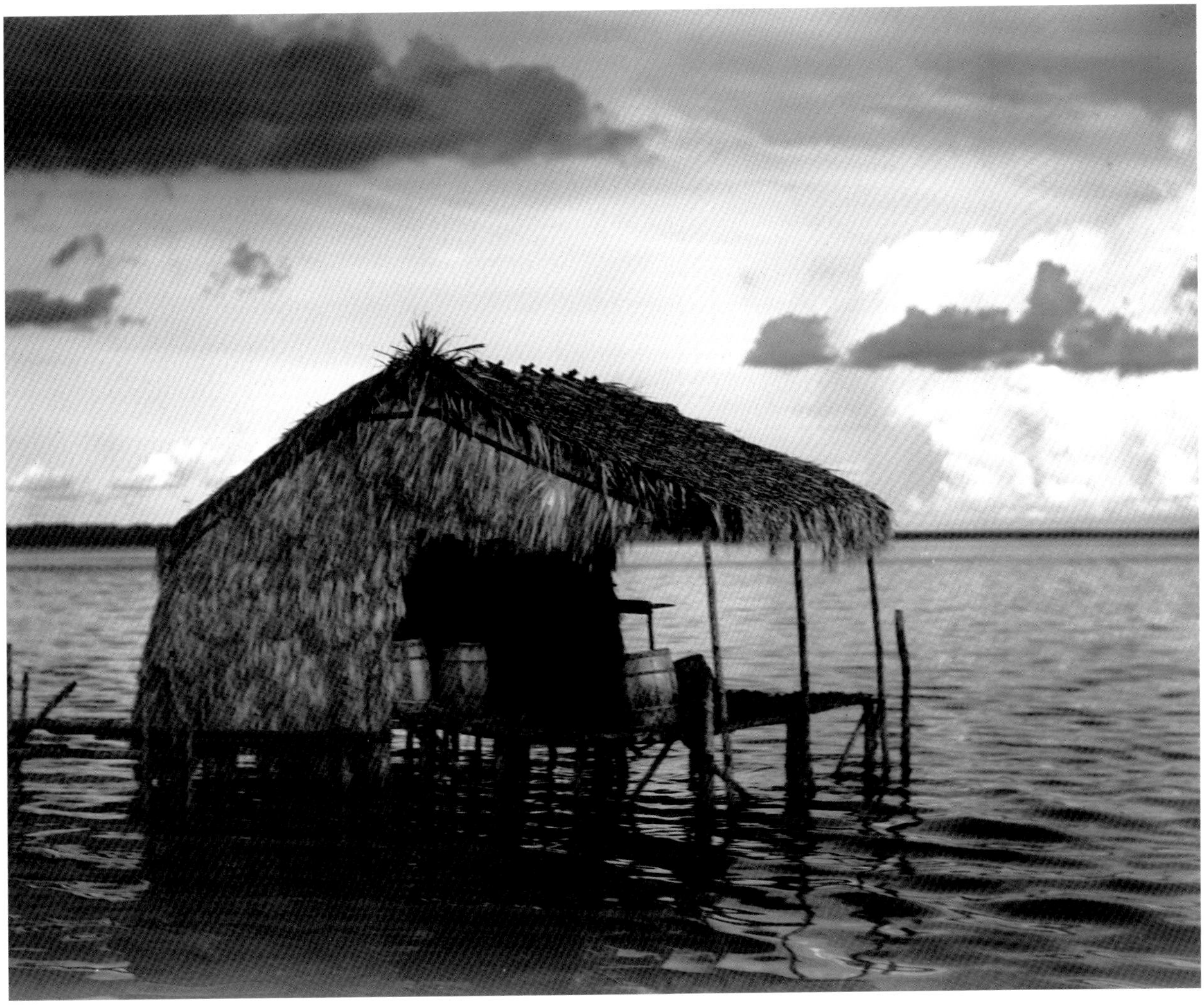

A "fish house," as Julian called it, near the mouth of Halfway Creek, Chokoloskee Bay.
August 1, 1908; 48460.

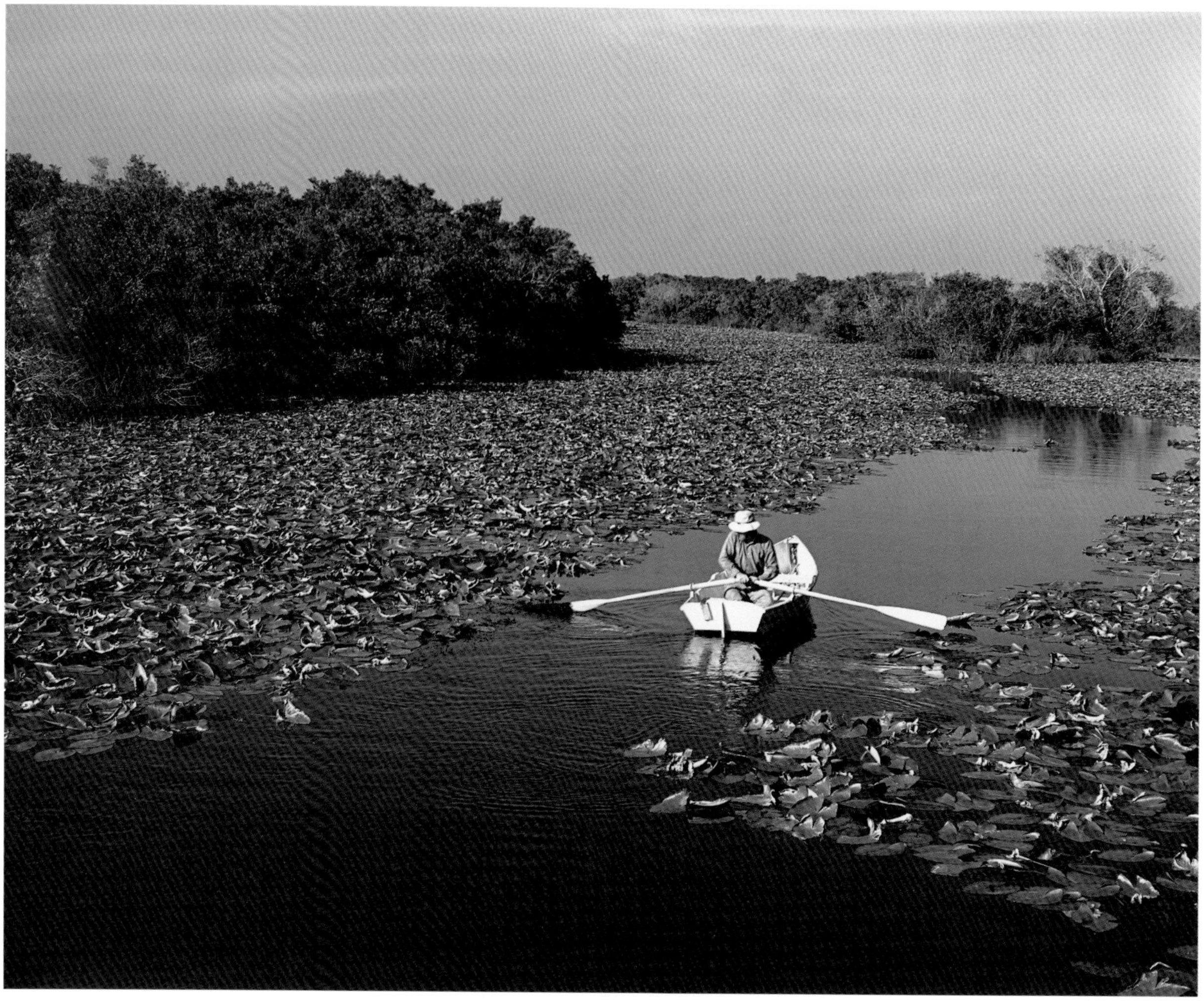

Paddling the skiff in one of the rivers that flowed through the Ten Thousand Islands. It may have been up this river that the Dimocks traveled to reach the moonshine still that Julian photographed later the same day. In "The Passing of a Wilderness" (1907), A. W. described the Ten Thousand Islands as "a labyrinth. The big rivers fork into smaller streams which divide and subdivide into creeks that, although deep, will for miles give passage only to skiffs for which a way must frequently be cleared with knives through vines and overhanging bushes. Often these creeks branch out into hundreds of shallow channels, making a thousand tiny mangrove keys in each square mile. Within these mazes are occasional blazed trails, upon one of which I found hanging to a tree an old shoe containing a bit of paper on which was penciled 'ef u want Sum grub tom has got it.'" April 26, 1906, 48263.

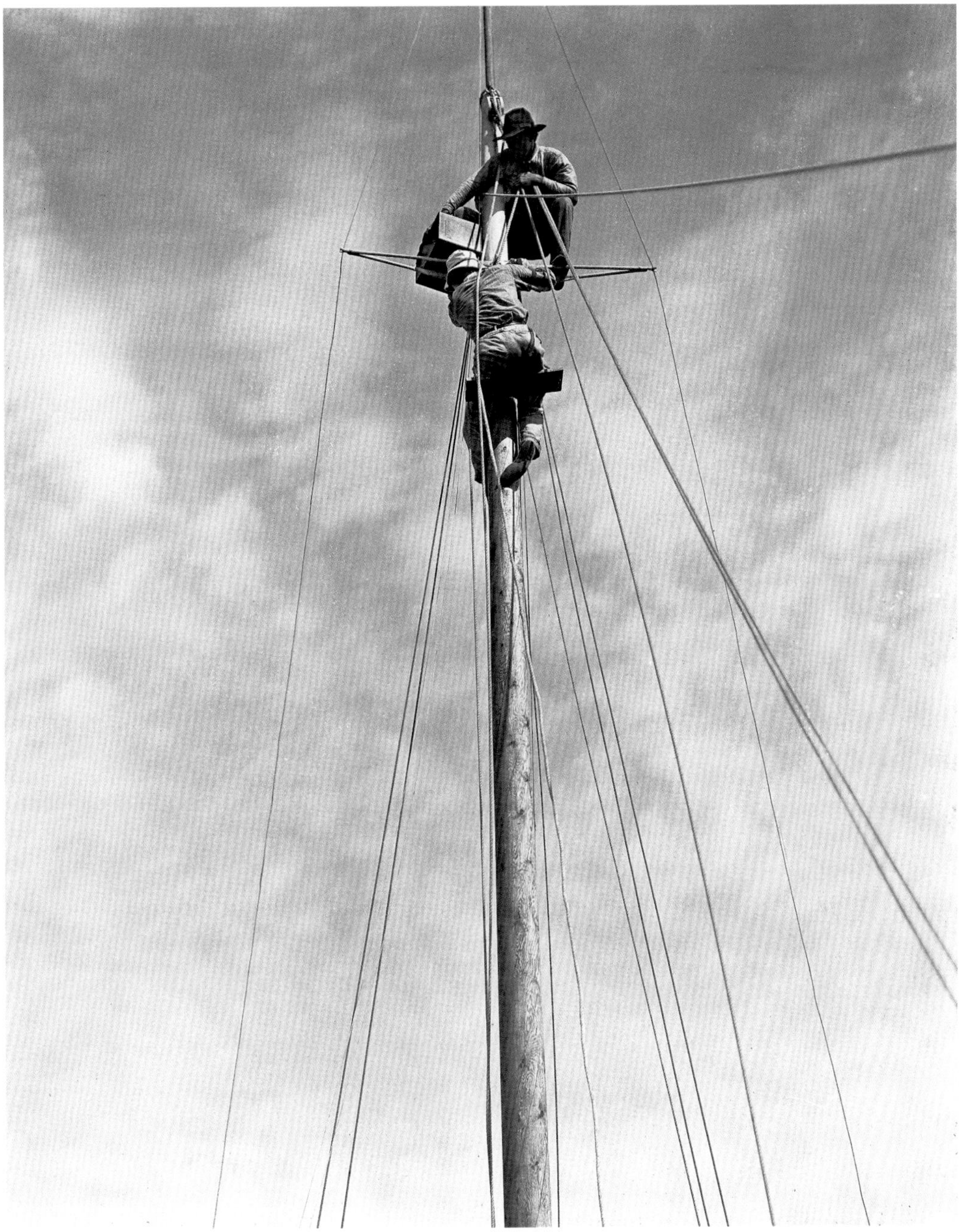

On one of their voyages to explore the Ten Thousand Islands, the Dimocks took the *Irene* up the Harney River as far as they could go, and then sent Julian up the mast to photograph the Everglades in the distance. February 8, 1906; 48303.

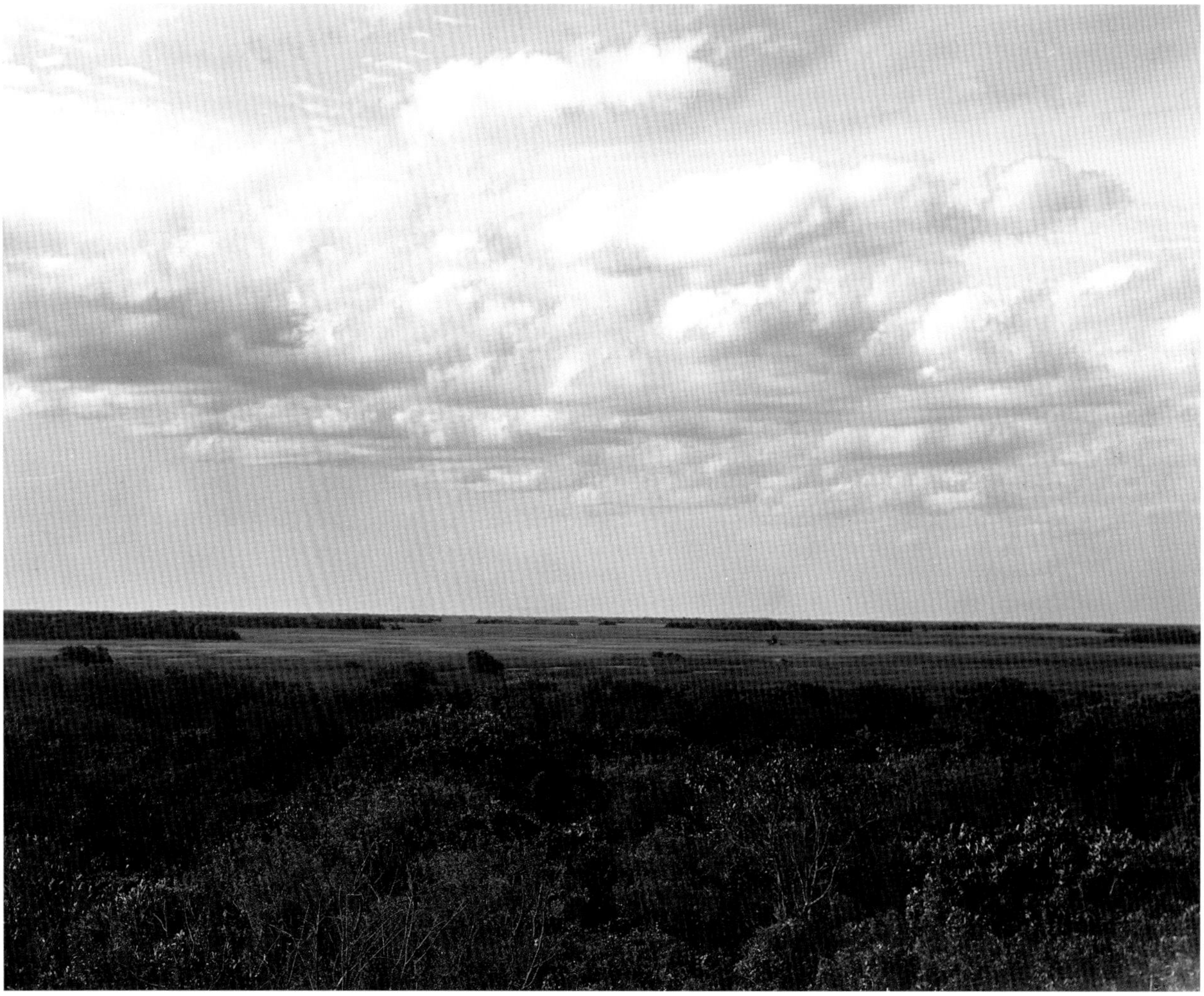

Julian's view of the Everglades from the masthead of the *Irene*.
February 8, 1906; 48301.

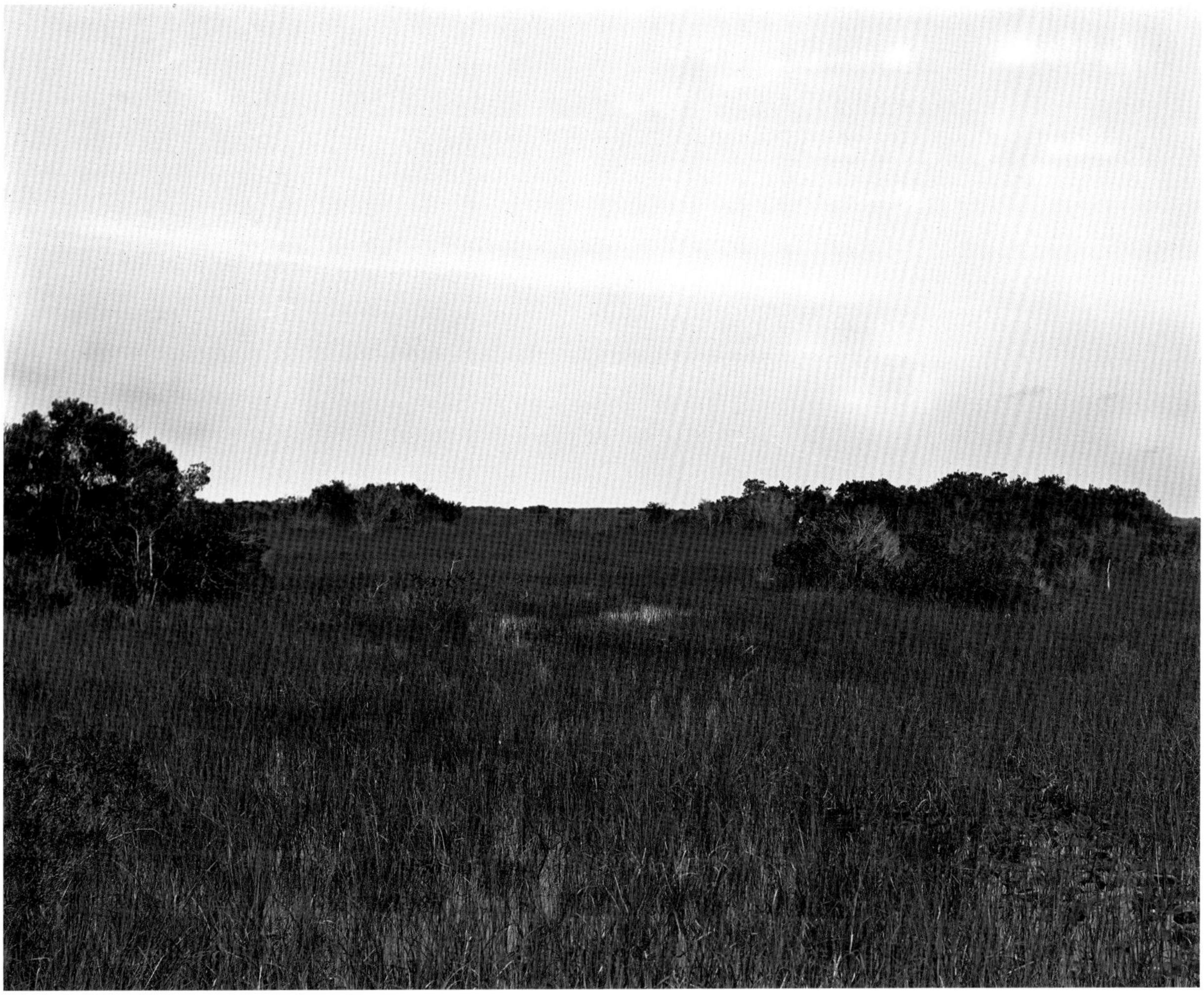

"The Everglades . . . lay before me. From the head of Harney's River I looked out upon them, and, instead of an interminable stretch of impenetrable saw-grass, beheld a multitude of islands" (Julian Dimock, "In the Everglades—With Camera and Canoe," 1907). January 27, 1906; 48535.

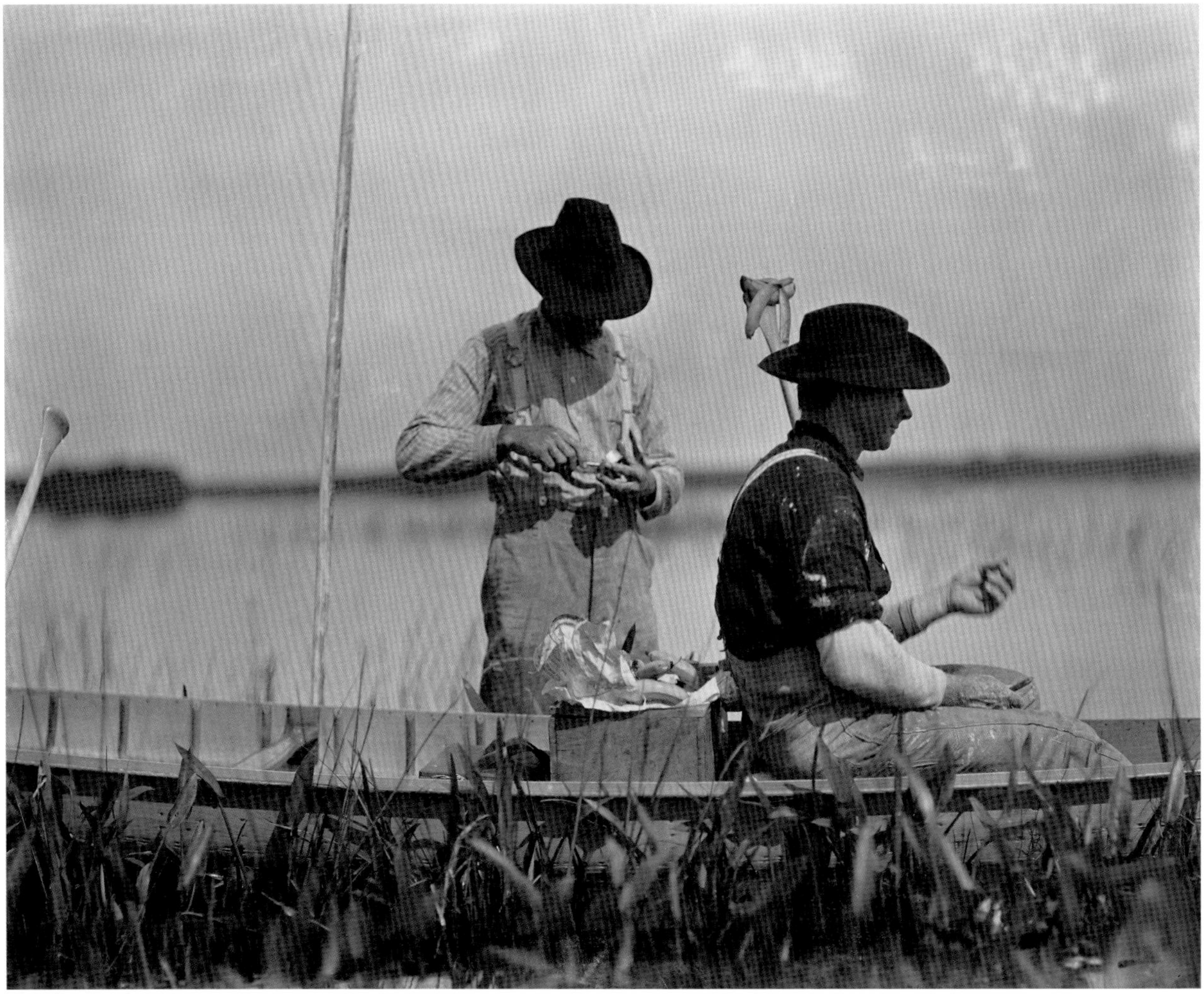

"Stopping for Lunch." The two men probably were residents of Everglades City whom the Dimocks hired to guide them up the Harney River. February 5, 1906; 48310.

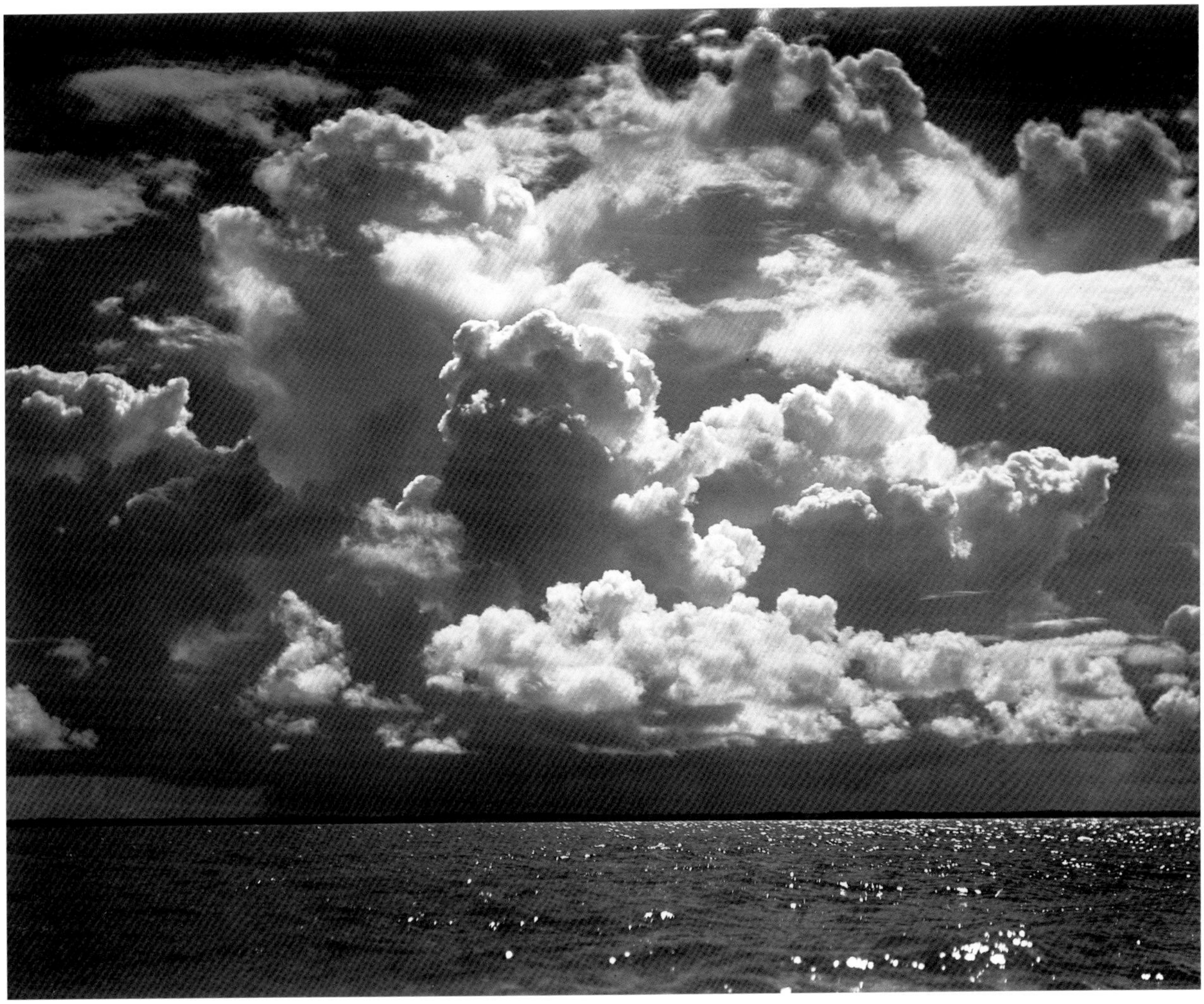

A spectacular summer thunderstorm over the Ten Thousand Islands seen from the deck of the *Irene*. August 28, 1908; 48457.

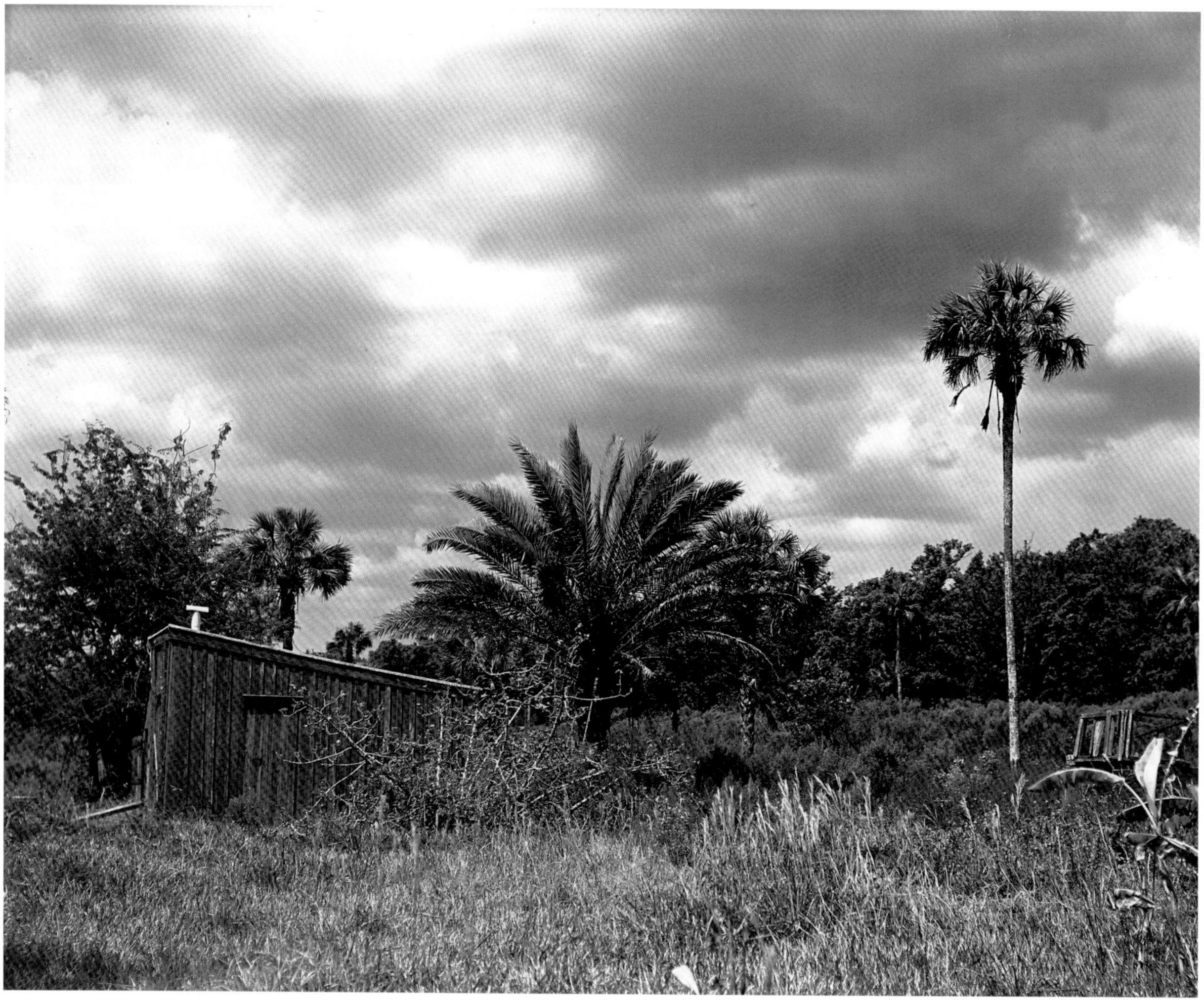

A house on the Rodgers River.
April 4, 1906; 48618.

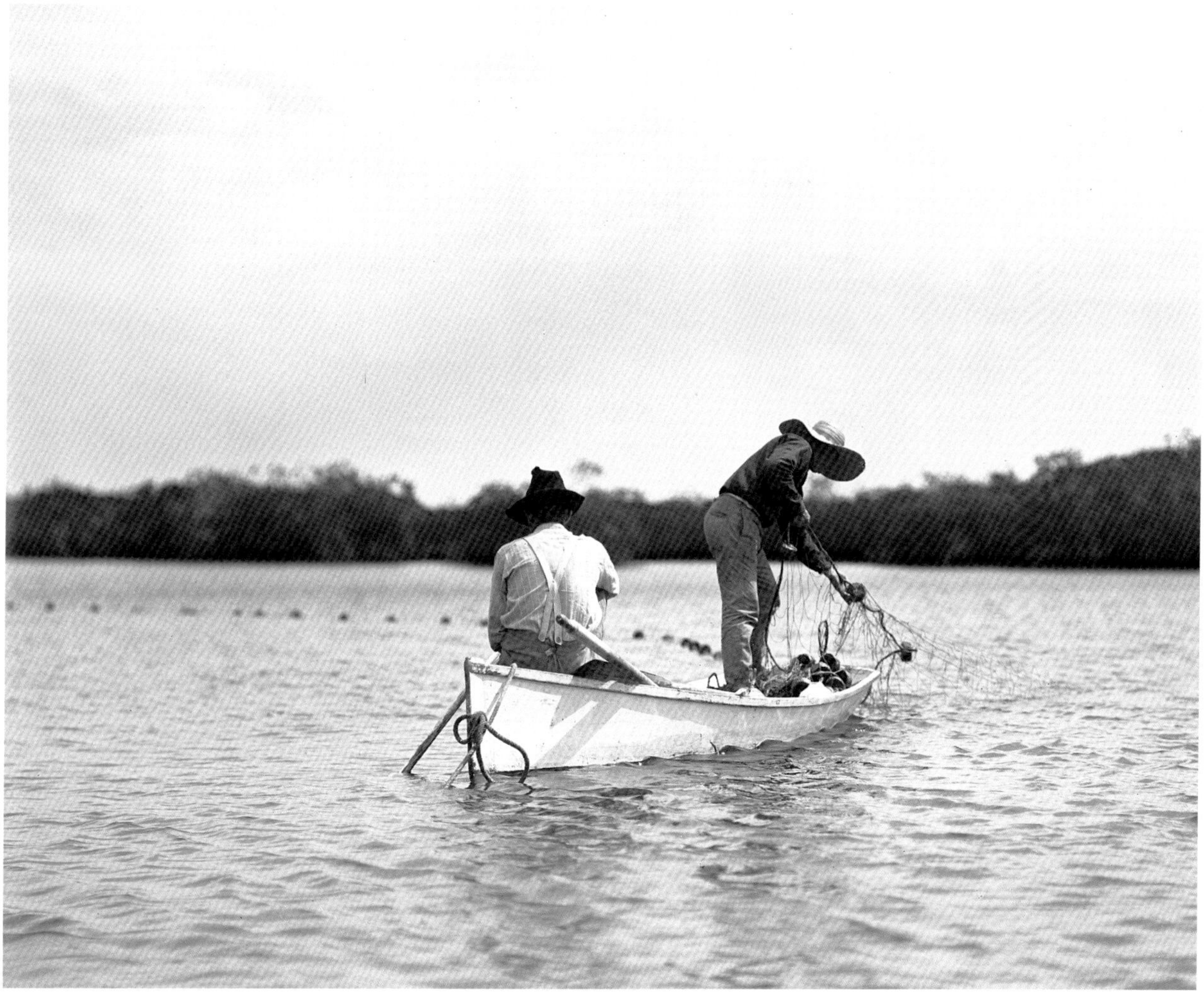

Fishermen taking in a seine net on the Shark River.
March 28, 1906; 48862.

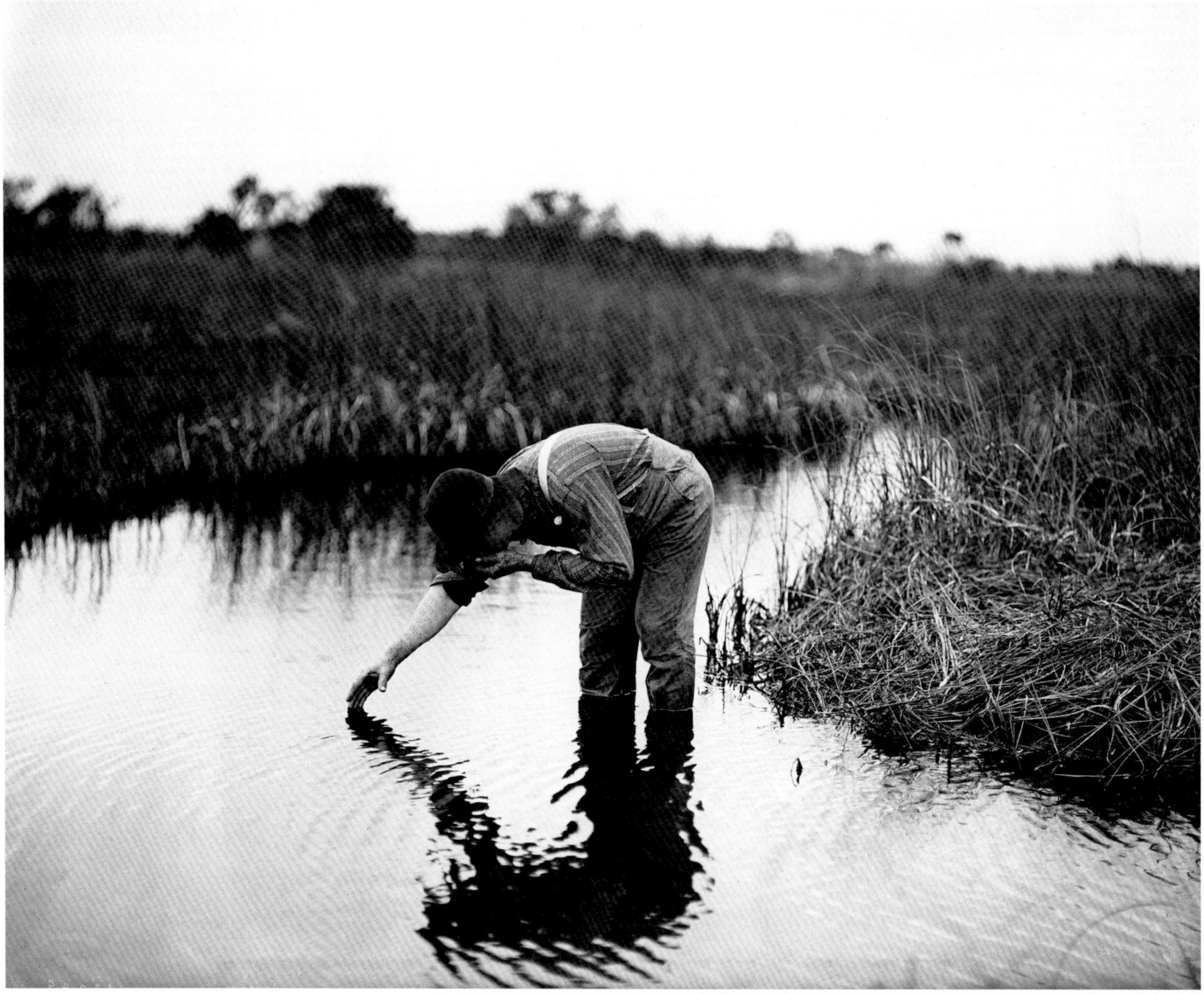

"No 'gator, large or small, can resist a peculiar call that resembles the grunt of a pig. Let a hunter grunt a few times at the side of a pond, and if there is an alligator in it, he will slowly raise his head above the surface and gaze curiously around" (Julian Dimock, "A Hunt for Baby Alligators," 1907). Harry, a young boy, demonstrates his grunting technique in a small pond near the Broad River. He was successful in catching several baby gators that were then collected by a herpetologist traveling with the Dimocks. April 19, 1906; 46758.

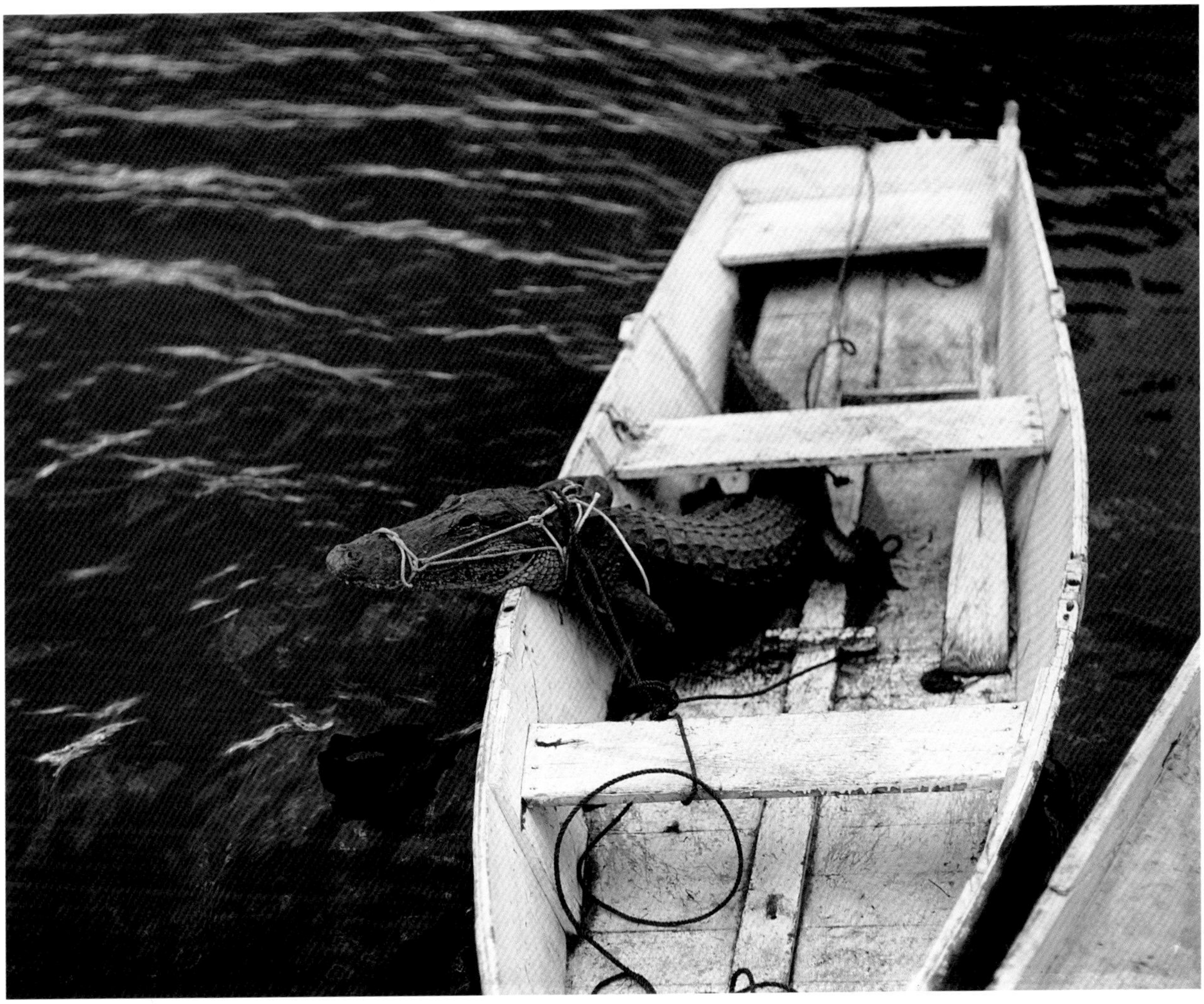

A captive alligator in the Dimocks' rowboat on the Broad River. The trussed-up alligator did not remain long in the boat. April 16, 1906; 46709.

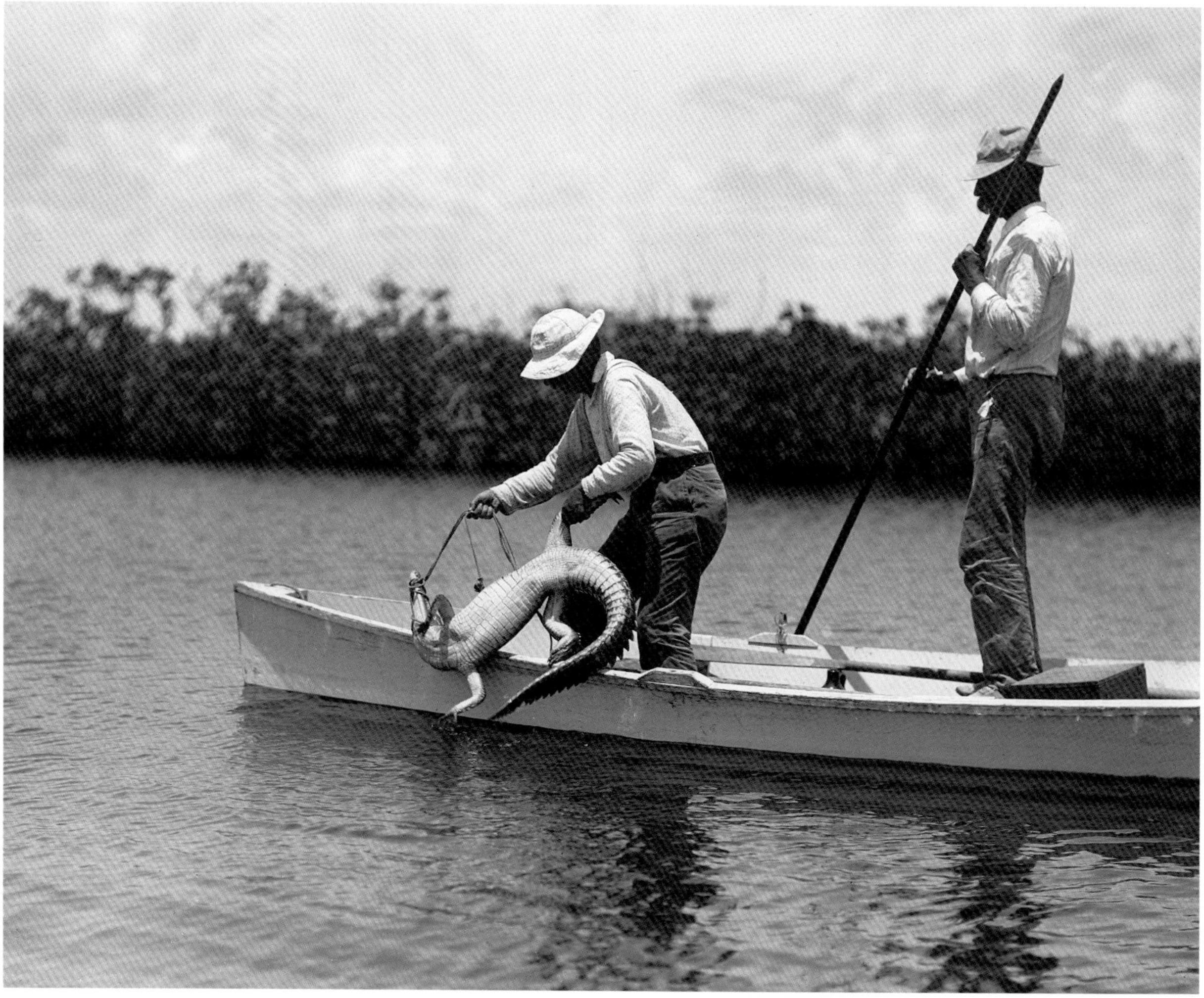

A. W. Dimock with a crocodile captured at Madeira Bay, a small inlet at the north side of Florida Bay in southernmost Florida. In 1906, he sent two live crocodiles from Florida to the New York Zoological Park, an event he wrote about in 1909 in a children's magazine ("How the Crocodiles Came to the Bronx"). May 3, 1905; 46836.

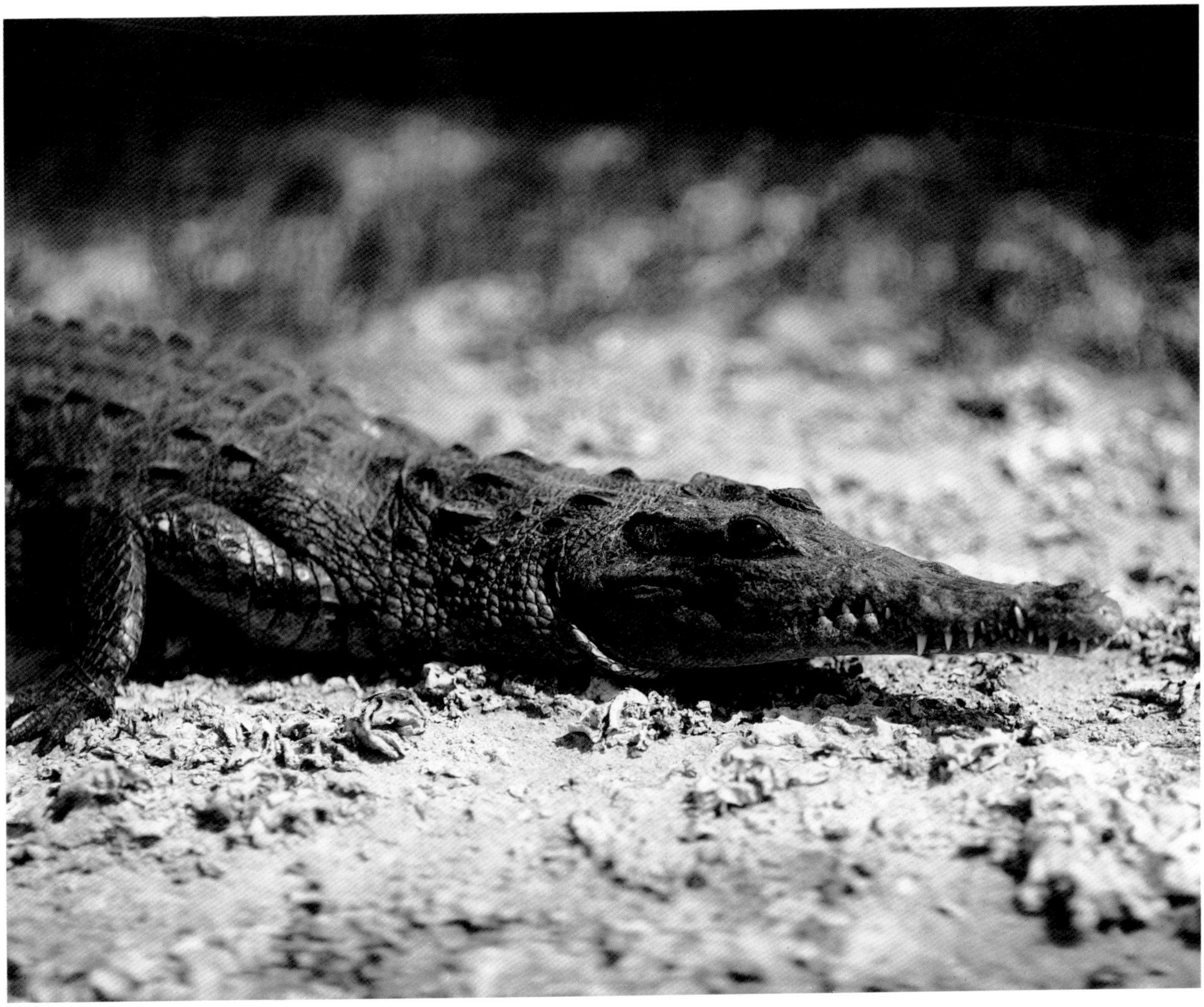

This crocodile, photographed at Madeira Bay, measured 5½ feet in length. In a 1918 article ("The Florida Crocodile"), A. W. stated that in 1889 (before he gave up hunting animals), he shot a specimen that was just over 14 feet long. Purportedly, the dead animal or its hide was sent to Yale University. The smaller crocodile photographed here was one of a "colony" of crocodiles that lived in and around Madeira Bay. May 3, 1905; 46837.

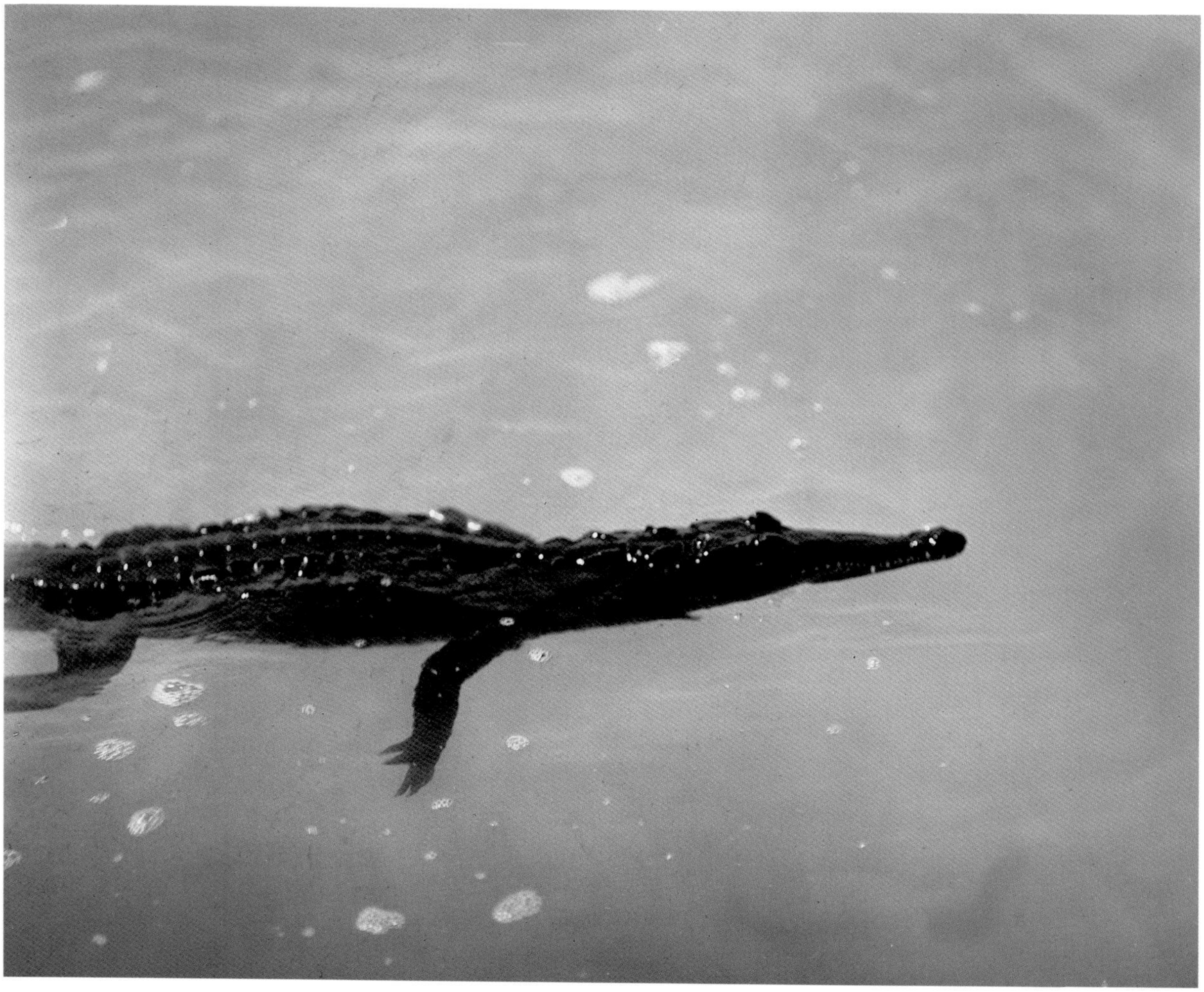

Crocodile swimming in Florida Bay. A.W. claimed that in 1889 he took the first photograph ever made of a Florida crocodile. Unfortunately, all of A.W.'s photographs and negatives stored at a cabin in the Catskills were destroyed in a fire. After that incident, Julian became the "camera man" for his and his father's adventures. March 10, 1906; 49348.

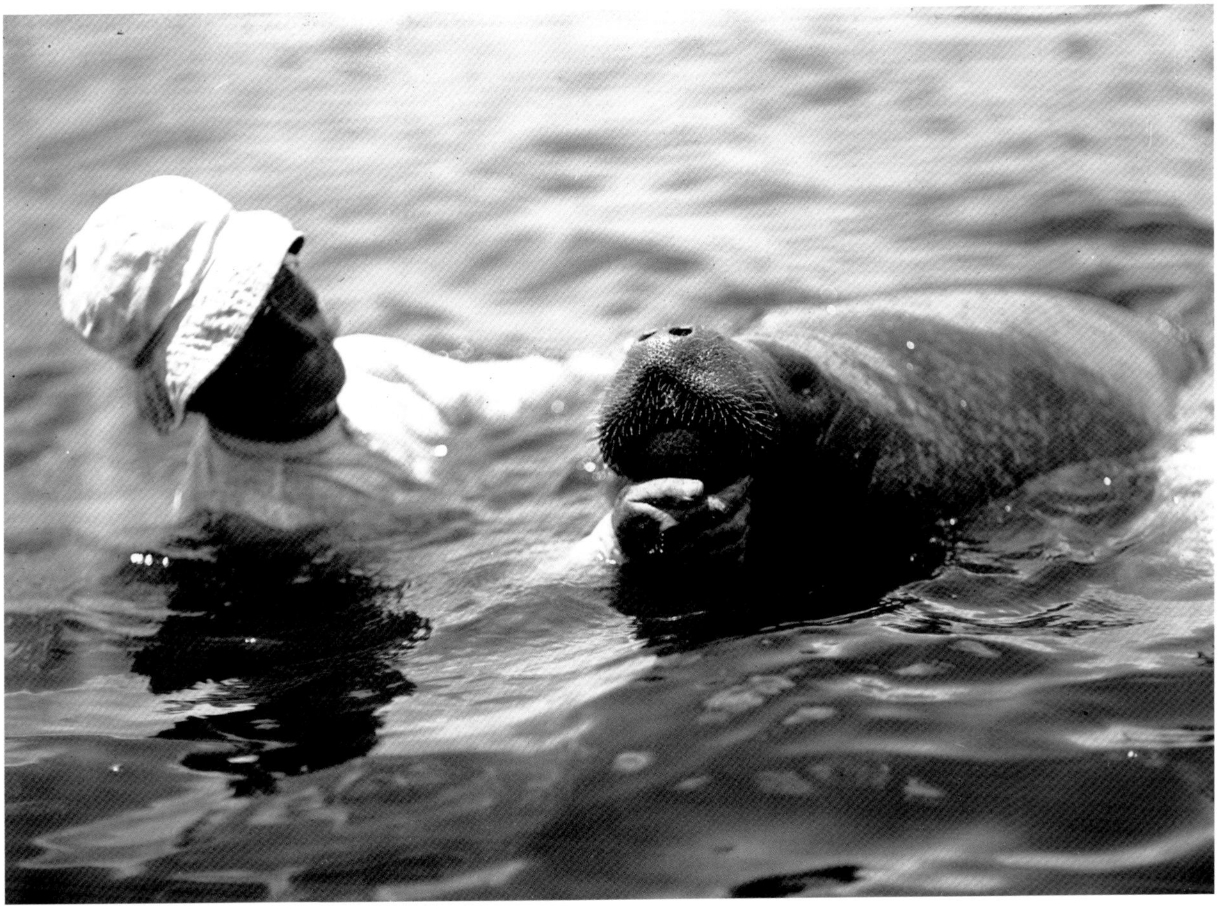

On two occasions, the Dimocks captured live manatees and sent them to the New York Aquarium. The first, an adult weighing 910 pounds, lived only a few weeks. Its skeleton today is curated at the American Museum of Natural History. The second, a much younger and smaller manatee, was still alive eighteen months later. A.W. and Julian both wrote several magazine articles about their adventures with manatees, and the animals were featured in chapters in *Florida Enchantments*. September 6, 1906; 49068.

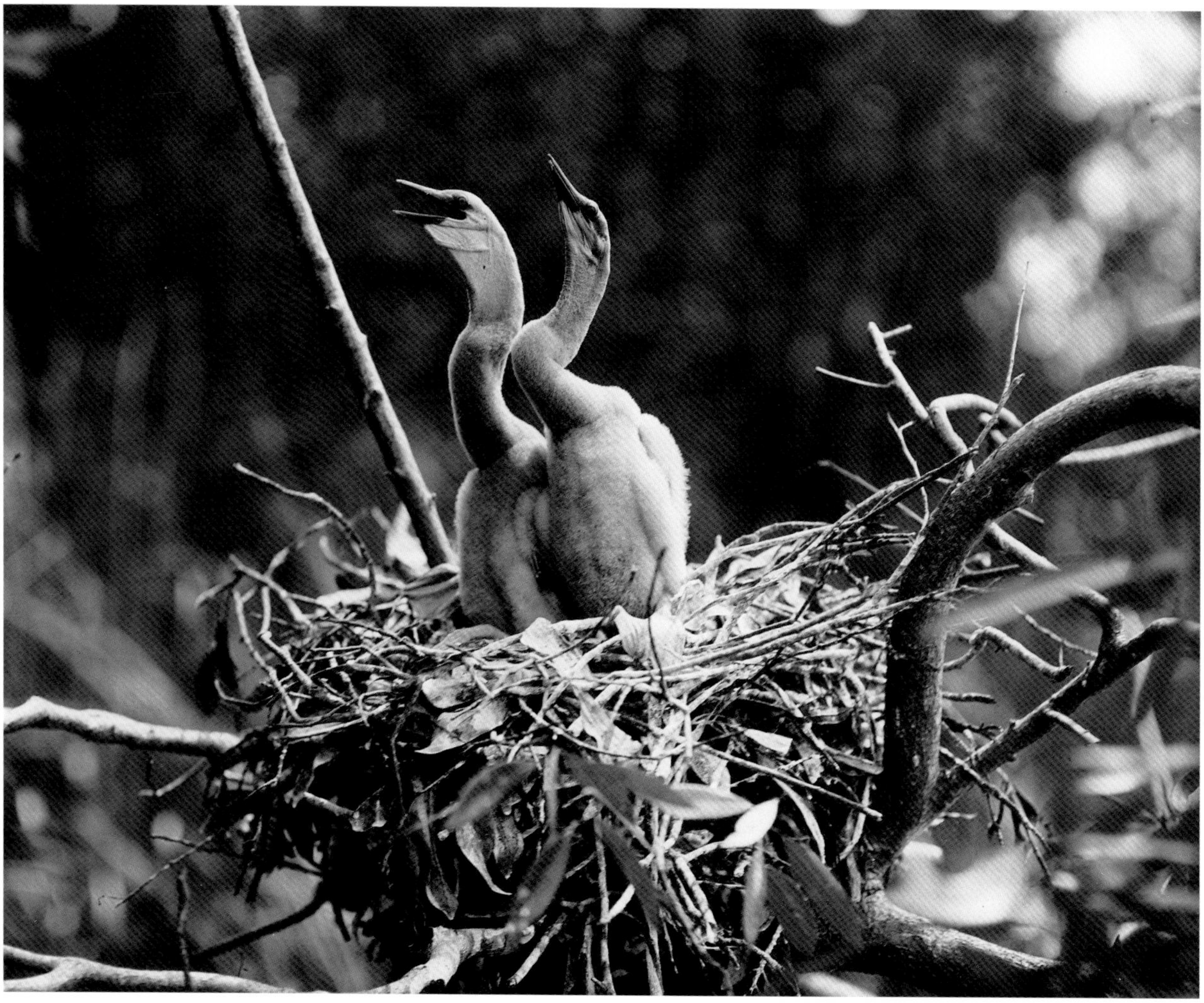

Young water turkeys (anhingas) in a rookery on the Harney River. In a wonderfully descriptive article about the rookery, A.W. recorded that he and Julian "spent [a] week, among fifteen thousand nests of squawking infants" ("Life in a Bird Rookery"). May 27, 1906; 47471.

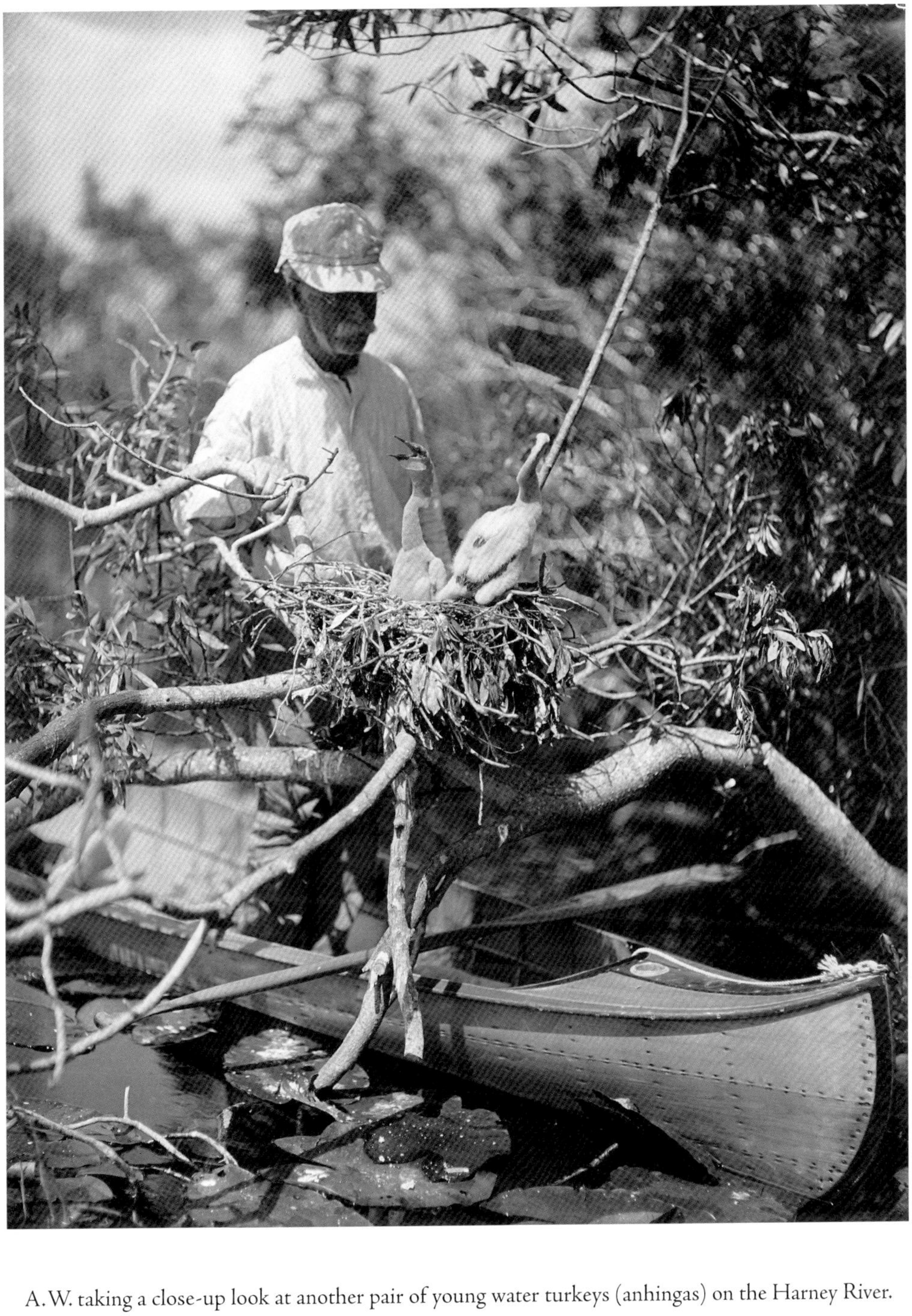

A.W. taking a close-up look at another pair of young water turkeys (anhingas) on the Harney River.
May 28, 1906; 47478.

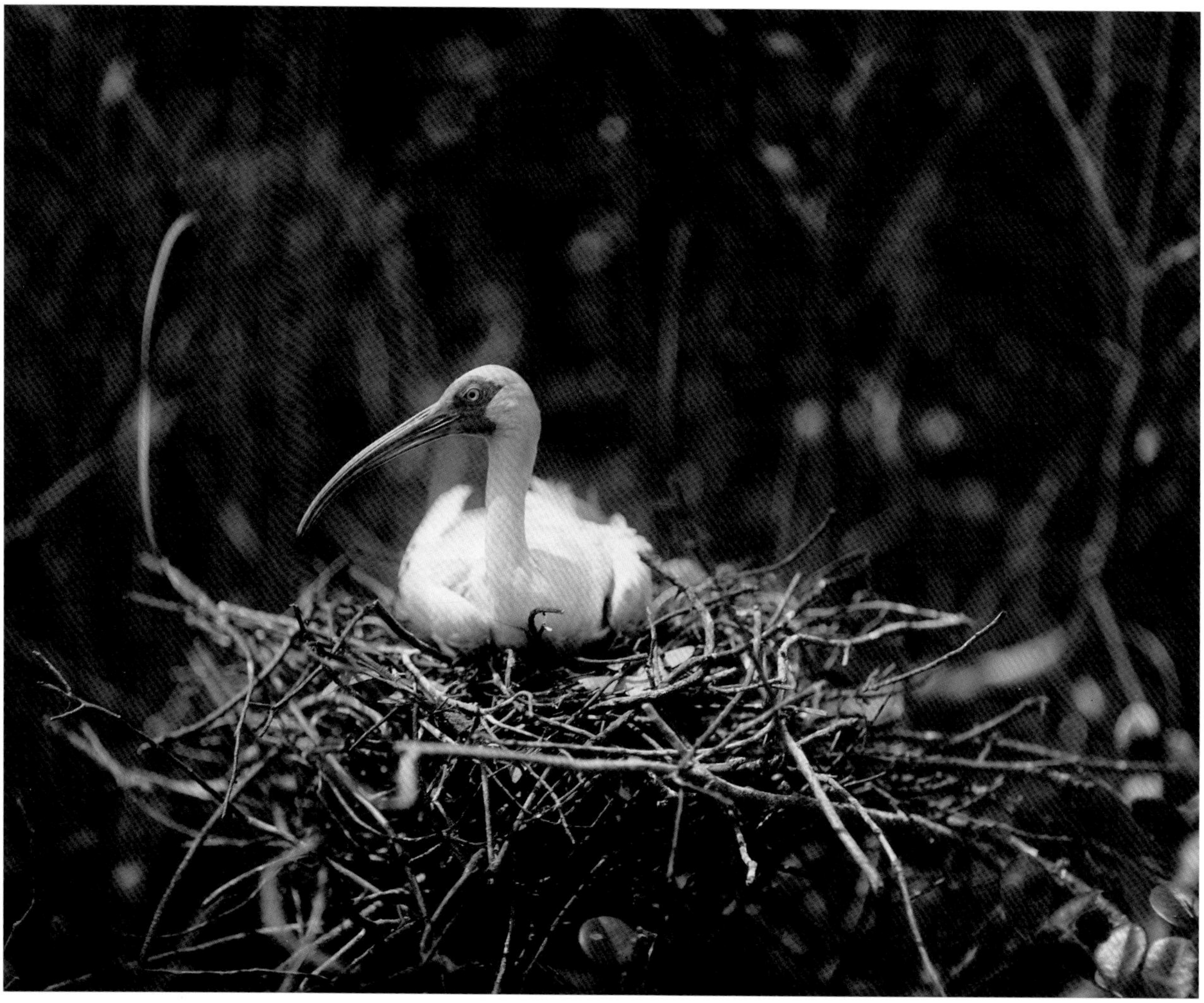

A nesting white ibis (Julian called it a "curlew"), Harney River. In "Life in a Bird Rookery," A. W. wrote, "We lived upon our boat, sleeping on the cabin roof under the stars, soothed to slumber each night by the composite *chack, chack, chack* resulting from the mingled cries of a thousand birds of many species." May 31, 1906; 47503.

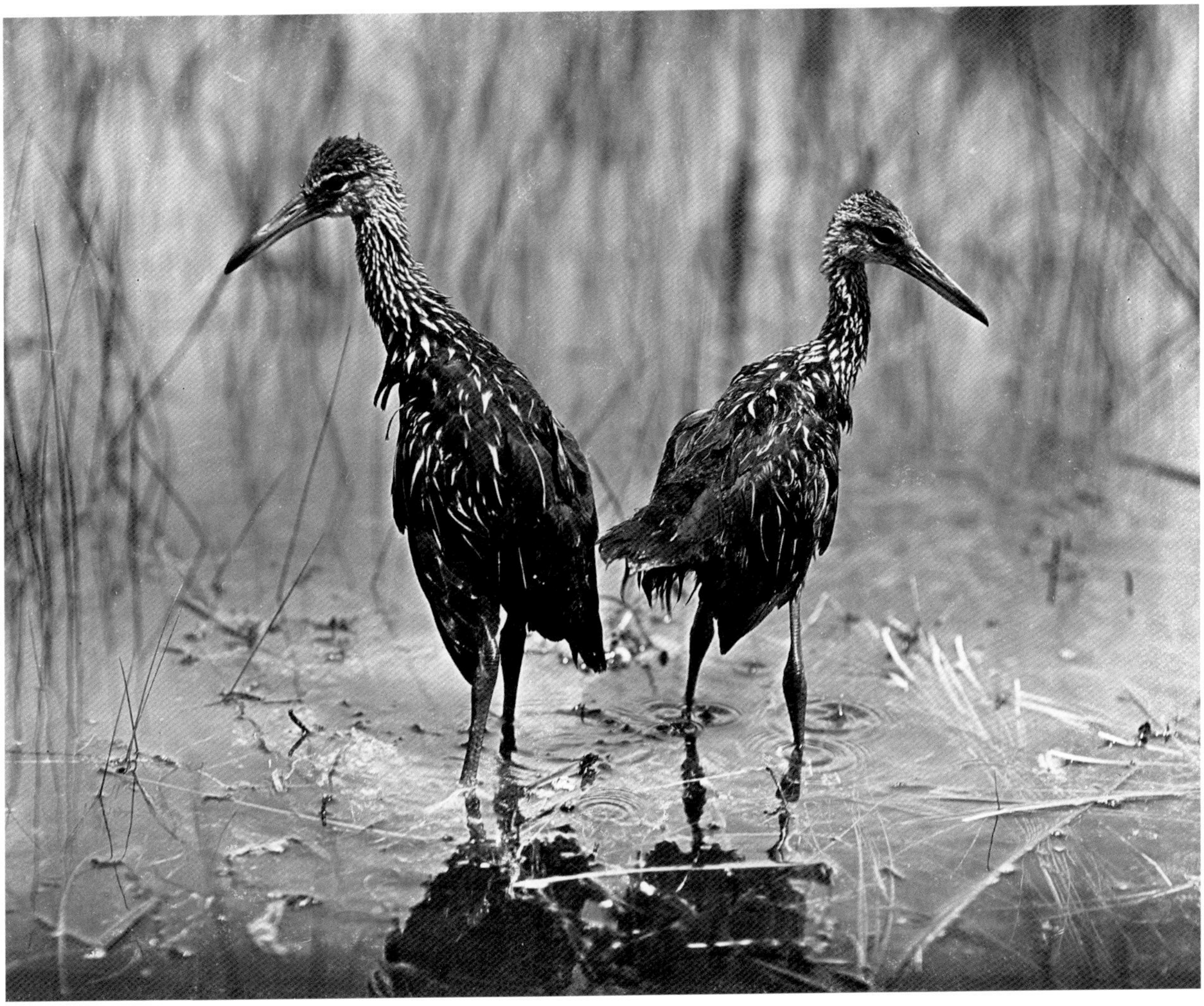

Limpkins, Harney River. Over six days, Julian Dimock took nearly one hundred photographs of birds along the river. Julian "waded and climbed trees, cut poles and made long legs for his camera, until he got the views he wanted of eggs and young birds." May 30, 1906; 47539.

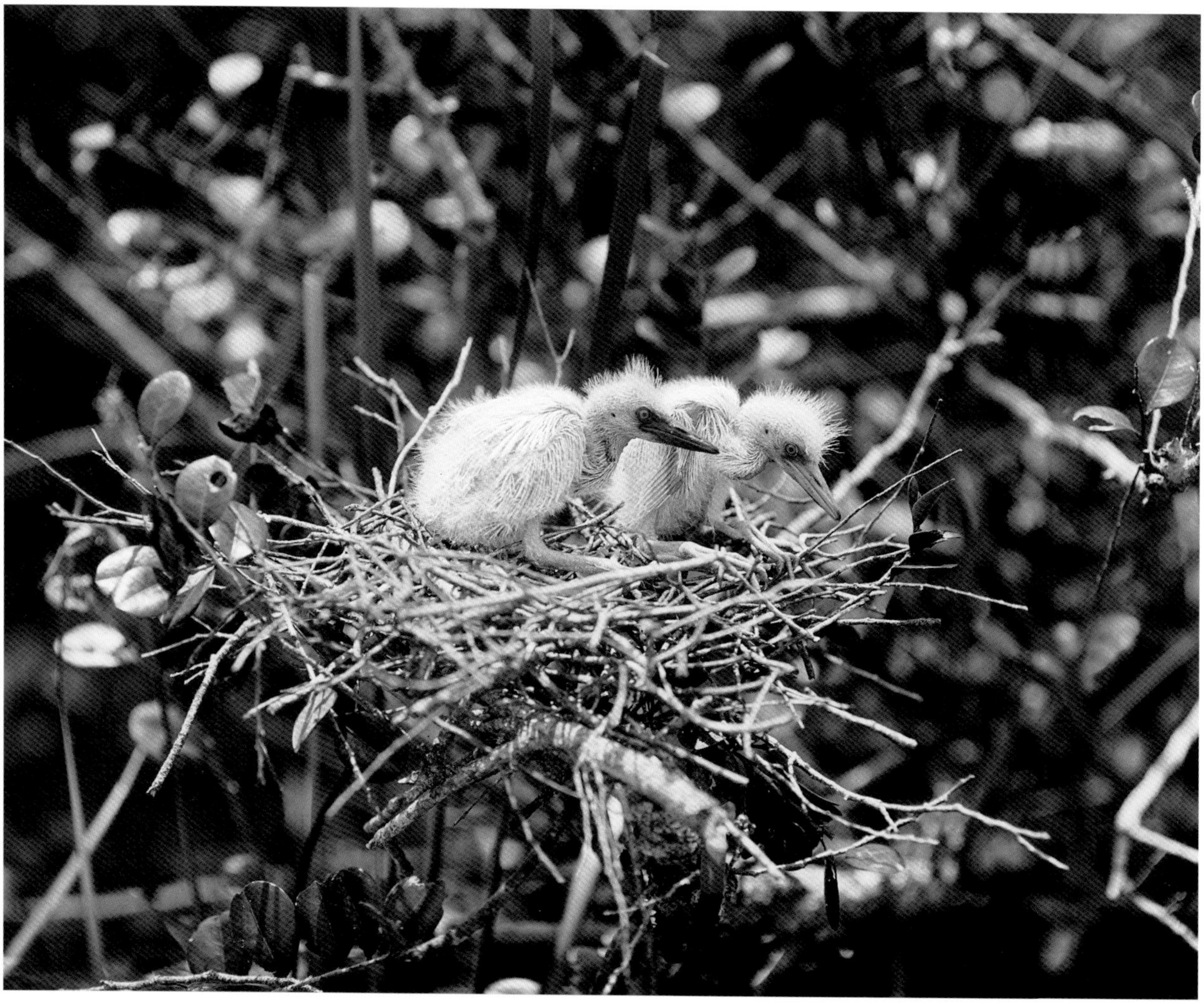

Baby blue herons in their nest, Harney River. Julian Dimock would publish a series of illustrated articles in *Field and Stream, Country Life in America, Illustrated London News,* and *Country Life* condemning the wholesale slaughter of egrets and herons to obtain feathers for the fashion industry. May 27, 1906; 47626.

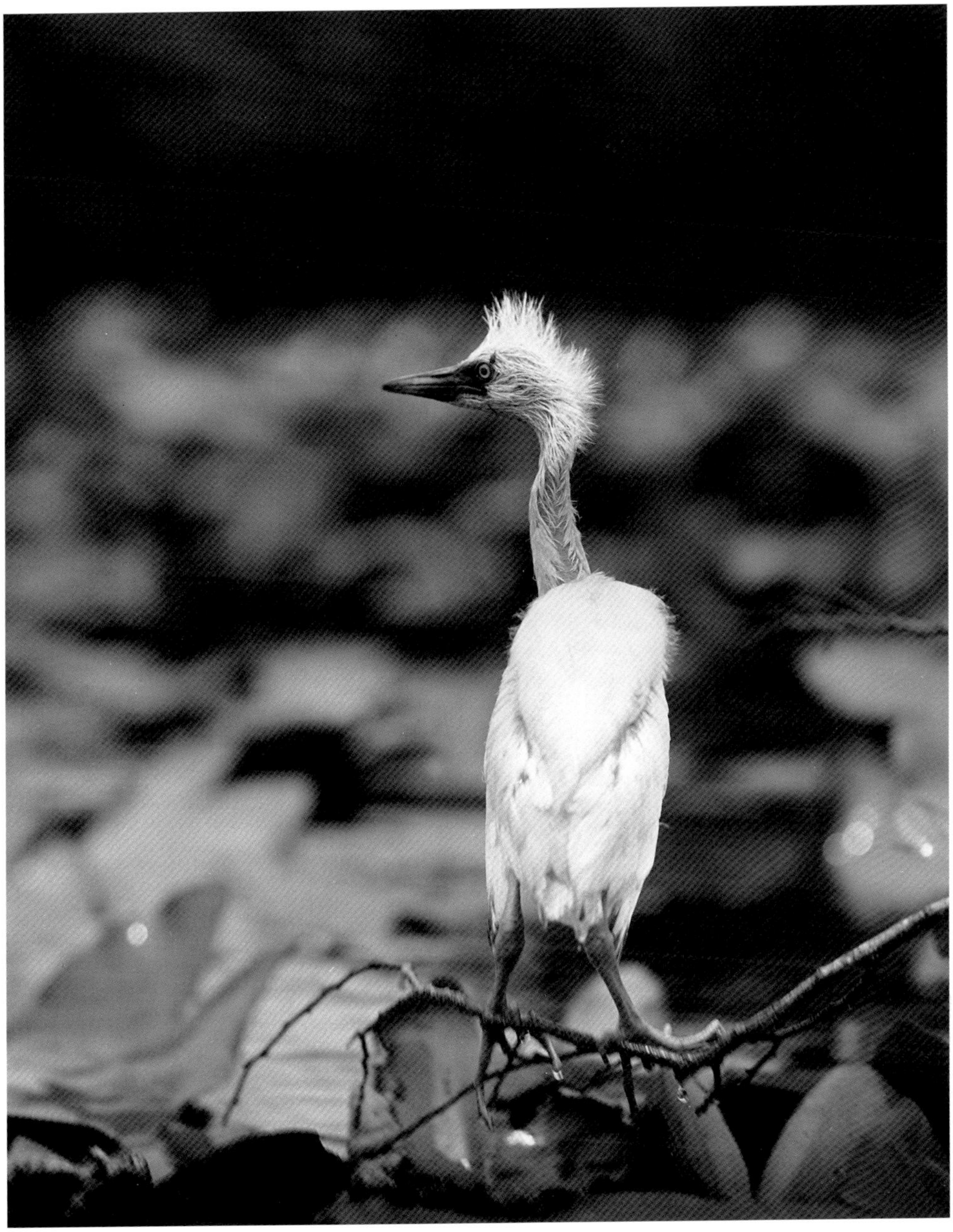

Young blue heron at the Harney River. According to A.W. ("Life in a Bird Rookery"): "We had little chance here to study the egret or long-white [great white heron]. The plume-hunters had visited the rookery ahead of us, and of fifteen thousand nests, not fifteen were occupied by these birds. . . . I now look back upon that bustling colony of beautiful birds with the sorrowful knowledge that it is doomed. The tourist-with-a-gun will destroy what the plume-hunter has left." May 27, 1906; 47632.

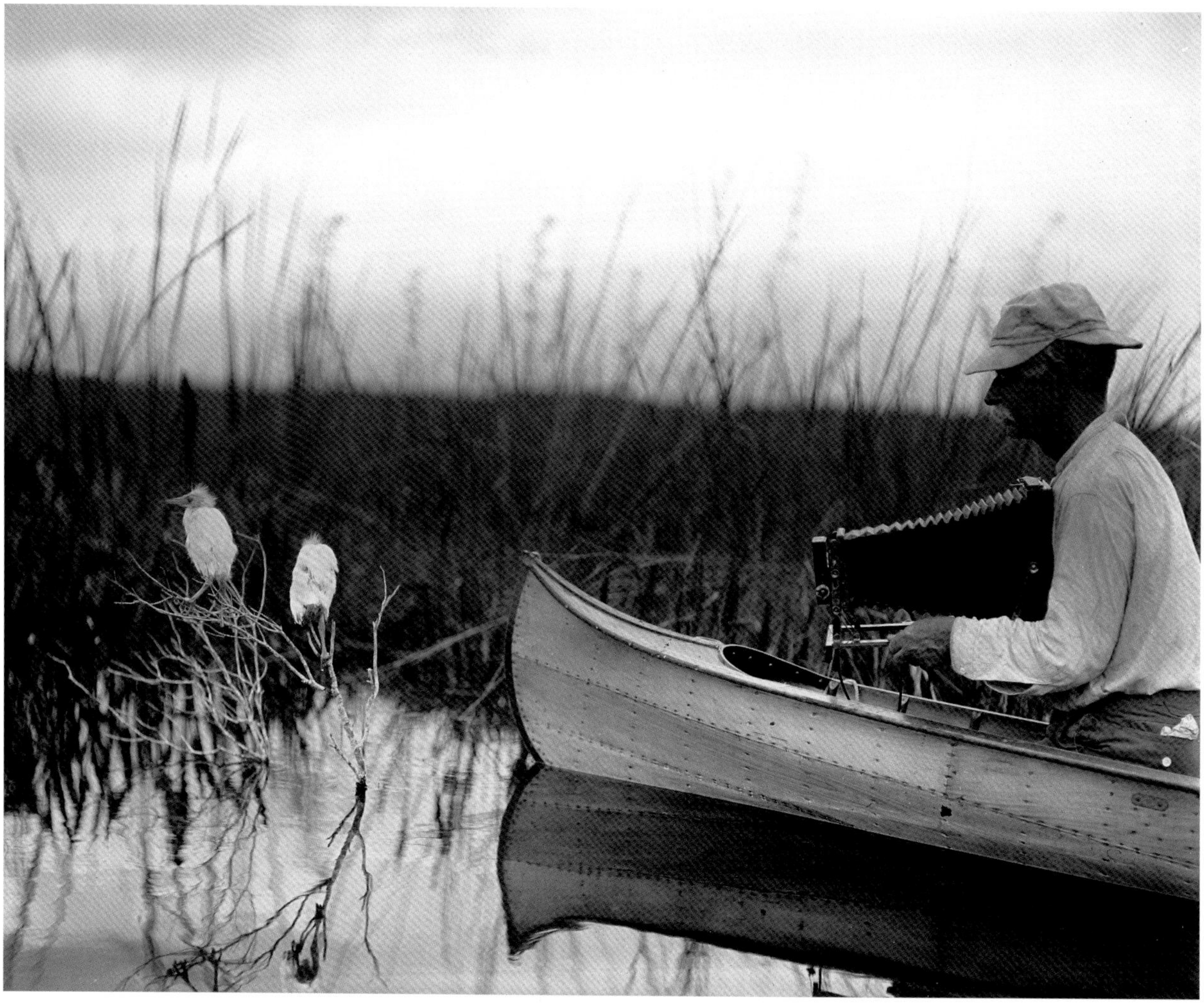

A. W. moves in for a close-up of two young blue herons at the Harney River. In his guidebook *Outdoor Photography* (1912), Julian wrote, "For ten years I have used a 6" × 8" Reflex camera for eighty-five per cent of my work and for the other fifteen per cent an ordinary tripod view camera of the folding type—so ordinary that it has not even the maker's name. The same lens and plate-holders fit both these instruments." Here A. W. is holding the folding camera while Julian photographs the scene with the other camera. May 28, 1906; 47641.

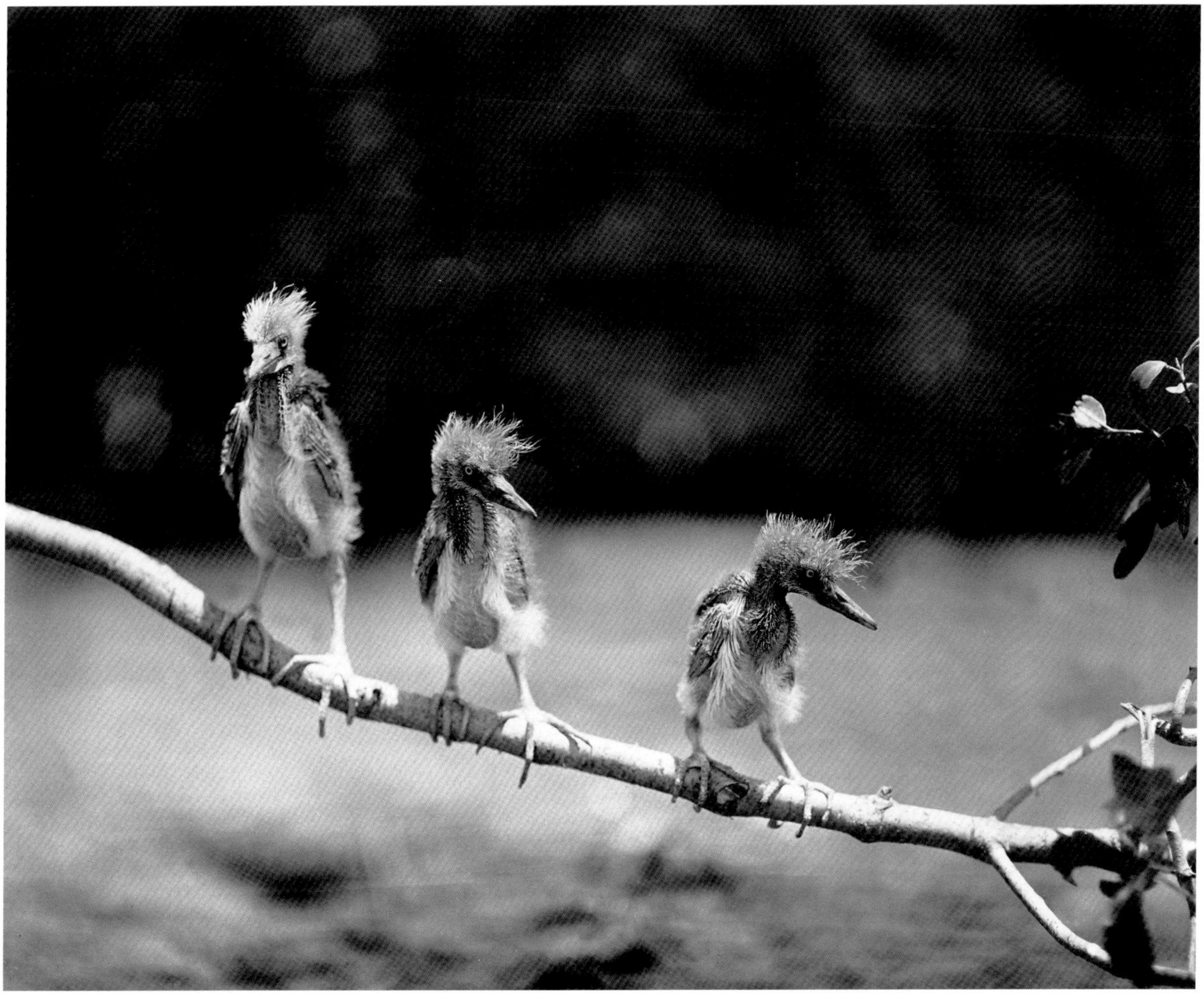

Three young tricolored herons, Sandfly Pass. (Julian called them by their former name: Louisiana heron.) May 15, 1906; 47548.

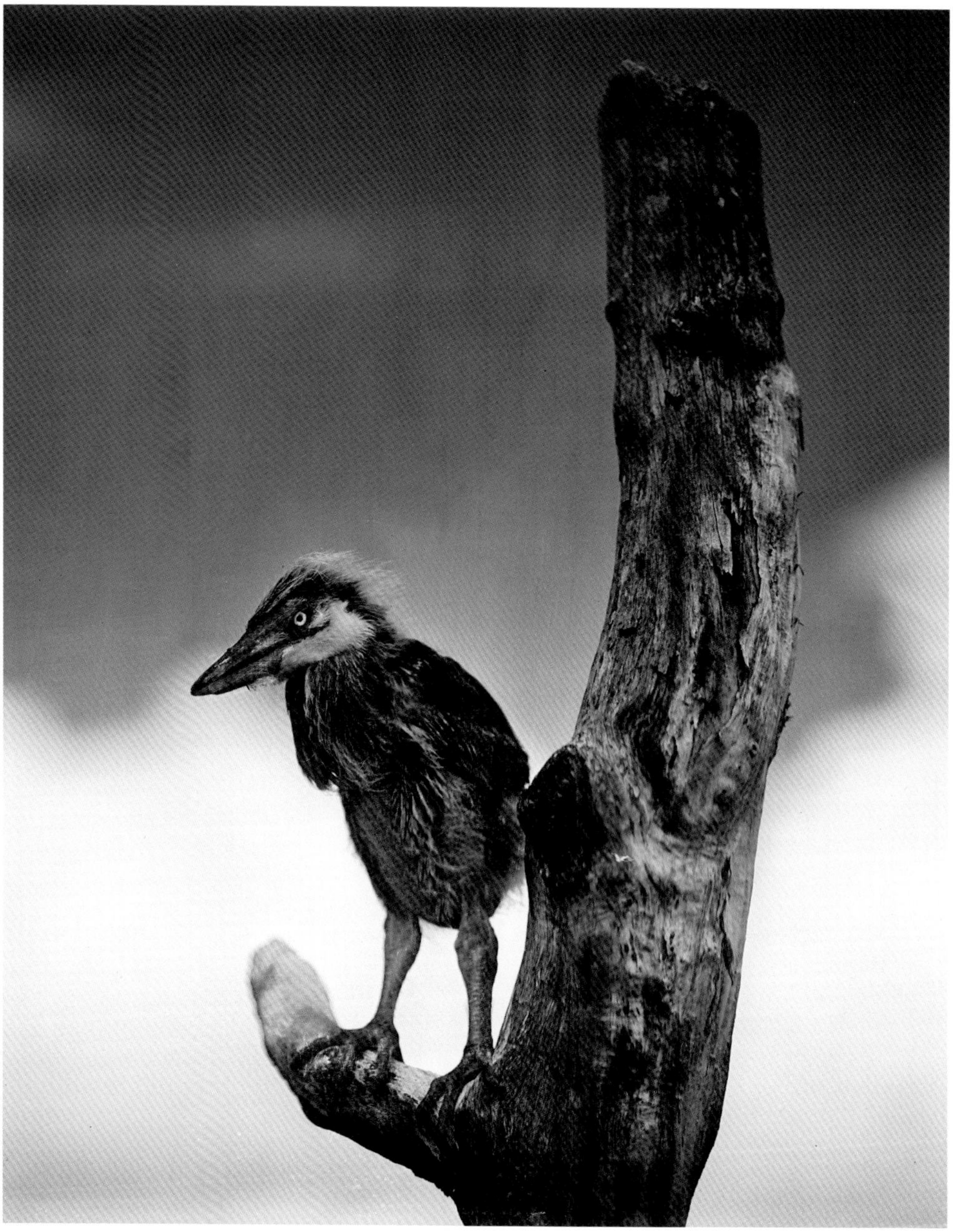

Young blue heron, Cape Sable.
March 15, 1906; 47597.

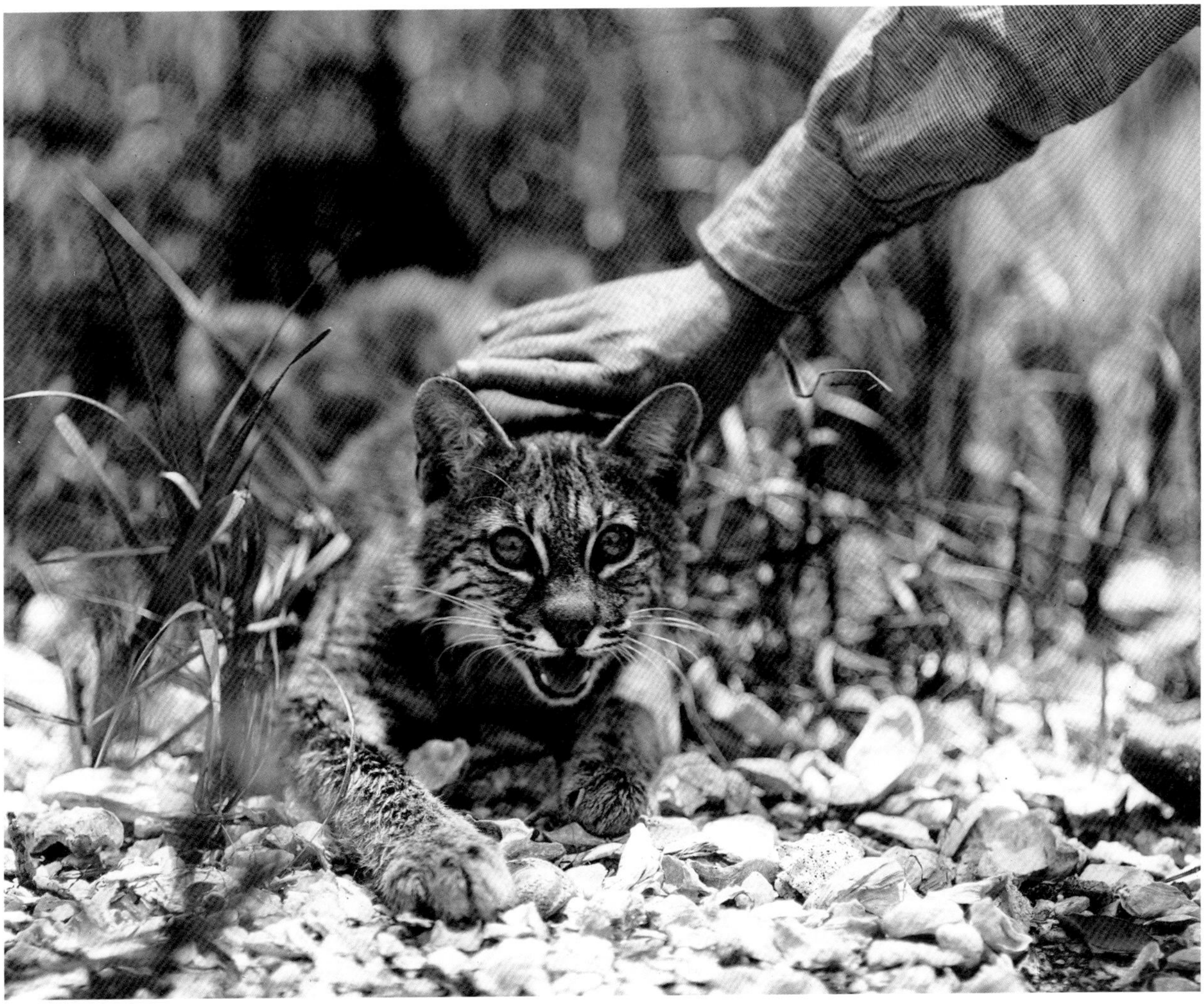

At Fakahatchee (Julian calls it "Figahatchee"), the Dimocks met a boy and his pet bobcat. Somewhere near Chokoloskee Bay, the Dimocks obtained another pet bobcat from Seminole Indians. They kept the animal aboard the *Irene* for about two weeks before the animal swam ashore. (A. W. said it jumped overboard when the bobcat heard a rooster crow at a house nearby on the mainland.) April 18, 1905; 47750.

Moonshiners

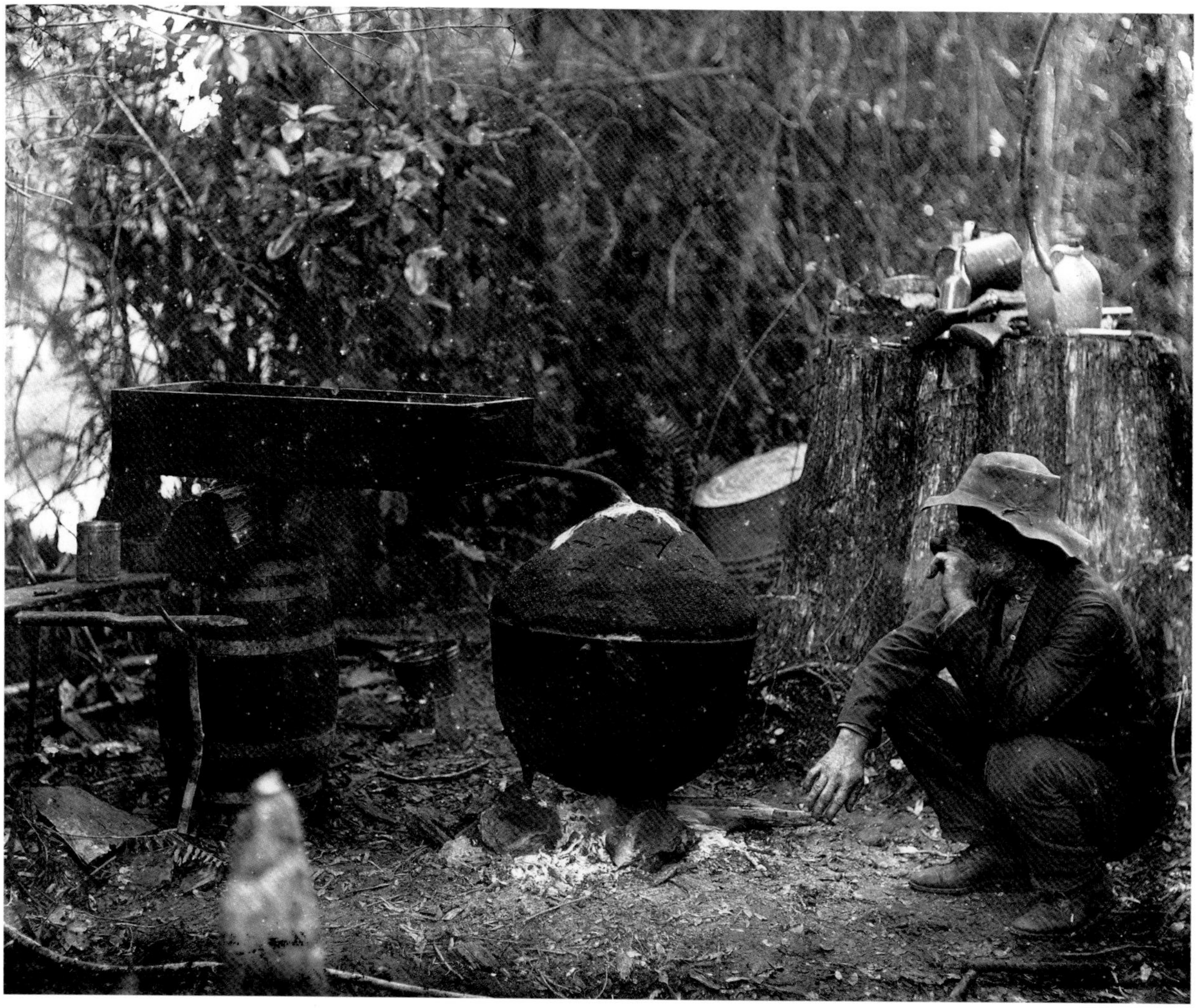

In the spring of 1906, the Dimocks convinced a friend they had met on their southwest Florida travels to guide them to a moonshine still somewhere in the Big Cypress Swamp. A.W. wrote about their adventure in 1909 ("Makers of Moonshine"): "The big iron kettle over the fire was fitted with a wooden top, deftly fashioned from a section of a cypress tree three feet in diameter, the stump of which served as a table within the glade. An iron pipe led from the cypress cover of the kettle through a wooden box of water, and from its projecting end poured a tiny stream of the potent product of the still."
April 27, 1906; 48810.

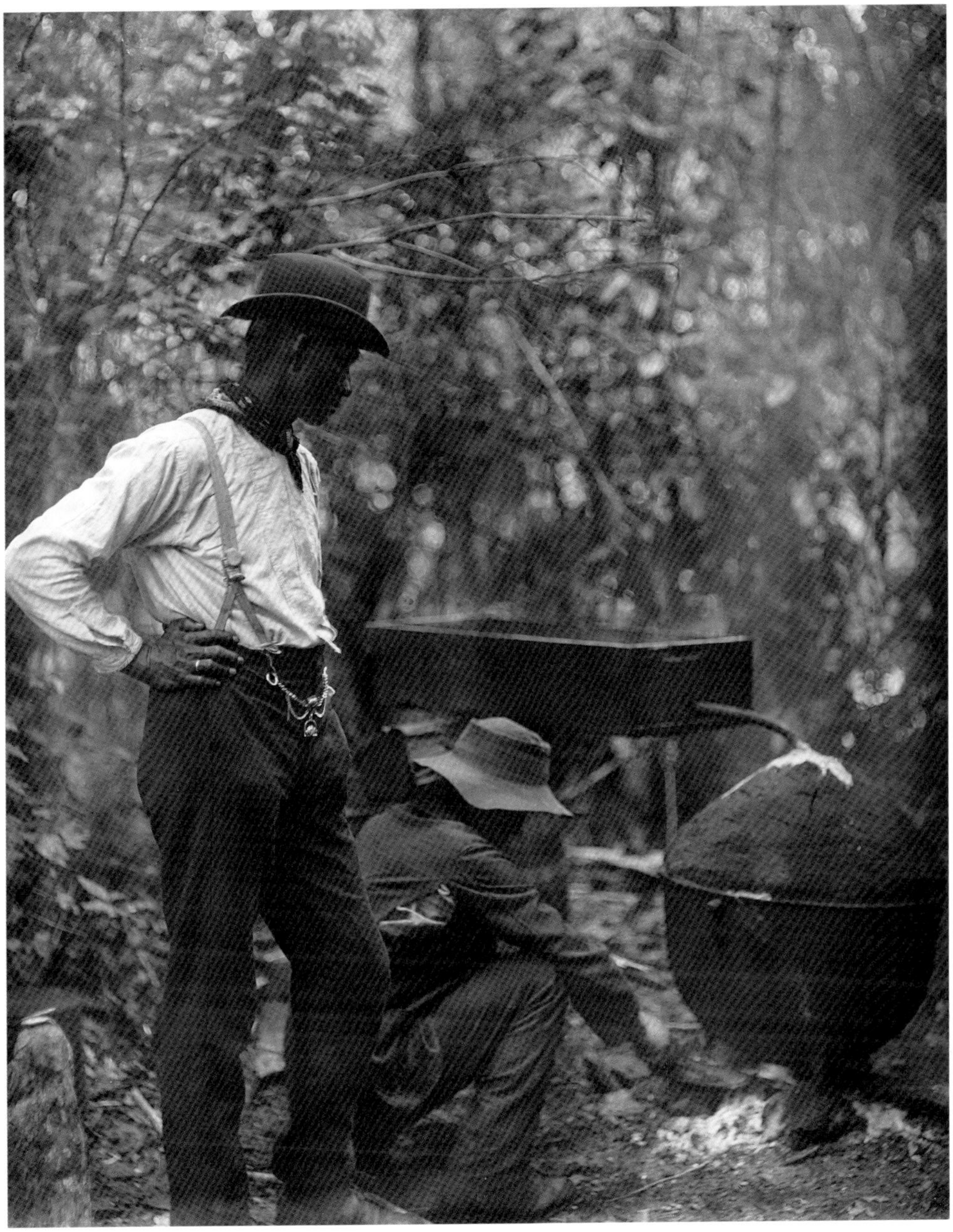

The moonshine operation was run by three armed men, only one of whom consented to be photographed. When the Dimocks inquired who the man above on the left was, they were told he was a Seminole Indian customer. The Seminole man told the Dimocks that the Big Cypress still's moonshine was better than that made near Miami. Julian photographed a sugarcane grinder somewhere nearby, probably the source of the mash used in the still. As A.W. noted in "The Passing of a Wilderness": "Sometimes in the [Ten Thousand Islands] a modest shack may be seen surrounded by a field of cane. In its final stage the cultivation of this crop is conducted by the light of the moon and its product attracts its own market."
April 27, 1906; 48813.

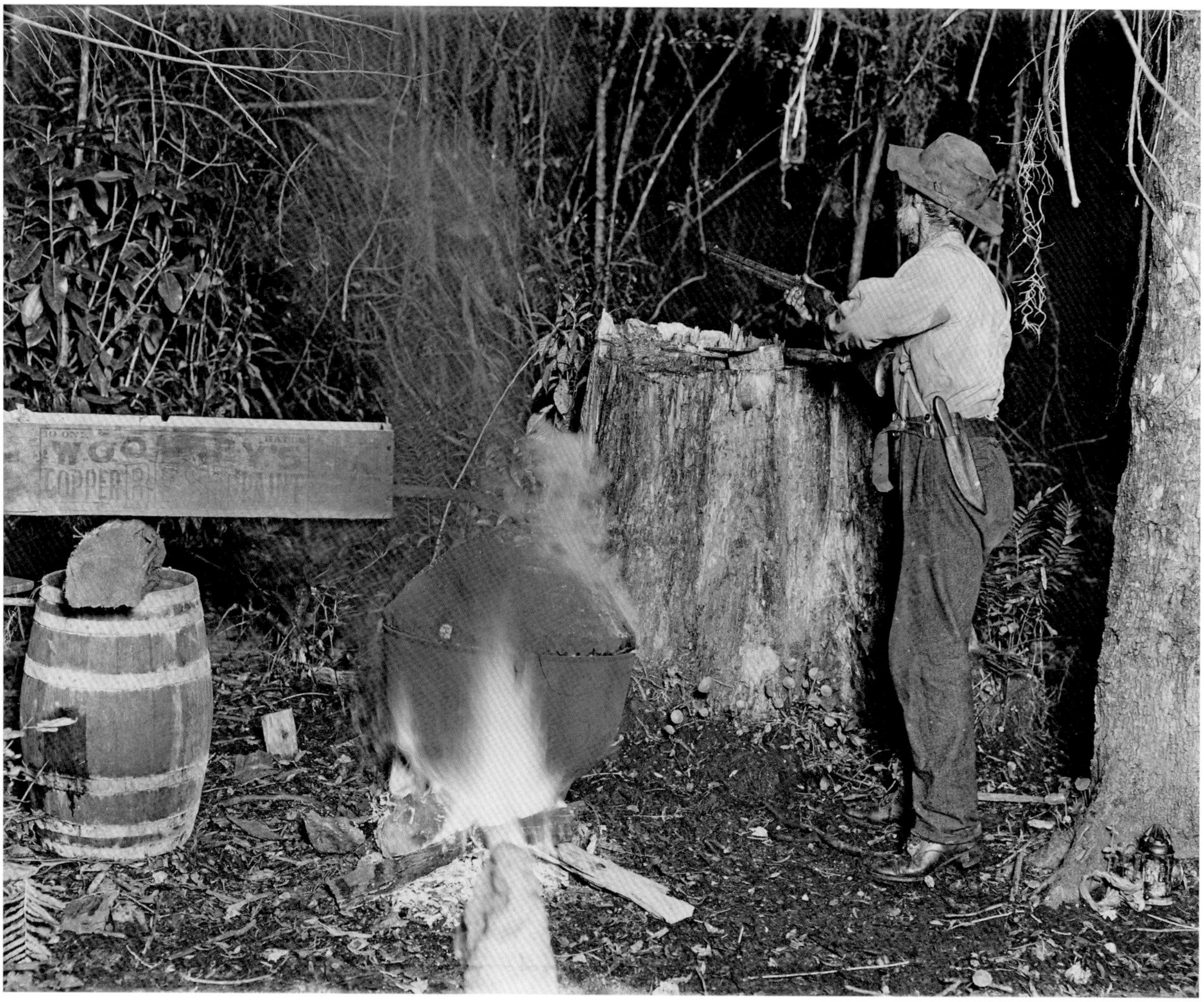

Because it was dark when they arrived, Julian used "flash lights" to illuminate the scene so he could take photographs. The moonshiners, unsure who the Dimocks were, were leery of them and jumped at every noise they heard coming from the nearby swamp. The Dimocks returned the following day in daylight to take more photographs. The printing on the wooden box reads "Woolsey's Copper Paint." April 26, 1906; 48809.

The Infamous Mr. Watson (Before and After)

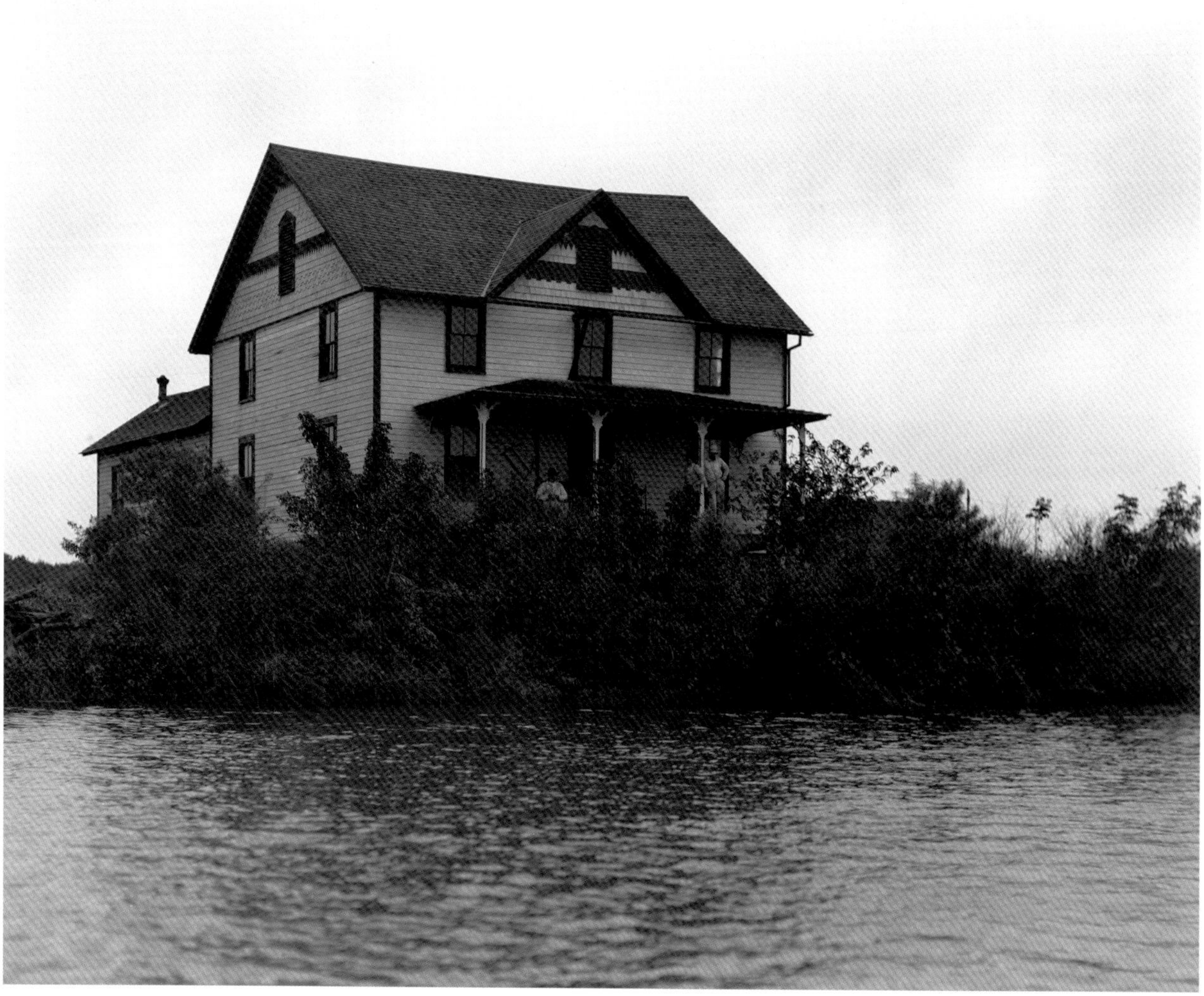

The Dimocks certainly knew the reputation of Edgar J. Watson when Julian took this photograph in 1905, apparently showing Watson seated on the front porch of his house at Chatham Bend in the Ten Thousand Islands. Watson, whose notorious exploits in southwest Florida are recounted in Peter Matthiessen's books *Killing Mister Watson* and *Shadow Country*, was killed by his Chokoloskee Bay neighbors in 1910. January 3, 1905; 48584.

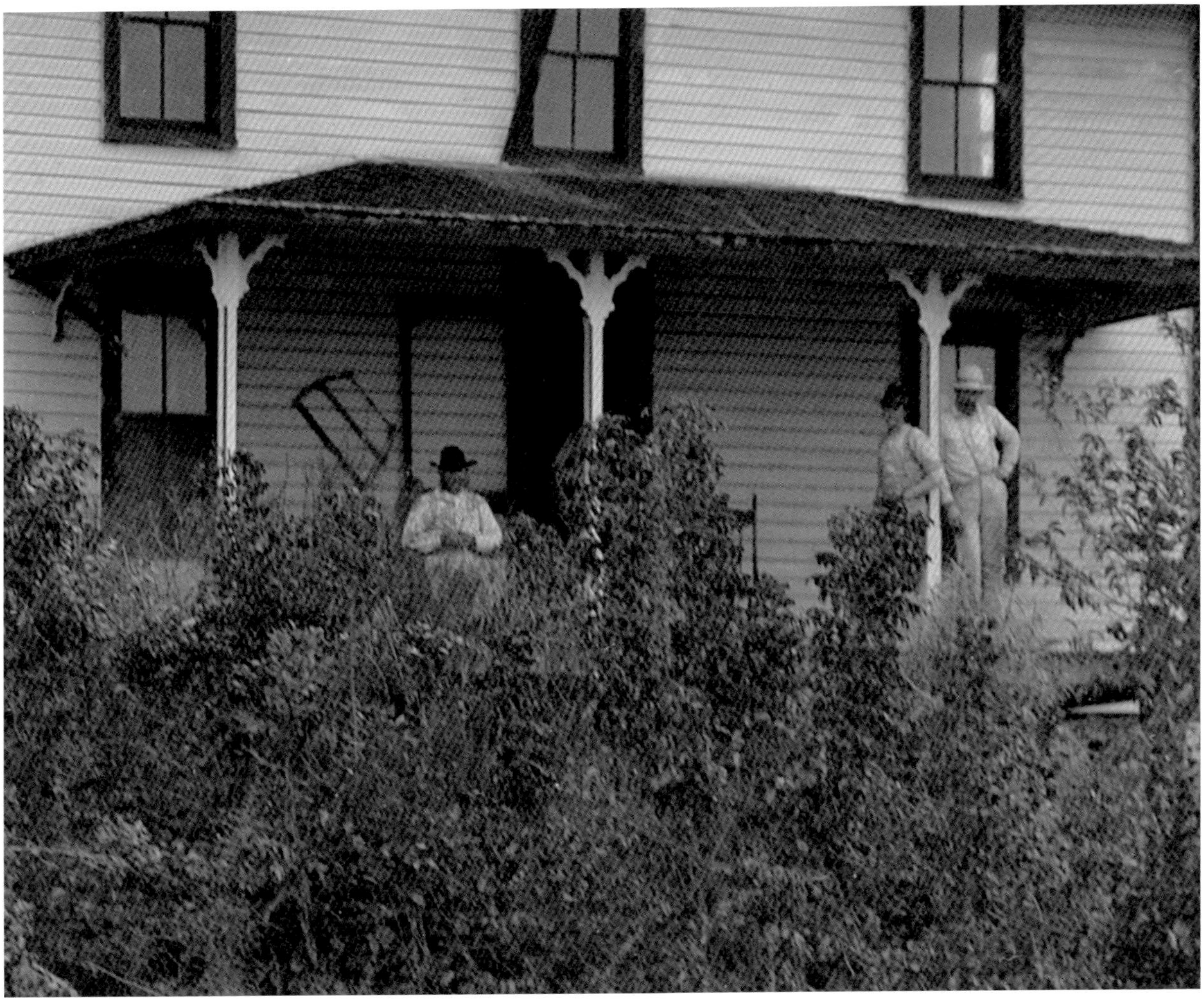

In a 1907 magazine article, "The Passing of a Wilderness," in which A.W. wrote about Mr. Watson (calling him J. E. Wilson), he unknowingly foretold Watson's 1910 murder by his neighbors: "He was a genial man, but mothers made use of his name to scare their babies into good behavior, and men who were looking for trouble found him most accommodating. . . . One of the principal men on the coast told me that court justice was too expensive and uncertain for that country, and that people were expected to settle their own quarrels—a homicidal custom. . . . Sometimes these settlements started little feuds which soon ran out for lack of material, and occasionally the participants violated the code of ethics of the community, which was apt to be bad for them." January 3, 1905; 48584 enlarged.

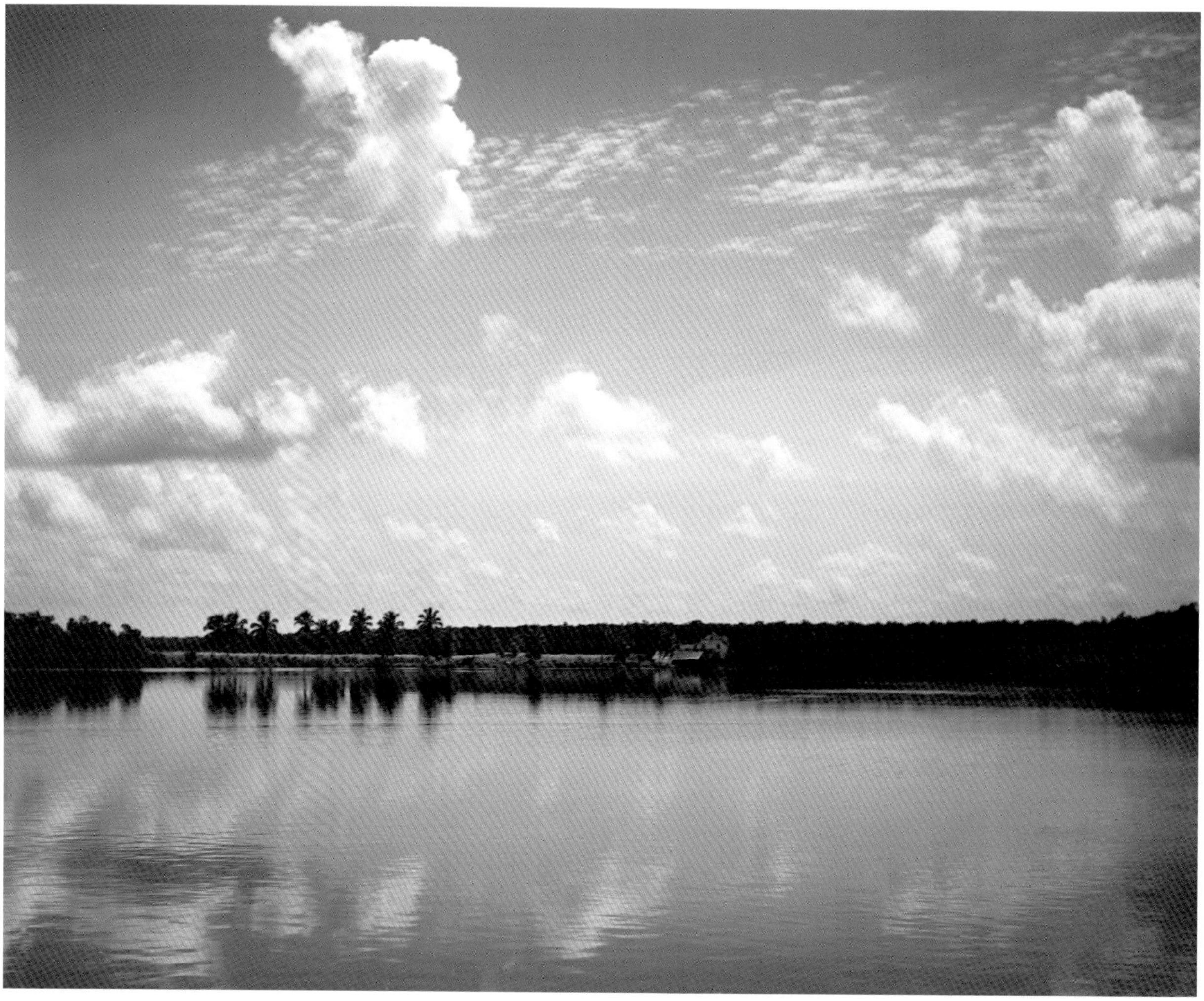

In 1913, the Dimocks again took photographs of Watson's buildings and fields. Six years earlier (in "Crossing the Everglades in a Power-boat"), A. W. had noted: "Some plantations in the Ten Thousand Islands have their private graveyards, but all have histories, and as we continued our placid voyage my companion told me of the one we had left, which was known by the name of its founder [Jean Chevelier]. He was a harmless individual who once weakly consented to join two of his associates . . . in arresting his nearest neighbor, one Wilson, upon a bogus warrant. Arresting Wilson upon a genuine warrant had long been recognized as a form of suicide, and it is believed that nervousness arising from his acquaintance with the man induced the leader of the trio to begin the service of the warrant at long range. The return shot neatly shaved off one side of his mustache, and he fled, followed by his fellow conspirators. Mr. Wilson chased them as far as Cape Sable in his boat, and is believed to be still on the lookout for their return." August 25, 1913; 49325.

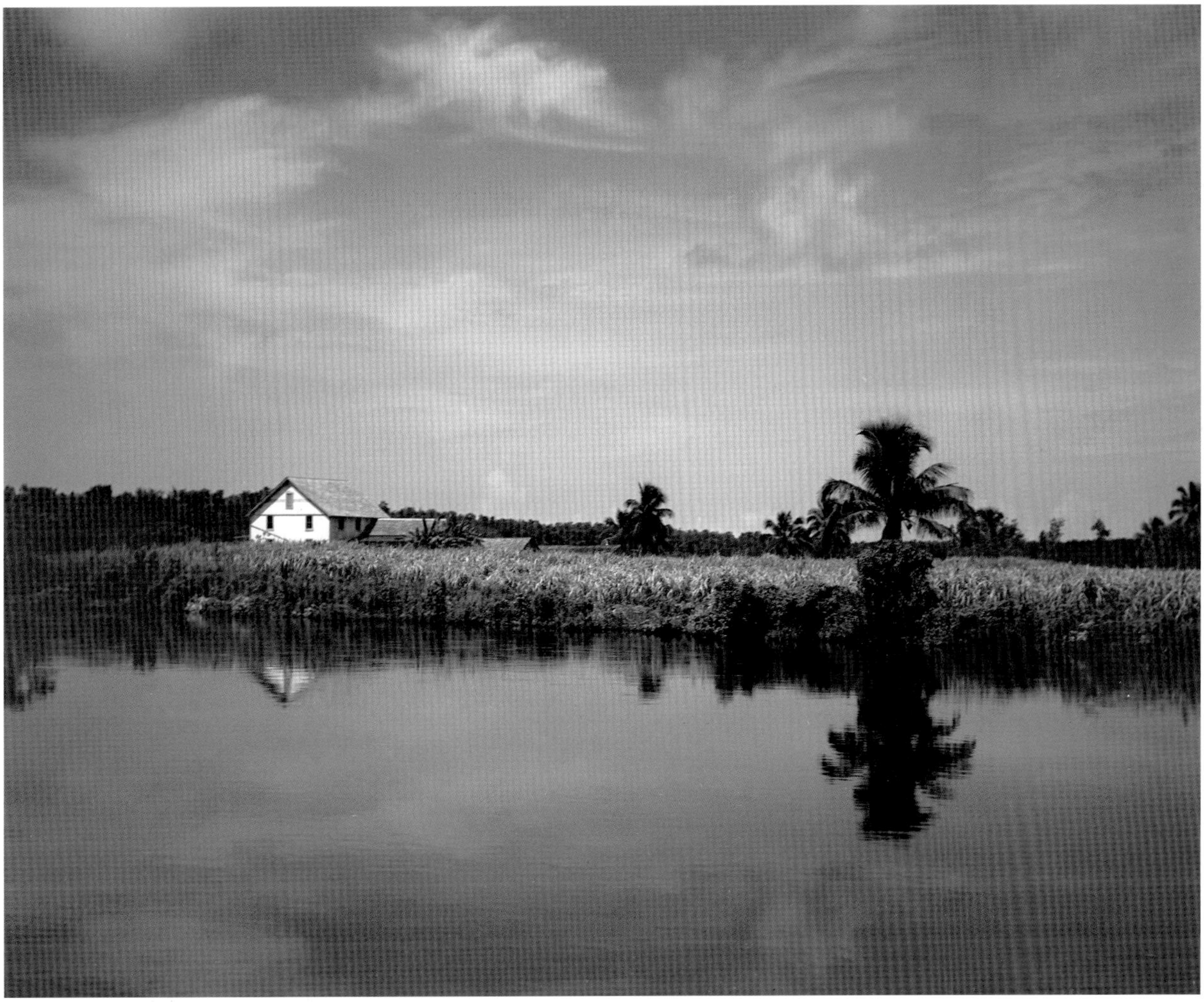

Watson's house, fields, and outbuildings. When Julian took this photograph in 1913, he and his father were well aware that in 1910 Watson had been "eliminated by a bunch of fourteen of his nearest neighbors." (*Florida Enchantments*, 1915 ed.). Peter Matthiessen likely drew on A. W. Dimock's anecdotes about "J. E. Wilson" for his book about the killing of Edgar Watson. August 25, 1913; 49327.

The Last Florida Adventure

The Last Photographs

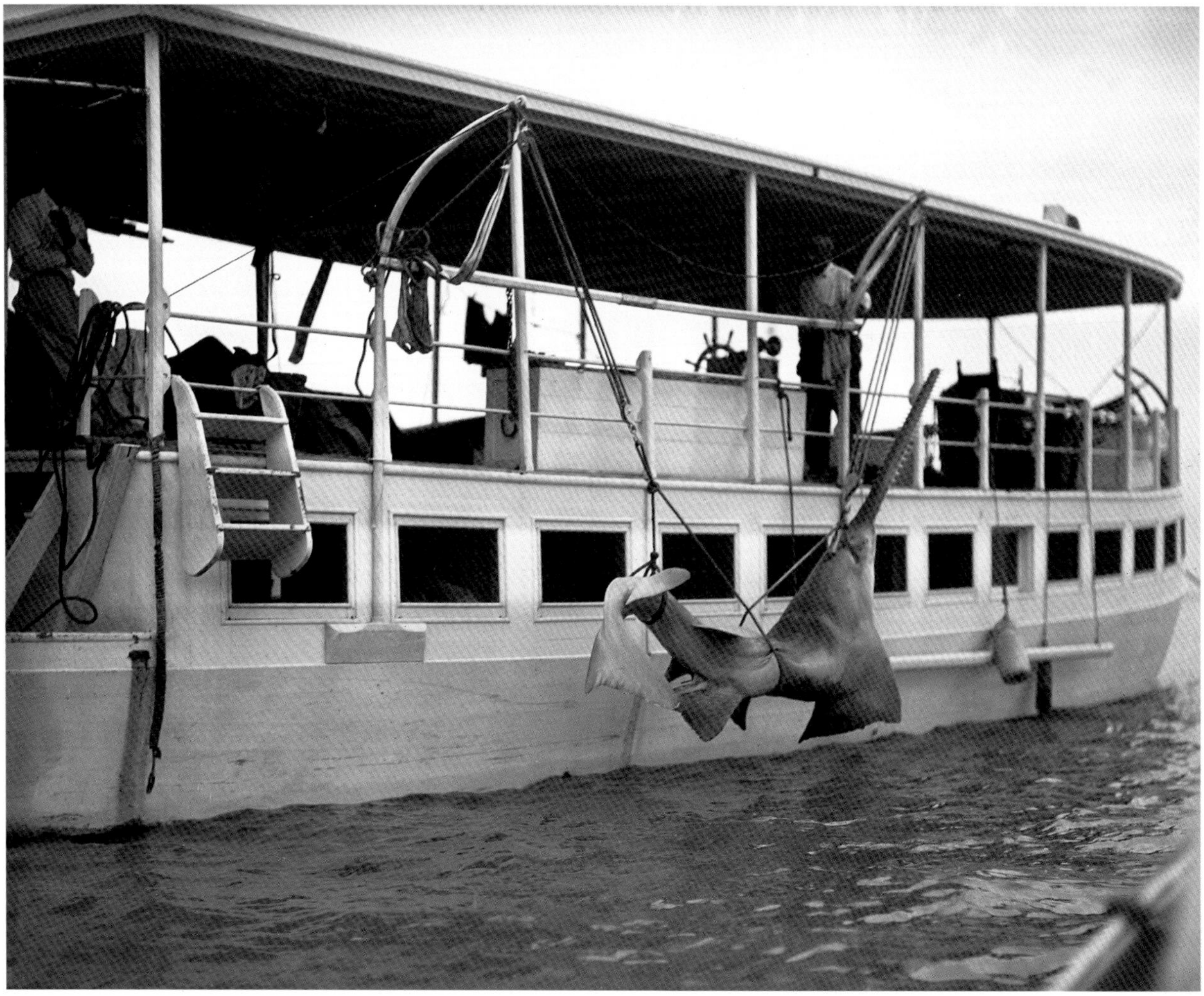

In 1913, A.W. and Julian Dimock returned to southwest Florida for the last time, bringing with them friends from New York. The Dimocks' spouses might also have come (Julian had married in 1912, and A.W., whose first spouse had died in 1901, had remarried in 1909). A 51-foot passenger vessel/houseboat, the *Kennesaw*, that had been built in 1910 on Marco Island (almost certainly at Collier's boatyard) was rented for a month in August and September. In the *Kennesaw*, the group first motored to Pine Island Sound, then down through the Ten Thousand Islands past Cape Sable, then back north to Boca Grande. Along the way the guests caught tarpon, sharks, and this sawfish. At one point, the *Kennesaw* anchored at Marco Island, where the Dimocks and their guests dined with the Olds family, friends from previous visits. Another dinner guest was the famed conservationist William T. Hornaday, who was staying on the island. At the time, Hornaday was head of the New York Zoological Society. September 4, 1913; 49082.

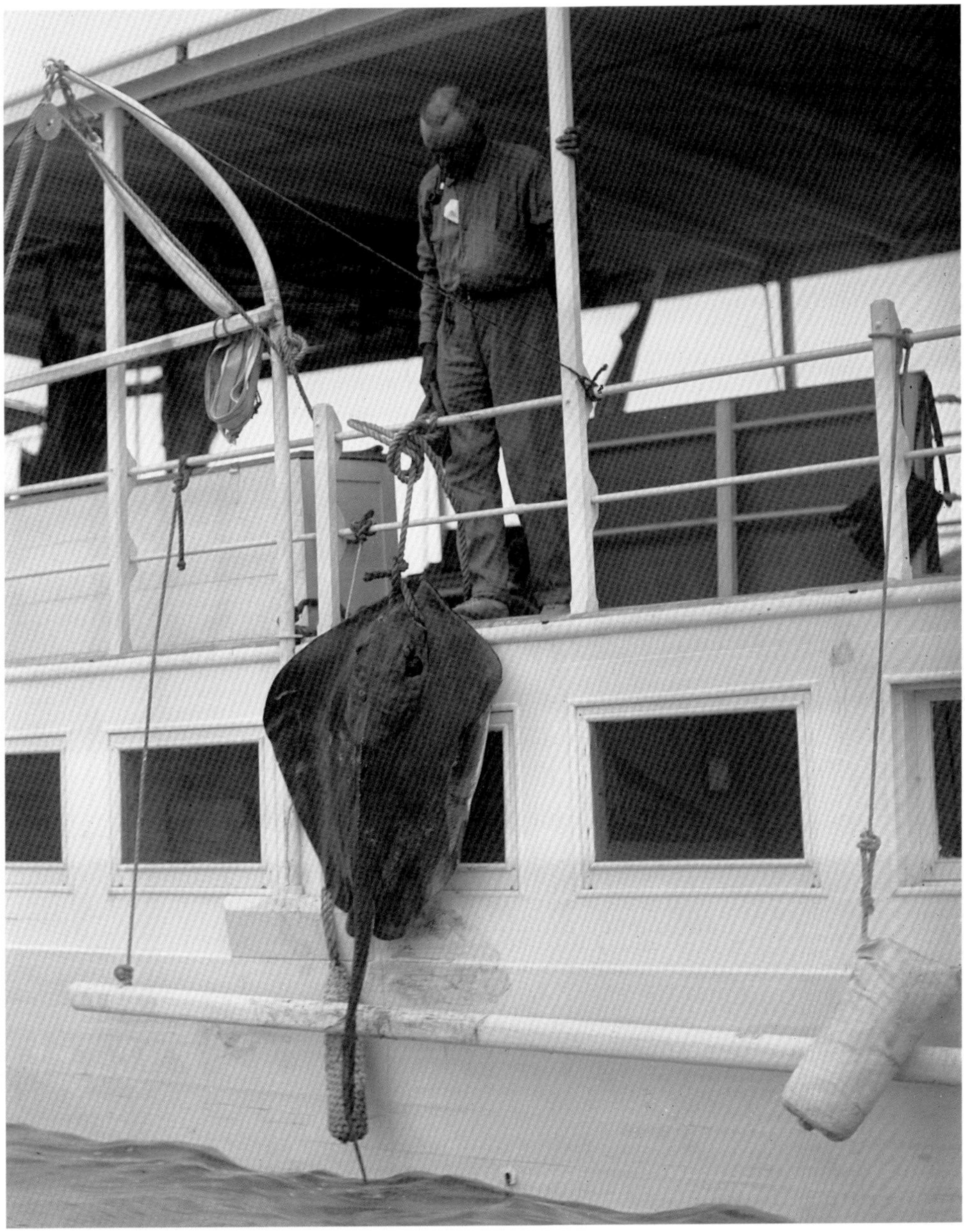

A.W., then 71, likely was not enamored of the experience of travel aboard the large houseboat with an entourage to match. In 1907, in "Cruising on the Gulf Coast of Florida," he had disparaged vessels like the *Kennesaw*, calling them "floating houses, with every attribute of a home, from a *chef* to a canary, from a library to a pet cat . . . which suggests yachting rather than the cruising I care for" (*Harper's Monthly*). He also might have not approved of the taking of marine life purely for sport (like this stingray caught off Joe Kemps Key). Julian's last Florida photograph was taken on September 10 on the Caloosahatchee River before disembarking the *Kennesaw* at Fort Myers. September 4, 1913; 49081.

ACKNOWLEDGMENTS

The authors wish to thank Tom Baione; Harold Boeschenstein, Director of the Department of Library Services at the American Museum of Natural History (AMNH); and Barbara Mathe, head of Special Collections, for their help and cooperation. Alexa Metrick, Digital Lab Manager in the Research Library at the AMNH, and her predecessors, Kelli Anderson and Lane Diko, facilitated the scanning of the Dimock glass negatives and our access to them. Ms. Metrick also digitally retouched the images to make them more presentable.

We are especially grateful to Craig R. Woodward of Marco Island for his careful reading of the manuscript and his suggestions and observations. Betsy Perdichizzi, also a Marco Island resident, graciously shared information about the Olds family, who once lived on the island and who knew the Dimocks.

Publication of this book in part was made possible by a grant from the Everglades Society for Historic Preservation (ESHP). We are indebted to the ESHP and the Marco Island Historical Society for their support.

BIBLIOGRAPHY

Works by A. W. Dimock

"An Alligator Hunt." *Country Life in America*, February 1903, cxix–cxx.

"An Alligator Hunter in the Making." *Country Life in America*, September 1909, 487–90.

"The Art of Catching the Manatee." *Century Illustrated Monthly Magazine*, April 1907, 848–53.

Be Prepared; or, The Boy Scouts in Florida. New York: Frederick A. Stokes, 1912.

The Book of the Tarpon. New York: Outing Publishing, 1911.

"The By-Products of Tarpon Fishing." *Van Norden's Magazine*, July 1909, 379–86.

"Camera and Rifle." *Photographic Mosaics*, 1890, 75–78.

"Canoeing in the Surf." *Pall Mall*, June 1909, 747–50.

"Canoeing in the Surf." *Recreation*, August 1908, 55–57.

"The Chase of the Dolphin." *Country Life in America*, January 1907, 291–97.

"Crossing the Everglades in a Power-boat." *Harper's Monthly*, January 1907, 213–20.

"The Cruise of the Kids." *Yachting*, July 1909, 23–26, 68.

"Cruising on the Gulf Coast of Florida." *Harper's Monthly*, March 1907, 520–28.

"A Despoiled People." *Outlook*, January 28, 1911, 201–6.

Dick among the Seminoles. New York: Frederick A. Stokes, 1911.

Dick in the Everglades. New York: Frederick A. Stokes, 1909.

"The Dolphin's Pedigree." *Country Life in America*, January 1907, 334.

"The Evolution of *Irene*: A Story of a Florida Cruise." *Recreation*, October 1907, 149–52.

"The Florida Crocodile." *American Museum Journal*, October 1918, 447–52.

Florida Enchantments. New York: Outing Publishing, 1908.

Florida Enchantments. 2nd ed. Peekamose, N.Y.: A. W. Dimock, 1915.

"Four Kinds of Tarpon Fishing." *Recreation*, March 1908, 99–103.

"How One Manatee Escaped the Zoo." *Youth's Companion*, July 7, 1910, 347.

"How the Crocodiles Came to the Bronx." *Youth's Companion*, August 5, 1909, 375.

"How the Pelicans Came to the Zoo." *Harper's Weekly*, October 30, 1909, 30, 32.
"In the Depths of the Everglades." *Travel*, January 1911, 116–19, 141–43.
"King Tarpon, The High Leaper of the Sea." *Outing*, March 1909, 703–17.
"Life in a Bird Rookery." *Harper's Monthly*, July 1907, 262–68.
"Lodging with a Rattlesnake." *Van Norden's Magazine*, February 1910, 509–12.
"Makers of Moonshine." *Recreation*, December 1909, 276–79.
"A Night with a Manatee." *Recreation*, April 1909, 163–68.
"On to Marco Pass: A Trip That Failed." *Outing*, January 1909, 397–412.
"An Overlooked River in Florida." *Travel*, November 1907, 65–67.
"The Passing of a Wilderness." *Scribner's Magazine*, March 1907, 358–64.
"The Passing of the Florida Alligator." *Harper's Monthly*, April 1908, 669–76.
"The Professor and the Prairie Schooner." *Outing*, January 1911, 387–97.
"Salt-Water Fly-Fishing." *Country Life in America*, January 1908, 303–6, 342, 344.
"A Southern Industrial Experiment." *Harper's Monthly*, July 1905, 302–8.
"Sponge-fishing in Florida." *Country Life in America*, July 1903, 176–77.
"A Square Deal: The Sport of Tarpon-Fishing from a Canoe Wherein the Roles of Pursued and Pursuer Sometimes Change." *Harper's Weekly*, November 3, 1906, 1572–74.
"Studying the Savage Seminoles In the Everglades of Florida." *Washington Post*, magazine section, February 20, 1916, 1, 5.
"The Tarpon and the Shark." *Appleton's Magazine*, January 1908, 3–16.
"The Tarpon and the Shark." *Country Life*, December 21, 1907, 900–904.
"Tarpon Fishing in Florida." *Country Life in America*, April 1903, 225–26.
"Turkey Tracks in the Big Cypress." *Outing*, October 1909, 13–21.
"Turtling, An Exciting Sport." *Country Life in America*, November 1903, 54–55.
"A Vanishing Race." *Collier's*, October 17, 1908, 16–17.
"The Wrecker," *Bob Taylor's Magazine*, June 1906, 275–81.
"Yachting in a Canoe." *Outing*, September 1908, 721–33.

Works by Julian A. Dimock

"After Tarpon with a Camera." *Country Life in America*, February 1905, 401–5.
"Babyhood of a Blue Heron." *Country Life*, January 25, 1908, 122–23.
"Big Game at Sea—No. IV: Hunting the Manatee." *Illustrated London News*, London ed., September 5, 1908, 332–33.
"The Bloodstained Aigrette." *Field and Stream*, August 1911, 355–60.
"By-Products of Tarpon-Fishing: Added Thrills to the Finest Aquatic Sport in the World." *Illustrated London News*, London ed., October 15, 1921, 494–95.
"Capturing the Crocodile." *Scientific American Supplement*, September 5, 1908, 156.
"Casting a Net for Mullet." *Country Life in America*, June 1903, 136.

"Crocodiling with a Camera." *American Illustrated Magazine*, 1906, 269–80.
"A Crusade and What Came of It." *Country Life in America*, February 1908, 422, 424.
"Egret Murder: A Protest and a Crusade." *Country Life in America*, February 1907, 418–20.
"Feathers Forbidden in America! The Question of the Plume-Birds." *Illustrated London News*, London ed., October 11, 1913, 564.
"Fly-Fishing in Florida." *Illustrated Sporting & Dramatic News for Town and Country*, February 1908, 959–60.
"The Gambols of the Tarpon: A Huge Quarry for Fishermen." *Illustrated London News*, London ed., February 8, 1908, 202.
"The Herons of Florida." *Country Life in America*, February 1908, 434, 436.
"A Hunt for Baby Alligators." *Outlook*, March 23, 1907, 680–86.
"Hunting Alligators and Crocodiles in Florida." *Country Life in America*, January 1903, 99–102.
"In the Everglades—With Camera and Canoe." *Outlook*, May 25, 1907, 181–89.
"The Lay of the Loggerhead." *Country Life in America*, April 1909, 612–14.
"The Mangrove as an Island Builder." *Country Life in America*, November 1905, 40–41.
"The New Florida: I—Florida Farming." *Country Life in America*, November 1910, 33–36.
"The New Florida: II—The Idyll of an Orange Grove." *Country Life in America*, December 1910, 137–42.
"The New Florida: III—Where Celery Is King." *Country Life in America*, January 1911, 219–22.
"The New Florida: IV—Two Acres Enough." *Country Life in America*, February 1911, 279–81.
"La Pesca Del Tarpon." *La Hacienda*, May 1909, 239–41.
"No Sport on Earth Offers Greater Excitement: A Day's Tarpon-Fishing in the Gulf of Mexico." *Illustrated London News*, London ed., July 17, 1920, 102–3.
"Photographing Tarpon." In *American Annual of Photography 1908*, 73–86. New York: Tennant and Word, 1907.
"Un sport emocionante." *Caras y Caretas*, March 13, 1909 (unpaginated).
"Sport Extraordinary—No. VI: Bagging a Crocodile Alive." *Illustrated London News*, London ed., October 3, 1908, 468–69.
"A Struggle with a Tarpon: The Biggest Fish Caught with Rod and Line." *Illustrated London News*, London ed., February 8, 1908, 203.
"A Summer Florida Vacation." *Country Life in America*, July 1905, 345.
"Where the Tarpon Leaps." *Travel*, June 1914, 9–13, 56–58.
"The Wild Excitement of Fishing for the Saw-Fish: A Fish that Turns upon the Fisherman." *Illustrated London News*, London ed., August 24, 1908, 268–69.
"With Camera and Canoe in the Everglades." *Wide World*, November 1907, 65–71.

INDEX

Jerald T. Milanich is professor emeritus of the University of Florida and contributing editor at *Archaeology* magazine. He is the author or editor of many books including *Florida Indians from Ancient Times to the Present* and *Laboring in the Fields of the Lord: Spanish Missions and Southeastern Indians*. In 2010 he was inducted into the American Academy of Arts and Sciences.

Nina J. Root is director emerita of the Research Library of the American Museum of Natural History in New York City. Before coming to the museum she was head of reference, Science and Technology Division, Library of Congress. She is the author of numerous books and articles on the history of natural history and on the AMNH Library's collections and is the coeditor of *Camera Man's Journey: Julian Dimock's South*. With Jerald T. Milanich she coauthored *Hidden Seminoles: Julian Dimock's Historic Florida Photographs*.

The University Press of Florida is the scholarly publishing agency for the State University System of Florida, comprising Florida A&M University, Florida Atlantic University, Florida Gulf Coast University, Florida International University, Florida State University, New College of Florida, University of Central Florida, University of Florida, University of North Florida, University of South Florida, and University of West Florida.